DAVID HERBERT was educated at Rugby and Trinity College, Cambridge. For short periods he was a bookseller, a stage manager (at the Maddermarket Theatre, Norwich), a teacher of English in Spain and of Spanish and French at Eton. From 1955 to 1961 he taught English at Christ's Hospital, where he produced and acted in a great many plays. But for most of his working life he has been in publishing, first with Penguin and later as Publisher at Studio Vista and then at Rainbird. In 1976 he and his wife formed their own company, The Herbert Press. Books he has written or edited for other publishers include *The Operas of Benjamin Britten, Romeo and Juliet* (in the Kennet Shakespeare series), *Everymans's Book of Evergreen Verse, The Gallery of World Photography: The Human Figure* and selections of *John Keats, George Herbert* and *Comic Verse*.

The Everyman Book of Narrative Verse

Edited by David Herbert

J. M. Dent & Sons Ltd
EVERYMAN'S LIBRARY

Phototypeset in 9½ on 10 point Bembo by
Deltatype Ltd, Ellesmere Port, Cheshire

Made in Great Britain by
The Guernsey Press Co. Ltd, Guernsey, C.I. for
J. M. Dent & Sons Ltd
91 Clapham High Street, London sw4 7ta

First published in Everyman's Library, 1990

British Library Cataloguing in Publication Data
The Everyman book of narrative verse.
1. Narrative poetry in English, 1300–1980 –
Anthologies
I. Herbert, David, *1927*–
821′.03′008

ISBN 0–460–87006–8 Paperback
0–460–87016–5 Hardback

CONTENTS

CONTENTS

INTRODUCTION

Once upon a time, good stories were always told or sung in verse, being passed on from court to court or tavern to tavern and down through generations until one variant or another was recorded in writing. The rhythm and shape of verse helped to put over the story and keep it in the memory. By no means all narrative verse is part of this continuing oral tradition, although much is indebted to it and influenced by it directly or indirectly. But even after three centuries of accumulating prose fiction, many of the best stories we have are in verse form. Likewise, many of the world's greatest poems are narrative. Homer's *Iliad* and *Odyssey* are examples of both. Aristotle held that the noblest form of literature was the epic, a heroic story poem on a grand scale; and to many people today narrative verse, whether part of an oral tradition or not, is the poetry they most often read or remember.

Paradise Lost, Christmas Day in the Workhouse, Don Juan, The Dong with a Luminous Nose, Clerk Saunders, The Pied Piper, The Eve of St Agnes, Horatius, The Green Eye of the Yellow God: these are all narrative poems, however different. There is so much good narrative verse (and so many poems are long) that it would be easy to fill a book twice the length of this without greatly lowering the overall standard. Anthologists, of course, often make things easier by limiting the basis of selection – either severely or marginally; to long or short poems, for example, to the well known or little known, to certain categories of story or types of poem. In an earlier publication (now long out of print), where my brief was to provide a narrative introduction to English poetry in general, selection was sometimes deliberately influenced by the need to represent an important poet's work or a particular fashion in verse writing.

For this Everyman volume, no such limitations were set. I have aimed at as much variety as possible, ranging widely through all kinds of narrative verse and choosing what I think the best of every kind, regardless of authorship or popularity. There are light poems here as well as serious, ballads, romances, adventure stories, heroic poems, burlesques, moral stories, incidents from epics, poems that simply tell a story and others which use the narrative form as a vehicle for something else (reflection, satire, social comment). The longest poem (*Sohrab and Rustum*) has 900 lines, the shortest (*I Saw a Jolly Hunter*) has twenty. Rhythms vary from irregular blank verse to the simple ballad metre, style from the rich diffuse imagery of *Hero and Leander* to the tight texture of *King Harald's Trance* or the colloquial looseness of *The Shooting of Dan McGrew*. The range in time is from Chaucer to the present day. Poets earlier than Chaucer are difficult for most people to enjoy without a large and unappealing glossary; and I have stopped short of the younger poets alive now only because a book has to end somewhere.

All extracts from longer works tell stories which are complete in themselves. I have avoided cuts in the middle of a poem or extract as far as possible; where these have been necessary (to save space), I have taken care to omit nothing which is part of the main action or which in any way makes a difference to the rest of the story. For this reason *Sohrab and Rustum*, a single episode whose slow movement is part of its quality, remains intact; whereas *The Rape of the Lock* – in a version that is a compromise between Pope's first and final drafts – retains the 'machinery' that gives this exquisite burlesque most of its delicacy, but leaves out the description of Belinda's morning toilet, all mention of Umbriel and his visit to the Cave of Spleen, and a long speech by Clarissa just before the fight. A number (but not all) of Byron's asides have been omitted from *Juan and Haidée*, as have some verses, including all references to Sextus, from *Horatius*.

Many poems were read many times before anthology-making was complete, and inevitably rejections in the final rounds of this process were painful. I hope only that what is here makes up a collection that will appeal to modern readers of any age, who will be glad to find old favourites side-by-side with poems of a similar standard that they had forgotten or did not know. I particularly regret the absence of an excerpt from Shakespeare's *The Rape of Lucrece*. But I'm particularly glad to have included part of the unfashionable *Hiawatha*, *The Stage-Driver's Story*, *King Harald's Trance* and, among all too few ballads, the long, beautiful and little-known *Robin Hode and the Munke* – as well as, I think, a good variety of twentieth-century examples. Finally, I would like to acknowledge my debt to Philip Larkin, whose *Oxford Book of Twentieth Century Verse* was the source of Muriel Stuart's *In the Orchard*, a poignant Hardyesque dialogue that I did not know.

Note on the Text

The poets are in chronological order. Ballads have been printed in a group between Chaucer and Spenser, even though some are obviously later in the form in which we have them and others may well be earlier. For the texts of the ballads I have gone to F. J. Child's *English and Scottish Popular Ballads*, Sir Walter Scott's *Minstrelsy of the Scottish Border*, and Bishop Percy's *Reliques*. Where Child printed several versions of the same ballad, I have made, out of a combination of them, what I think is the best single version; where the version in this book is that supplied by Scott or Percy, I have retained their modernized spelling. In neither case have I altered or added to the text.

The passages in square brackets in *Robin Hode and the Munke* are Sir

Arthur Quiller-Couch's suggestions for lines missing in the original. For the poem by Chaucer and for those ballads where the text used is an early one, I have kept the original spelling although to some extent regularizing it in *Robin Hode and the Munke*. But in the hundred and fifty years between the death of Chaucer and the birth of Spenser, English changed considerably, to become very much the same language that it is today. For this reason, and because for generations we have been accustomed to reading Shakespeare without the peculiarities of Elizabethan spelling, I have modernized all spelling from the sixteenth century onwards, except where rhythm or some definite purpose of the author's has demanded the old form.

Single incidents or extracts from larger works have been given an editor's title, which appears in square brackets after the title of the poem itself. A row of dots denotes that a passage in the poem has been omitted by the editor, and an asterisk that the author has indicated a pause or break in the action.

DAVID HERBERT

GEOFFREY CHAUCER

From *The Pardoner's Tale*

[THE THREE RIOTERS]

In Flaundres whilom was a compaignye
Of yongė folk, that haunteden folye,   *indulged in*
As riot, hasard, stiwes and tavernes,   *gambling; brothels*
Whereas with harpes, lutes and giternes,   *guitars*
They daunce and pleyen at dees, bothe day and night,   *dice*
And eten also, and drinken over hir might,   *their*
Thurgh which they doon the devel sacrifise
Withinne that develes temple, in cursed wise,
By superfluitee abhominable.
Hir othes been so grete and so dampnable   *oaths*
That it is grisly for to heere hem swere.
Oure blissed Lordes body they to-tere –
Hem thoughte that Jewes rente him noght ynough –   *they thought*
And ech of hem at otheres sinnė lough.

    . . .

Thise riotoures three, of whiche I telle,
Long erst er primė rong of any belle,   *before Prime*
Were set hem in a taverne for to drinke;
And, as they sat, they herde a bellė clinke
Biforn a cors, – was caried to his grave.   *corpse*
That oon of hem gan callen to his knave: *servant*
'Go bet,' quod he, 'and axė redily   *quickly/ask*
What cors is this, that passeth heer forby,
And looke that thou reporte his namė weel.'
    'Sire,' quod this boy, 'it nedeth never-a-deel;   *it is not a bit necessary*
It was me toold, er ye cam heer, two houres.
He was, *pardee*, an old felawe of youres,
And sodeynly he was yslain to-night,
Fordronke, as he sat on his bench upright.   *completely drunk*
Ther cam a privee theef, men clepeth Deeth,   *name*
That in this contree al the peplė sleeth,   *slays*
And with his spere he smoot his herte a-two,
And wente his wey withouten wordes mo.
He hath a thousand slain this pestilence;   *plague*
And, maister, er ye come in his presence,
Me thinketh that it werė necessarye
For to be war of swich an adversarye.
Beth redy for to meete him everemoore;
Thus taughtė me my dame; I seye namoore.'   *mother*

'By seintė Marie!' seyde this taverner,
'The child seith sooth, for he hath slain this yeer
Henne over a mile, withinne a greet village,   *hence*
Bothe man and womman, child, and hine, and page.   *servant*
I trowe his habitacioun be there;   *believe*
To been avised, greet wisdom it were,   *warned*
Er that he dide a man a dishonour.'
   'Ye, Goddes armes!' quod this riotour,
'Is it swich peril with him for to meete?
I shal him seke, by wey and eek by strete,   *on every path*
I make avow to Goddes dignė bones!   *worthy*
Herkneth, felawes, we three been al ones,
Lat ech of us holde up his hand til oother,   *to*
And ech of us bicomen otheres brother,
And we wol sleen this falsė traitour, Deeth;   *slay*
He shal be slain, he that so many sleeth,
By Goddes dignitee, er it be night!'
   To-gidres han thise three hir trouthes plight   *together; troths*
To live and dyen ech of hem for oother,
As though he were his owene yborė brother.
And up they stirte, al dronken, in this rage;   *sprang*
And forth they goon towardes that village
Of which the taverner had spoke biforn.
And many a grisly ooth thanne han they sworn;
And Cristes blessed body al to-rente,   *rent in pieces*
Deeth shal be deed, if that they may him hente.   *catch*
   Whan they han goon nat fully half a mile,
Right as they wolde han troden over a stile,
An oold man and a pourė with hem mette.   *them*
This oldė man ful mekėly hem grette,   *greeted*
And seydė thus: 'Now, lordes, God you see!'   *bless you*
   The proudeste of thise riotoures three
Answerde again, 'What! carl, with sory grace,
Why artou al forwrapped, save thy face?   *are you; wrapped up*
Why livestou so longe in so greet age?'
   This oldė man gan looke in his visage,
And seydė thus: 'For I ne kan nat finde   *because I cannot*
A man, though that I walked into Inde,   *as far as India*
Neither in citee, ne in no village,
That woldė chaunge his youthė for myn age;
And therfore moot I han myn agė stille,   *must*
As longė time as it is Goddes wille;
Ne Deeth, allas! ne wol nat han my lyf.
Thus walke I, lyk a restelees caitif.
And on the ground, which is my moodres gate,   *mother's*
I knokkė with my staf, bothe erly and late,
And seyė: "Leevė mooder, leet me in!   *dear*

Lo, how I vanishe, flesh and blood and skin;　　　　*waste away*
Allas! whan shul my bones been at reste?
Mooder, with you wolde I chaunge my cheste　　　　*strong-box*
That in my chambrė longė time hath be,
Ye, for an heyrė-clout to wrappe in me!"　　　　*shroud*
But yet to me she wol nat do that grace,
For which ful pale and welked is my face.　　　　*withered*
　　'But, sires, to you it is no curteisye
To speken to an old man vileynye,　　　　*rudeness*
But he trespasse in word, or elles in dede.　　　　*unless*
In Hooly Writ ye may yourself wel rede,
"Agains an oold man, hoor upon his heed,　　　　*hoary-headed*
Ye sholde arise"; wherfore I yeve you reed,　　　　*give; advice*
Ne dooth unto an oold man noon harm now,
Namoore than that ye wolde men did to you
In agė, if that ye so longe abide:
And God be with you, where ye go or ride;　　　　*wherever; walk*
I moot go thider as I have to go.'
　　'Nay, oldė cherl, by God, thou shalt nat so!'
Seyde this oother hasardour anon;　　　　*gambler*
'Thou partest nat so lightly, by seint John!
Thou spak right now of thilkė traitour, Deeth,　　　　*that*
That in this contree alle oure freendes sleeth;
Have heer my trouthe, as thou art his espye,　　　　*spy*
Telle where he is, or thou shalt it abye,　　　　*pay for*
By God and by the hooly sacrement!
For soothly, thou art oon of his assent
To sleen us yongė folk, thou falsė theef!'
　　'Now, sires,' quod he, 'if that ye be so leef　　　　*desirous*
To findė Deeth, turne up this croked wey,
For in that grove I laftė him, by my fey,　　　　*faith*
Under a tree, and there he wole abide;
Noght for youre boost he wole him nothing hide.
See ye that ook? Right there ye shal him finde.　　　　*oak*
God savė you, that boghte again mankinde,
And you amende!' thus seyde this oldė man;
　　And everich of thise riotoures ran
Til he cam to that tree, and ther they founde,
Of florins fine, of gold ycoined rounde,　　　　*coined*
Wel ny an eightė bushels, as hem thoughte.　　　　*nearly*
No lenger thannė after Deeth they soughte,
But ech of hem so glad was of that sighte,
For that the florins been so faire and brighte,
That down they sette hem by this precious hoord.
The worste of hem he spak the firste word.
　　'Bretheren,' quod he, 'taak kepe what I seye;　　　　*take heed of*
My wit is greet, though that I bourde and pleye.　　　　*jest; fool about*

3

This tresor hath Fortune unto us yiven
In mirthe and jolitee our lyf to liven;
And lightly as it comth, so wol we spende. *comes*
By, Goddes precious dignitee! who wende *guessed*
To-day, that we sholde han so fair a grace?
But mighte this gold be caried fro this place
Hoom to myn hous, or elles unto youres, –
For wel ye woot that al this gold is oures, – *know*
Thanne werė we in heigh felicitee.
But trewėly, by daye it may nat be;
Men woldė seyn that we were theves stronge,
And for oure owenė tresor doon us honge. *hang us*
This tresor moste ycaried be by nighte
As wisely and as slyly as it mighte.
Wherfore, I rede that cut among us alle *lots*
Be drawe, and lat see wher the cut wol falle;
And he that hath the cut, with hertė blithe,
Shal rennė to the town, and that ful swythe, *quickly*
And bringe us breed and wyn ful privėly, *very secretly*
And two of us shul kepen subtilly *cunningly guard*
This tresor wel; and, if he wol nat tarie,
Whan it is night, we wol this tresor carie
By oon assent where-as us thinketh best.'
    That oon of hem the cut broughte in his fest, *fist*
And bad hem drawe, and looke where it wol falle;
And it fil on the yongeste of hem alle,
And forth toward the town he wente anon.
    And also soonė as that he was gon, *immediately*
That oon of hem spak thus unto that oother:
'Thou knowest wel thou art my sworen brother;
Thy profit wol I tellė thee anon; *will*
Thou woost wel that oure felawe is agon,
And heere is gold, and that ful greet plentee,
That shal departed been among us three; *shared*
But nathėlees, if I kan shape it so
That it departed were among us two,
Hadde I nat doon a freendes turn to thee?'
    That oother answerde, 'I noot how that may be; *know not*
He woot wel that the gold is with us tweye; *two*
What shal we doon? what shal we to him seye?'
    'Shal it be conseil?' seyde the firstė shrewe, *a secret; rogue*
'And I shal tellen in a wordes fewe
What we shal doon, and bringe it wel aboute.'
    'I grauntė,' quod that oother, 'out of doute,
That by my trouthe I wol thee nat biwreye.' *betray*
    'Now,' quod the firste, 'thou woost wel we be tweye, *knowest*

4

And two of us shul strenger be than oon.
Looke whan that he is set, that right anoon — *sat down*
Arys, as though thou woldest with him pleye, — *play at wrestling*
And I shal ryve him thurgh the sides tweye, — *stab*
Whil that thou strogelest with him as in game,
And, with thy daggere, looke thou do the same;
And thanne shal al this gold departed be,
My deere freend, bitwixen me and thee.
Thanne may we bothe our lustes all fulfille, — *pleasures*
And pleye at dees right at our owene wille.'
And thus acorded been thise shrewes tweye, — *agreed*
To sleen the thridde, as ye han herd me seye.
    This yongeste, which that wente unto the town
Ful ofte in herte he rolleth up and down
The beautee of thise florins newe and brighte.
'O Lord,' quod he, 'if so were that I mighte
Have al this tresor to myself allone,
Ther is no man that liveth under the trone — *throne*
Of God, that sholde live so murie as I!' — *merry*
And atte laste the feend, oure enemy, — *at the; devil*
Putte in his thought that he sholde poison beye, — *buy*
With which he mighte sleen his felawes tweye;
For-why the feend foond him in swich livinge, — *because; state of life*
That he hadde leve him to sorwe bringe, — *permission*
For this was outrely his fulle entente — *utterly*
To sleen hem bothe and nevere to repente.
    And forth he gooth, no lenger wolde he tarye,
Into the town, unto a pothecarye,
And preyede him that he him wolde selle
Som poison, that he mighte his rattes quelle; — *rats*
And eek ther was a polcat in his hawe, — *hedge*
That, as he seyde, his capouns hadde yslawe; — *chickens*
And fain he wolde wreke him, if he mighte, — *avenge*
On vermin, that destroyed him by night.
    The pothecarye answerde, 'And thou shalt have
A thing that – also God my soule save! –
In al this world ther is no creature,
That eten or dronken hath of this confiture, — *mixture*
Noght but the montance of a corn of whete, — *amount; grain of*
That he ne shal his lyf anon forlete; — *wheat; yield up*
Ye, sterve he shal, and that in lasse while — *perish go at walking pace*
Than thou wolt goon a-paas nat-but a mile; — *only*
This poisoun is so strong and violent.'
    This cursed man hath in his hond yhent — *seized*
This poisoun in a box, and sith he ran — *then*

5

Into the nexté strete unto a man,
And borwed of him largé botelles three,
And in the two his poison poured he;
The thridde he kepté clené for his drinke;   *third*
For al the night he shoop him for to swinke   *he intended; labour*
In caryinge of the gold out of that place.
And whan this riotour, with sory grace,   *evil intention*
Hadde filled with wyn his greté botels three,
To his felawes again repaireth he.
    What nedeth it to sermone of it moore?
For right as they hadde cast his deeth bifoore,   *planned*
Right so they han him slain, and that anon,
And whan that this was doon, thus spak that oon:
'Now lat us sitte and drinke, and make us merie,
And afterward we wol his body berie';
And with that word it happed him, *par cas*,   *he happened*
To take the botel ther the poison was,
And drank, and yaf his felawe drinke also,
For which anon they storven bothé two.   *died*
    But certes, I suppose that Avicen   *Avicenna (an Arab*
Wroot nevere in no Canon, ne in no fen,   *doctor); chapter*
Mo wonder signes of empoisoning
Than hadde thise wrecches two, er hir ending.
Thus ended been thise homicides two,
And eek the false empoisonere also.
    O cursed sinne of allé cursednesse!
O traitours homicide! O wikkednesse!
O glotonye, luxurye, and hasardrye!   *lust; gambling*
Thou blasphemour of Crist with vileynye,
And othes grete, of usage and of pride!   *both of habit and*
Allas! mankindé, how may it bitide   *insolence*
That to thy Creatour, which that thee wroghte,
And with his precious herté-blood thee boghte,
Thou art so fals and so unkinde, allas!

ANONYMOUS

Robin Hode and the Munke

In somer, when the shawes be sheyne,   *woods; bright*
    And leves be large and long,
It is full mery in feyre foreste
    To here the fowlis song:

To see the dere draw to the dale,
   And leve the hilles hee,
And shadow hem in the leves green,
   Under the grene-wode tree.

It befel on Whitsontide,
   Erly in a May morning,
The son up feyre can shine,
   And the briddis mery can sing.

'This is a mery morning,' seid Litull John,
   'Be Him that died on tree;
A more mery man than I am one
   Lives not in Cristiante.

'Pluk up thy hert, my dere maister,'
   Litull John can sey,
'And think it is a full faire time
   In a morning of May.'

'Ye, on thing greves me,' seid Robin,
   'And does my hert much woo;
That I may not no solem day
   To mass nor matins goo.

'It is a fourtnet and more,' seid he,
   'Syn I my Saviour see;
To day wil I to Notingham,' seid Robin,
   'With the might of milde Marye.'

Than spake Moche, the milner son, –   *miller's son*
   Ever more wel him betide!
'Take twelve of thy wight yemen,   *sturdy*
   Well weppynd, be thy side.
Such on wolde thy selfe slon,   *slay*
   That twelve dar not abide.'

'Of all my mery men,' seid Robin,
   'Be my feith I wil non have,
But Litull John shall beyre my bow,
   Til that me list to drawe.'   *I want*

'Thou shall beyre thin own,' seid Litull John,
   'Maister, and I wil beyre mine,
And we wil shete a peny,' seid Litull John,   *shoot a penny*
   'Under the grene-wode lyne.'   *linden*

'I wil not shete a peny,' seid Robin Hode,
  'In feith, Litull John, with thee,
But ever for on as thou shetis,' seid Robin,
  'In feith I holde thee three.'   *wager*

Thus shet they forth, these yemen two,
  Bothe at buske and brome,   *bush*
Til Litull John wan of his maister
  Five shillings to hose and shone.

A ferly strife fel them betwene,   *strange*
  As they went by the wey;
Litull John seid he had won five shillings,
  And Robin Hode seid schortly nay.

With that Robin Hode lied Litull John,
  And smote him with his hande;
Litull John waxed wroth therwith,
  And pulled out his bright bronde.

'Were thou not my maister,' seid Litull John,
  'Thou shuldis be hit ful sore;
Get thee a man wher thou wilt,
  For thou getis me no more.'

Then Robin goes to Notingham,
  Him selfe mourning allone,
And Litull John to mery Scherwode,
  The pathes he knew ilkone.   *each one*

Whan Robin came to Notingham,
  Sertenly withouten layn,   *concealment*
He prayed to God and mild Mary
  To bring him out save again.

He gos in to Seint Mary church,
  And kneled down before the rode;
Alle that e'er were the church within
  Beheld wel Robin Hode.

Beside him stod a gret-hedid munke,
  I pray to God woo he be!
Ful sone he knew gode Robin,
  As sone as he him see.

Out at the durre he ran,
  Ful sone and anon;

Alle the yatis of Notingham   *gates*
  He made to be sparred everychon.   *barred*

'Rise up,' he seid, 'thou proude Schereff,
  Buske thee and make thee bowne;   *prepare; ready*
I have spied the Kingis felon,
  For sothe he is in this town.

'I have spied the false felon,
  As he stondis at his masse;
It is long of thee,' seide the munke,   *thy fault*
  'And ever he fro' us passe.

'This traitur name is Robin Hode,
  Under the grene-wode lynde;   *linden*
He robbit me onys of a hundred pound,
  It shall never out of my minde!'

Up then rose this proude Schereff,
  And radly made him yare;   *quickly; ready*
Many was the moder son
  To the kirk with him can fare.

In at the durres they throly thrast,   *stubbornly*
  With staves ful gode wone;   *in plenty, a good*
'Alas! alas!' seid Robin Hode,   *number*
  'Now misse I Litull John.'

But Robin toke out a two-hond sworde,
  That hangit down be his knee;
Ther as the Schereff and his men stode thickust,
  Thethurwarde wolde he.

Thries throout them he ran then,
  Forsothe as I you sey,
And woundit mony a moder son,
  And twelve he slew that day.

His sworde upon the Schereff hed
  Sertenly he brake in two;
'The smith that thee made,' seid Robin,
  'I pray to God wyrke him woo!

'For now am I weppynlesse,' seid Robin,
  'Alas! again my wille;
But if I may flee these traitors fro,   *unless*
  I wot they wil me kill.'

Robin into the churche ran,
   Throout hem everilkon . . .
[Then word is gone to his yemen
   In grene-wode wher they wone.]   *dwelt*

Sum fel in swoning as they were dede,
   And lay stil as any stone;
Non of theym were in her minde   *in their right minds*
   But only Litull John.

'Let be your rule,' seid Litull John,   *lamenting*
   'For his luf that died on tree;
Ye that shulde be dughty men,
   It is gret shame to see.

'Oure maister has bene harde bistode
   And yet scapid away;
Pluk up your hertis, and leve this mone,
   And harkin what I shal say.

'He has servid Oure Lady many a day,
   And yet wil, securly;
Therfor I trust in hir specialy
   No wickud deth shal he die.

'Therfor be glad,' seid Litull John,
   'And let this mourning be;
And I shal be the munkis gide,
   With the might of milde Mary.'

[Then spake Moche, the milner son,]
   'We wil go but we two.'
'And I mete him,' seid Litull John,
   ['I trust to wyrke him woo.]

'Loke that ye kepe wel oure tristil-tree,   *trysting-tree*
   Under the leves smale,   *small*
And spare non of this venison,
   That gose in this vale.'

Forth then went these yemen two,
   Litull John and Moche on fere,   *together*
And lokid on Moch' emys hous, –   *uncle's*
   The hie-way lay full nere.

Litull Jo·n stode at a window in the morning,
   And lokid forth at a stage;   *from an upper storey*
He was war wher the munke came riding,
   And with him a litul page.

'Be my feith,' seid Litull John to Moch,
   'I can thee tel tithingus gode;
I see wher the munke cumis riding,
   I know him be his wide hode.'

They went into the way, these yemen bothe,
   As curtes men and hende;   *civil*
They spyrred tithingus at the munke,   *inquired news from*
   As they hade bene his frende.

'Fro whens come ye?' seid Litull John,
   'Tel us tithingus, I you pray,
Of a false outlay, called Robin Hode,
   Was takin yisterday.

'He robbit me and my felowes bothe
   Of twenty marke in serten;
If that false outlay be takin,
   For sothe we wolde be fain.'

'So did he me,' seid the munke,
   'Of a hundred pound and more;
I laide furst hande him apon,
   Ye may thonke me therfore.'

'I pray God thanke you,' seid Litull John,
   'And we wil when we may;
We wil go with you, with your leve,
   And bring you on your way.

'For Robin Hode hase many a wilde felow,
   I tell you in serten;
If they wist ye rode this way,
   In feith ye shulde be slain.'

As they went talking be the way,
   The munke and Litull John,
John toke the munkis horse be the hede,
   Ful sone and anon.

John toke the munkis horse be the hed,
   For sothe as I you say;

So did Much the litull page,
   For he shulde not scape away.

Be the golett of the hode   *throat*
   John pulled the munke down;
John was nothing of him agast,   *frightened*
   He lete him falle on his crown.

Litull John was sore agrevid,
   And drew out his swerde in hie;   *haste*
This munke saw he shulde be ded,
   Loud mercy can he crye.

'He was my maister,' seid Litull John,
   'That thou hase brought in bale;   *to trouble*
Shalle thou never cum at our King,
   For to telle him tale.'

John smote off the munkis hed,
   No longer wolde he dwell;
So did Moch the litull page,
   For ferd lest he wolde tell.

Ther they beried hem bothe,
   In nouther mosse nor ling,
And Litull John and Much in fere
   Bare the letturs to oure King.

[When John came unto oure King]
   He knelid down upon his knee:
'God you save, my lege lorde,
   Jhesus you save and see!

'God you save, my lege King!'
   To speke John was full bolde;
He gaf him the letturs in his hond,
   The King did it unfold.

The King red the letturs anon,
   And seid, 'So mot I the,   *as I hope to thrive*
Ther was never yemen in mery Inglond
   I longut so sore to see.

'Wher is the munke that these shuld have brought?'
   Oure King can say:
'Be my trouth,' seid Litull John,

'He died after the way.'   *on*

The King gaf Moch and Litull John
   Twenty pound in serten,
And made theim yemen of the crown,
   And bade theim go again.

He gaf John the seel in hand,
   The Schereff for to bere,
To bring Robin him to,
   And no man do him dere.   *harm*

John toke his leve at oure King,
   The sothe as I you say;
The next way to Notingham
   To take, he yede the way.   *went*

Whan John came to Notingham
   The yatis were sparred ychon;
John callid up the porter,
   He answerid sone anon.

'What is the cause,' seid Litull John,
   'Thou sparris the yates so fast?'
'Because of Robin Hode,' seid the porter,
   'In depe prison is cast.

'John and Moch and Will Scathlok,
   For sothe as I you say,
They slew oure men upon our wallis,
   And sawten us every day.'   *assault*

Litull John spyrred after the Schereff,
   And sone he him fonde;
He oppyned the Kingus prive seell,
   And gaf him in his honde.

Whan the Schereff saw the Kingus seell,
   He did of his hode anon: *took off*
'Wher is the munke that bare the letturs?'
   He seid to Litull John.

'He is so fain of him,' seid Litull John   *taken with him*
   'For sothe as I you say,
He has made him abot of Westminster,
   A lorde of that abbay.'

The Schereff made John gode chere,
   And gaf him wine of the best;
At night they went to her bedde,   *their*
   And every man to his rest.

When the Schereff was on slepe,
   Dronken of wine and ale,
Litull John and Moch for sothe
   Toke the way unto the jale.

Litull John callid up the jailer,
   And bade him rise anon;
He seid Robin Hode had brokin prison,
   And out of it was gon.

The porter rose anon serten,
   As sone as he herd John calle;
Litull John was redy with a swerd,
   And bare him to the walle.

'Now wil I be porter,' seid Litull John,
   'And take the keyes in honde':
He toke the way to Robin Hode,
   And sone he him unbonde.

He gaf him a gode swerd in his hond,
   His hed therwith for to kepe,
And ther as the walle was lowist
   Anon down can they lepe.

Be that the cok began to crow,
   The day began to spring,
The Schereff fond the jailer ded;
   The comyn bell made he ring.

He made a crye throout al the town,
   Wheder he be yoman or knave,
That couthe bring him Robin Hode,
   His warison he shuld have.   *reward*

'For I dar never,' seid the Schereff,
   'Cum before oure King;
For if I do, I wot serten
   For sothe he wil me heng.'

The Schereff made to seke Notingham,
   Bothe be strete and stye,   *path, alley*

And Robin was in mery Scherwode,
  As light as lef on lynde.

Then bespake gode Litull John,
  To Robin Hode can he say,
'I have done thee a gode turne for an evill,
  Quite thee whan thou may.

'I have done thee a gode turne,' seid Litull John,
  'For sothe as I you say;
I have brought thee under grene-wode lyne;
  Fare wel, and have gode day.'

'Nay, be my trouth,' seid Robin Hode,
  'So shall it never be;
I make thee maister,' seid Robin Hode,
  'Of alle my men and me.'

'Nay, be my trouth,' seid Litull John,
  'So shalle it never be;
But lat me be a felow,' seid Litull John,
  'No noder kepe I be.'   *I want nothing more*

Thus John gate Robin Hode out of prison,
  Serten withoutin layn;   *without lying*
Whan his men saw him hol and sounde,
  For sothe they were full faine.   *glad*

They filled in wine, and made hem glad,
  Under the leves smale,
And yete pastes of venison,   *ate*
  That gode was with ale.

Then worde came to oure King
  How Robin Hode was gon,
And how the Schereff of Notingham
  Durst never loke him upon.

Then bespake oure cumly King,
  In an angur hie:
'Litull John hase begiled the Schereff,
  In faith so hase he me.

'Litull John has begiled us bothe
  And that full wel I see;
Or ellis the Schereff of Notingham
  Hie hongut shulde he be.

'I made hem yemen of the crowne,
   And gaf hem fee with my hond;
I gaf hem grith,' seid oure King,   *safety*
   'Thorowout all mery Inglond.

'I gaf theim grith,' then seid oure King;
   'I say, so mot I the,
For sothe soch a yeman as he is on
   In all Inglond ar not three.

'He is trew to his maister,' seid our King;
   'I sey, be swete Seint John,
He lovis better Robin Hode
   Then he dose us ychon.

'Robin Hode is ever bond to him,
   Bothe in strete and stalle;
Speke no more of this mater,' seid oure King,
   'But John has begiled us alle.'

Thus endis the talking of the munke
   And Robin Hode ywisse;
God, that is ever a crowned king,
   Bring us all to his blisse!

Clerk Saunders

PART I

Clerk Saunders and May Margaret
   Walked owre yon graveld green;
And sad and heavy was the love
   That fell thir twa between.

'A bed, a bed,' Clerk Saunders said,
   'A bed for you and me!'
'Fye na, fye na,' said May Margaret,
   'Till anes we married be!

'For in may come my seven bauld brothers,
   Wi' torches burning bright;
They'll say – "We hae but ae sister,
   And behold she's wi' a knight!"'

'Then take the sword frae my scabbard
  And slowly lift the pin;
And you may swear, and safe your aith,
  Ye never let Clerk Saunders in.

'And take a napkin in your hand,
  And tie up baith your bonny een;
And you may swear, and safe your aith,
  Ye saw me na since late yestreen.

'Ye'll take me in your armes twa,
  And carry me into your bed;
And ye may swear, and safe your aith,
  In your bower I never tread.'

It was about the midnight hour,
  When they asleep were laid,
When in and came her seven brothers,
  Wi' torches burning red:

When in and came her seven brothers,
  Wi' torches shining bright:
They said, 'We hae but ae sister,
  And behold her lying with a knight!'

Then out and spake the first o' them,
  'I bear the sword shall gar him die.'
And out and spake the second o' them,
  'His father has nae mair than he.'

And out and spake the third o' them,
  'I wot that they are lovers dear.'
And out and spake the fourth o' them,
  'They hae been in love this mony a year.'

Then out and spake the fifth o' them,
  'It were great sin true love to twain.'
And out and spake the sixth o' them,
  'It were shame to slay a sleeping man.'

Then up and gat the seventh o' them,
  And never a word spake he;
But he has striped his bright brown brand
  Out thro' Clerk Saunders' fair body.

Clerk Saunders he started, and Margaret she turned
  Into his arms as asleep she lay;

And sad and silent was the night
   That was atween thir twae.

And they lay still and sleepèd sound
   Until the day began to daw';
And kindly she to him did say,
   'It is time, true love, you were awa'.'

But he lay still, and sleepèd sound,
   Albeit the sun began to sheen;
She looked atween her and the wa',
   And dull and drowsie were his een.

Then in and came her father dear;
   Said, 'Let a' your mourning be;
I'll carry the dead corse to the clay,
   And I'll come back and comfort thee.'

'Comfort weel your seven sons,
   For comforted will I never be:
I ween 'twas neither knave nor loon
   Was in the bower last night wi' me.'

PART II

[A version of *Sweet William's Ghost*]

The clinking bell gaed thro' the toun,
   To carry the dead corse to the clay;
And Clerk Saunders stood at May Margaret's window,
   I wot, an hour before the day.

'Are ye sleeping, Margaret?' he says,
   'Or are ye waking presently?
Give me my faith and troth again,
   I wot, true love, I gied to thee.'

'Your faith and troth ye sall never get,
   Nor our true love sall never twin,   *break in two*
Until ye come within my bower,
   And kiss me cheik and chin.'

'My mouth it is full cold, Margaret;
   It has the smell, now, of the ground;
And if I kiss thy comely mouth,
   Thy days of life will not be lang.

'O cocks are crowing a merry midnight,
   I wot the wild fowls are boding day;
Give me my faith and troth again,
   And let me fare me on my way.'

'Thy faith and troth thou sall na get,
   And our true love sall never twin,
Until ye tell what comes o' women,
   I wot, who die in strong traivelling?'

'Their beds are made in the heavens high,
   Down at the foot of our good Lord's knee,
Weel set about wi' gillyflowers;
   I wot, sweet company for to see.

'O cocks are crowing a merry midnight,
   I wot the wild fowls are boding day;
The psalms of heaven will soon be sung,
   And I, ere now, will be missed away.'

Then she has ta'en a crystal wand,
   And she has stroken her troth thereon;
She has given it him out at the shot-window,
   Wi' mony a sad sigh and heavy groan.

'I thank ye, Margaret; I thank ye, Margaret;
   And ay I thank ye heartilie;
Gin ever the dead come for the quick,
   Be sure, Margaret, I'll come for thee.'

It's hosen and shoon, and gown alone,
   She climbed the wall, and followed him,
Until she came to the green forest,
   And there she lost the sight o' him.

'Is there ony room at your head, Saunders?
   Is there ony room at your feet?
Or ony room at your side, Saunders,
   Where fain, fain, I wad sleep?'

'There's nae room at my head, Margaret,
   There's nae room at my feet;
My bed it is fu' lowly now,
   Amang the hungry worms I sleep.

'Cauld mould is my covering now,
   But and my winding-sheet;

The dew it falls nae sooner down
   Than my resting-place is weet.

'But plait a wand o' bonny birk,
   And lay it on my breast;
And shed a tear upon my grave,
   And wish my saul gude rest.

'And fair Margaret, and rare Margaret,
   And Margaret o' veritie,
Gin e'er ye love another man,
   Ne'er love him as ye did me.'

Then up and crew the milk-white cock,
   And up and crew the gray;
Her lover vanished in the air,
   And she gaed weeping away.

Barbara Allan

In Scarlet Town, where I was born,
   There was a fair maid dwellin',
Made every youth cry *Well-a-day!*
   Her name was Barbara Allan.

'Twas in and about the Martinmas time,
   When the green leaves were fallin',
That Sir John Graeme in the West Country
   Fell in love with Barbara Allan.

He sent his man down through the town,
   To the place where she was dwellin';
'O haste and come to my master dear,
   Gin ye be Barbara Allan.'

O hooly, hooly raise she up,   *slowly*
   To the place where he was lyin',
And when she drew the curtain by –
   'Young man, I think you're dyin'.'

'O it's I am sick and very very sick,
   And it's a' for Barbara Allan.'
'O the better for me ye's never be,
   Tho' your heart's blood were spillin'!

'O dinna ye mind, young man,' said she,

'When ye the cups were fillin',
How ye made the healths go round and round,
    And slighted Barbara Allan?'

He turned his face unto the wall,
    And death was with him dealin';
'Adieu, adieu, my dear friends all,
    Be kind to Barbara Allan!'

Then hooly, hooly raise she up,
    And hooly, hooly left him,
And sighing said she could not stay,
    Since death of life had reft him.

She had not gane a mile but twa
    When she heard the dead-bell knellin';
And every jow the dead-bell geid   *beat, tolled*
    Cried 'Woe to Barbara Allan.'

'O mither, mither, make my bed,
    O make it saft and narrow:
Since my love died for me today,
    I'se die for him tomorrow.

'Farewell,' she said, 'ye virgins all,
    And shun the fault I fell in:
Henceforth take warning by the fall
    Of cruel Barbara Allan.'

Lord Randal

'O where hae you been, Lord Randal, my son?
And where hae you been, my handsome young man?'
'I hae been at the greenwood; mother, make my bed soon,
For I'm wearied wi' hunting, and fain wad lie down.'

'An wha met ye there, Lord Randal, my son?
And wha met ye there, my handsome young man?'
'O I met wi' my true-love; mother, make my bed soon,
For I'm wearied wi' hunting, and fain wad lie down.'

'And what did she give you, Lord Randal, my son?
And what did she give you, my handsome young man?'
'Eels fried in a pan; mother, make my bed soon,
For I'm wearied wi' hunting, and fain wad lie down.'

'And wha gat your leavins, Lord Randal, my son?
And wha gat your leavins, my handsome young man?'
'My hawks and my hounds; mother, make my bed soon,
For I'm wearied wi' hunting, and fain wad lie down.'

'And what became of them, Lord Randal, my son?
And what became of them, my handsome young man?'
'They stretched their legs out and died; mother, make my bed soon,
For I'm wearied wi' hunting, and fain wad lie down.'

'O I fear you are poisoned, Lord Randal, my son!
I fear you are poisoned, my handsome young man!'
'O yes, I am poisoned; mother, make my bed soon,
For I'm sick at the heart, and I fain wad lie down.'

'What d'ye leave to your mother, Lord Randal, my son?
What d'ye leave to your mother, my handsome young man?'
'Four and twenty milk kye; mother, make my bed soon,
For I'm sick at the heart, and I fain wad lie down.'

'What d'ye leave to your sister, Lord Randal, my son?
What d'ye leave to your sister, my handsome young man?'
'My gold and my silver; mother, make my bed soon,
For I'm sick at the heart, and I fain wad lie down.'

'What d'ye leave to your brother, Lord Randal, my son?
'What d'ye leave to your brother, my handsome young man?'
'My houses and lands; mother, make my bed soon,
For I'm sick at the heart, and I fain wad lie down.'

'What d'ye leave to your true-love, Lord Randal, my son?
What d'ye leave to your true-love, my handsome young man?'
'I leave her hell and fire; mother, make my bed soon,
For I'm sick at the heart, and I fain wad lie down.'

EDMUND SPENSER

From *The Faerie Queene*

[ARTHUR'S FIGHT WITH ORGOGLIO AND DUESSA]

They sadly travelled thus, until they came
  Nigh to a castle builded strong and high:
  Then cried the dwarf, 'Lo yonder is the same,

In which my lord my liege doth luckless lie,
  Thrall to that giant's hateful tyranny:
  Therefore, dear sir, your mighty powers assay.'
  The noble knight alighted by and by
  From lofty steed, and bade the lady stay,
To see what end of fight should him befall that day.

So with the squire, th' admirer of his might,
  He marchèd forth towards that castle wall;
  Whose gates he found fast shut, ne living wight
  To ward the same, nor answer comers' call.
  Then took that squire an horn of bugle small,
  Which hung adown his side in twisted gold,
  And tassels gay. Wide wonders over all
  Of that same horn's great virtues weren told,
Which had approvèd been in uses manifold.

Was never wight, that heard that shrilling sound,
  But trembling fear did feel in every vein;
  Three miles it might be easy heard around,
  And echoes three answered itself again:
  No false enchantment, nor deceitful train
  Might once abide the terror of that blast,
  But presently was void and wholly vain:
  No gate so strong, no lock so firm and fast,
But with that piercing noise flew open quite, or brast.

The same before the giant's gate he blew,
  That all the castle quakèd from the ground,
  And every door of freewill open flew.
  The giant self dismayèd with that sound,
  Where he with his Duessa dalliance found,
  In haste came rushing forth from inner bower,
  With staring countenance stern, as one astound,
  And staggering steps, to weet what sudden stowre
Had wrought that horror strange, and dared his dreaded power.

And after him the proud Duessa came,
  High mounted on her manyheaded beast,
  And every head with firey tongue did flame,
  And every head was crownèd on his crest,
  And bloody mouthèd with late cruel feast.
  That when the knight beheld, his mighty shield
  Upon his manly arm he soon addressed,
  And at him fiercely flew, with courage filled,
And eager greediness through every member thrilled.

Therewith the giant buckled him to fight,
  Inflamed with scornful wrath and high disdain,
  And lifting up his dreadful club on height,
  All armed with ragged snubs and knotty grain,
  Him thought at first encounter to have slain.
  But wise and wary was that noble peer,
  And lightly leaping from so monstrous main,
  Did fair avoid the violence him near;
It booted nought, to think, such thunderbolts to bear.

Ne shame he thought to shun so hideous might:
  The idle stroke, enforcing furious way,
  Missing the mark of his misaimèd sight,
  Did fall to ground, and with his heavy sway
  So deeply dinted in the driven clay,
  That three yards deep a furrow up did throw:
  The sad earth, wounded with so sore assay,
  Did groan full grievous underneath the blow,
And trembling with strange fear, did like an earthquake show.

As when almighty Jove in wrathful mood,
  To wreak the guilt of mortal sins is bent,
  Hurls forth his thundering dart with deadly food,
  Enrolled in flames, and smouldering dreriment,
  Through riven clouds and molten firmament;
  The fierce threeforkèd engine making way,
  Both lofty towers and highest trees hath rent,
  And all that might his angry passage stay,
And shooting in the earth, casts up a mount of clay.

His boisterous club, so buried in the ground,
  He could not rearen up again so light,
  But that the knight him at advantage found,
  And whiles he strove his cumbered club to quite
  Out of the earth, with blade all burning bright
  He smote off his left arm, which like a block
  Did fall to ground, deprived of native might;
  Large streams of blood out of the trunkèd stock
Forth gushèd, like fresh water stream from riven rock.

Dismayèd with so desperate deadly wound,
  And eke impatient of unwonted pain,
  He loudly brayed with beastly yelling sound,
  That all the fields rebellowèd again;
  As great a noise, as when in Cymbrian plain,
  An herd of bulls, whom kindly rage doth sting,
  Do for the milky mothers' want complain,

And fill the fields with troublous bellowing,
The neighbour woods around with hollow murmur ring.

That when his dear Duessa heard, and saw
  The evil stound, that dangered her estate,
  Unto his aid she hastily did draw
  Her dreadful beast, who swoll'n with blood of late
  Came ramping forth with proud presumptuous gait,
  And threatened all his heads like flaming brands.
  But him the squire made quickly to retrate,
  Encountering fierce with single sword in hand,
And 'twixt him and his lord did like a bulwark stand.

The proud Duessa full of wrathful spite,
  And fierce disdain, to be affronted so,
  Enforced her purple beast with all her might
  That stop out of the way to overthrow,
  Scorning the let of so unequal foe:
  But nathemore would that courageous swain
  To her yield passage, 'gainst his lord to go,
  But with outrageous strokes did him restrain,
And with his body barred the way atwixt them twain.

Then took the angry witch her golden cup,
  Which still she bore, replete with magic arts;
  Death and despair did many thereof sup,
  And secret poison through their inner parts,
  Th' eternal bale of heavy wounded hearts;
  Which, after charms and some enchantments said,
  She lightly sprinkled on his weaker parts;
  Therewith his sturdy courage soon was quayed,
And all his senses were with sudden dread dismayed.

So down he fell before the cruel beast,
  Who on his neck his bloody claws did seize,
  That life nigh crushed out of his panting breast:
  No power he had to stir, nor will to rise.
  That when the careful knight gan well avise,
  He lightly left the foe, with whom he fought,
  And to the beast gan turn his enterprise;
  For wondrous anguish in his heart it wrought,
To see his lovèd squire into such thraldom brought.

And high advancing his bloody-thirsty blade,
  Struck one of those deformèd heads so sore,
  That of his puissance proud ensample made;
  His monstrous scalp down to his teeth it tore,

And that misformèd shape mis-shapèd more:
A sea of blood gushed from the gaping wound,
That her gay garments stained with filthy gore,
And overflowèd all the field around;
That over shoes in blood he waded on the ground.

Thereat he roarèd for exceeding pain,
That to have heard, great horror would have bred,
And scourging th' empty air with his long train,
Through great impatience of his grievèd head
His gorgeous rider from her lofty sted
Would have cast down, and trod in dirty mire,
Had not the giant soon her succourèd;
Who all enraged with smart and frantic ire,
Came hurtling in full fierce, and forced the knight retire.

The force, which wont in two to be dispersed,
In one alone left hand he now unites,
Which is through rage more strong than both were erst;
With which his hideous club aloft he dights,
And at his foe with furious rigour smites,
That strongest oak might seem to overthrow:
The stroke upon his shield so heavy lights,
That to the ground it doubleth him full low:
What mortal wight could ever bear so monstrous blow?

And in his fall his shield, that covered was,
Did loose his veil by chance, and open flew:
The light whereof, that heaven's light did pass,
Such blazing brightness through the air threw,
That eye mote not the same endure to view.
Which when the giant spied with staring eye,
He down let fall his arm, and soft withdrew
His weapon huge, that heavèd was on high
For to have slain the man, that on the ground did lie.

And eke the fruitful-headed beast, amazed
At flashing beams of that sunshiny shield,
Became stark blind, and all his senses dazed,
That down he tumbled on the dirty field,
And seemed himself as conquerèd to yield.
Whom when his mistress proud perceived to fall,
Whiles yet his feeble feet for faintness reeled,
Unto the giant loudly she gan call,
'O help Orgoglio, help, or else we perish all.'

At her so piteous cry was much amoved

Her champion stout, and for to aid his friend,
 Again his wonted angry weapon proved:
 But all in vain: for he has read his end
 In that bright shield, and all their forces spend
 Themselves in vain: for since that glancing sight,
 He hath no power to hurt, nor to defend;
 As where th' Almighty's lightning brond does light,
It dims the dazed eyen, and daunts the senses quite.

Whom when the Prince, to battle new addressed,
 And threat'ning high his dreadful stroke did see,
 His sparkling blade about his head he blest,
 And smote off quite his right leg by the knee,
 That down he tumbled; as an agèd tree,
 High growing on the top of rocky clift,
 Whose heartstrings with keen steel nigh hewen be,
 The mighty trunk half rent, with ragged rift
Doth roll adown the rocks, and fall with fearful drift.

Or as a castle rearèd high and round,
 By subtle engines and malicious sleight
 Is underminèd from the lowest ground,
 And her foundation forced, and feebled quite,
 At last down falls, and with her heapèd height
 Her hasty ruin does more heavy make,
 And yields itself unto the victor's might;
 Such was this giant's fall, that seemed to shake
The steadfast globe of earth, as it for fear did quake.

The knight then lightly leaping to the prey,
 With mortal steel him smote again so sore,
 That headless his unwieldy body lay,
 All wallowed in his own foul bloody gore,
 Which flowèd from his wounds in wondrous store.
 But soon as breath out of his breast did pass,
 That huge great body, which the giant bore,
 Was vanished quite, and of that monstrous mass
Was nothing left, but like an empty bladder was.

Whose grievous fall, when false Duessa spied,
 Her golden cup she cast unto the ground,
 And crownèd mitre rudely threw aside;
 Such piercing grief her stubborn heart did wound,
 That she could not endure that doleful stound,
 But leaving all behind her, fled away:
 The light-foot squire her quickly turned around,
 And by hard means enforcing her to stay,
So brought unto his lord, as his deserved prey.

MICHAEL DRAYTON

'Fair Stood the Wind for France'

Fair stood the wind for France
When we our sails advance,
Nor now to prove our chance
    Longer will tarry;
But putting to the main,
At Caux, the mouth of Seine,
With all his martial train
    Landed King Harry.

And taking many a fort,
Furnished in warlike sort,
Marcheth towards Agincourt
    In happy hour;
Skirmishing day by day
With those that stopped his way,
Where the French general lay
    With all his power.

Which, in his height of pride,
King Henry to deride,
His ransom to provide
    Unto him sending;
Which he neglects the while
As from a nation vile,
Yet with an angry smile
    Their fall portending.

And turning to his men,
Quoth our brave Henry then,
'Though they to one be ten
    Be not amazed:
Yet have we well begun;
Battles so bravely won
Have ever to the sun
    By fame been raised.

'And for myself,' quoth he,
'This my full rest shall be;
England ne'er mourn for me
    Nor more esteem me.
Victor I will remain
Or on this earth lie slain;
Never shall she sustain

Loss to redeem me.

'Poitiers and Cressy tell,
When most their pride did swell,
Under our swords they fell,
   No less our skill is
Than when our grandsire great.
Claiming the regal seat,
By many a warlike feat
   Lopped the French lilies.'

The Duke of York so dread
The eager vaward led;
With the main Henry sped
   Among his henchmen.
Exeter had the rear,
A braver man not there;
O Lord, how hot they were
   On the false Frenchmen!

They now to fight are gone,
Armour on armour shone,
Drum now to drum did groan,
   To hear was wonder;
That with the cries they make
The very earth did shake.
Trumpet to trumpet spake,
   Thunder to thunder.

Well it thine age became,
O noble Erpingham,
Which didst the signal aim
   To our hid forces!
When from a meadow by,
Like a storm suddenly
The English archery
   Struck the French horses.

With Spanish yew so strong,
Arrows a cloth-yard long
That like to serpents stung,
   Piercing the weather;
None from his fellow starts,
But playing manly parts,
And like true English hearts
   Stuck close together.

When down their bows they threw,
And forth their bilbos drew,
And on the French they flew,
   Not one was tardy;
Arms were from shoulders sent,
Scalps to the teeth were rent,
Down the French peasants went.
   Our men were hardy!

This while our noble king,
His broadsword brandishing,
Down the French host did ding
   As to o'erwhelm it;
And many a deep wound lent,
His arms with blood besprent,
And many a cruel dent
   Bruised his helmet.

Gloster, that duke so good,
Next of the royal blood,
For famous England stood
   With his brave brother;
Clarence, in steel so bright,
Though but a maiden knight,
Yet in that furious fight
   Scarce such another.

Warwick in blood did wade,
Oxford the foe invade,
And cruel slaughter made
   Still as they ran up.
Suffolk his axe did ply,
Beaumont and Willoughby
Bare them right doughtily,
   Ferrers and Fanhope.

Upon Saint Crispin's Day
Fought was this noble fray,
Which fame did not delay
   To England to carry.
O when shall English men
With such acts fill a pen?
Or England breed again
   Such a King Harry?

CHRISTOPHER MARLOWE

From *Hero and Leander*

[LEANDER'S RETURN]

Home when he came, he seemed not to be there,
But, like exilèd air thrust from his sphere,
Set in a foreign place; and straight from thence,
Alcides-like, by mighty violence,
He would have chased away the swelling main,
That him from her unjustly did detain.
Like as the sun in a diameter
Fires and inflames objects removèd far,
And heateth kindly, shining laterally;
So beauty sweetly quickens when 'tis nigh,
But being separated and removed,
Burns where it cherished, murders where it loved.
Therefore even as an index to a book,
So to his mind was young Leander's look.
O, none but gods have power their love to hide!
Affection by the countenance is descried;
The light of hidden fire itself discovers,
And love that is concealed betrays poor lovers.
His secret flame apparently was seen:
Leander's father knew where he had been,
And for the same mildly rebuked his son,
Thinking to quench the sparkles new-begun.
But love resisted once, grows passionate,
And nothing more than counsel lovers hate;
For as a hot proud horse highly disdains
To have his head controlled, but breaks the reins,
Spits forth the ringled bit, and with his hooves
Checks the submissive ground; so he that loves,
The more he is restrained, the worse he fares:
What is it now but mad Leander dares?
'O Hero, Hero!' thus he cried full oft;
And then he got him to a rock aloft,
Where having spied her tower, long stared he on't,
And prayed the narrow toiling Hellespont
To part in twain, that he might come and go;
But still the rising billows answered, 'No.'
With that, he stripped him to the ivory skin,
And, crying, 'Love, I come,' leaped lively in:
Whereat the sapphire-visaged god grew proud,
And made his capering triton sound aloud,
Imagining that Ganymed, displeased,

31

Had left the heavens; therefore on him he seized.
Leander strived; the waves about him wound,
And pulled him to the bottom, where the ground
Was strewed with pearl, and in low coral groves
Sweet-singing mermaids sported with their loves
On heaps of heavy gold, and took great pleasure
To spurn in careless sort the shipwreck treasure;
For here the stately azure palace stood,
Where kingly Neptune and his train abode.
The lusty god embraced him, called him 'love',
And swore he never should return to Jove:
But when he knew it was not Ganymed,
For under water he was almost dead,
He heaved him up, and, looking on his face,
Beat down the bold waves with his triple mace,
Which mounted up, intending to have kissed him,
And fell in drops like tears because they missed him.
Leander, being up, began to swim,
And, looking back, saw Neptune follow him:
Whereat aghast, the poor soul gan to cry,
'O, let me visit Hero ere I die!'
The god put Helle's bracelet on his arm,
And swore the sea should never do him harm.
He clapped his plump cheeks, with his tresses played,
And, smiling wantonly, his love bewrayed;
He watched his arms, and, as they opened wide
At every stroke, betwixt them would he slide,
And steal a kiss, and then run out and dance,
And, as he turned, cast many a lustful glance –
And threw him gaudy toys to please his eye –
And dive into the water, and there pry
Upon his breast, his thighs, and every limb,
And up again, and close beside him swim,
And talk of love. Leander made reply,
'You are deceived; I am no woman, I.'
Thereat smiled Neptune, and then told a tale,
How that a shepherd, sitting in a vale,
Played with a boy so lovely-fair and kind,
As for his love both earth and heaven pined;
That of the cooling river durst not drink,
Lest water-nymphs should pull him from the brink;
And when he sported in the fragrant lawns,
Goat-footed Satyrs and up-staring Fauns
Would steal him thence. Ere half this tale was done,
'Ay me,' Leander cried, 'th'enamoured sun,
That now should shine on Thetis' glassy bower,
Descends upon my radiant Hero's tower:

O, that these tardy arms of mine were wings!'
And, as he spake, upon the waves he springs.
Neptune was angry that he gave no ear,
And in his heart revenging malice bare:
He flung at him his mace; but, as it went,
He called it in, for love made him repent:
The mace, returning back, his own hand hit,
As meaning to be venged for darting it.
When this fresh-bleeding wound Leander viewed,
His colour went and came, as if he rued
The grief which Neptune felt; in gentle breasts
Relenting thoughts, remorse, and pity rests;
And who have hard hearts and obdurate minds,
But vicious, hare-brained, and illiterate hinds?
The god, seeing him with pity to be moved,
Thereon concluded that he was beloved;
(Love is too full of faith, too credulous,
With folly and false hope deluding us;)
Wherefore, Leander's fancy to surprise,
To the rich ocean for gifts he flies;
'Tis wisdom to give much; a gift prevails
When deep-persuading oratory fails.
  By this, Leander, being near the land,
Cast down his weary feet, and felt the sand.
Breathless albeit he were, he rested not
Till to the solitary tower he got;
And knocked, and called: at which celestial noise
The longing heart of Hero much more joys,
Than nymphs and shepherds when the timbrel rings,
Or crooked dolphin when the sailor sings.
She stayed not for her robes, but straight arose,
And, drunk with gladness, to the door she goes;
Where seeing a naked man, she screeched for fear,
(Such sights as this to tender maids are rare)
And ran into the dark herself to hide.
Rich jewels in the dark are soonest spied.
Unto her was he led, or rather drawn
By those white limbs which sparkled through the lawn.
The nearer that he came, the more she fled,
And, seeking refuge, slipped into her bed;
Whereon Leander sitting, thus began,
Through numbing cold, all feeble, faint, and wan.
'If not for love, yet, love, for pity-sake,
Me in thy bed and maiden bosom take;
At least vouchsafe these arms some little room,
Who, hoping to embrace thee, cheerly swome:
This head was beat with many a churlish billow,

And therefore let it rest upon thy pillow.'
Herewith affrighted, Hero shrunk away,
And in her lukewarm place Leander lay;
Whose lively heat, like fire from heaven fet,

fetched

Would animate gross clay, and higher set
The drooping thoughts of base-declining souls,
Than dreary-Mars-carousing nectar bowls.
His hands he cast upon her like a snare:
She, overcome with shame and sallow fear,
Like chaste Diana when Actaeon spied her,
Being suddenly betrayed, dived down to hide her;
And, as her silver body downward went,
With both her hands she made the bed a tent,
And in her own mind thought herself secure,
O'ercast with dim and darksome coverture.
And now she lets him whisper in her ear,
Flatter, entreat, promise, protest, and swear:
Yet ever, as he greedily assayed
To touch those dainties, she the harpy played,
And every limb did, as a soldier stout,
Defend the fort, and keep the foeman out;
For though the rising ivory mount he scaled,
Which is with azure circling lines empaled,
Much like a globe (a globe may I term this,
By which Love sails to regions full of bliss)
Yet there with Sisyphus he toiled in vain,
Till gentle parley did the truce obtain.
Wherein Leander, on her quivering breast,
Breathless spoke something, and sighed out the rest;
Which so prevailed, as he, with small ado,
Enclosed her in his arms, and kissed her too:
And every kiss to her was as a charm,
And to Leander as a fresh alarm:
So that the truce was broke, and she, alas,
Poor silly maiden, at his mercy was.
Love is not full of pity, as men say,
But deaf and cruel where he means to prey.
Even as a bird, which in our hands we wring,
Forth plungeth, and oft flutters with her wing,
She trembling strove: this strife of hers, like that
Which made the world, another world begat
Of unknown joy. Treason was in her thought,
And cunningly to yield herself she sought.
Seeming not won, yet won she was at length:
In such wars women use but half their strength.
Leander now, like Theban Hercules,
Entered the orchard of th' Hesperides;

34

Whose fruit none rightly can describe, but he
That pulls or shakes it from the golden tree.
   And now she wished this night were never done,
And sighed to think upon th'approaching sun;
For much it grieved her that the bright day-light
Should know the pleasure of this blessed night,
And them, like Mars and Erycine, display
Both in each other's arms chained as they lay.
Again, she knew not how to frame her look,
Or speak to him, who in a moment took
That which so long, so charily she kept;
And fain by stealth away she would have crept,
And to some corner secretly have gone,
Leaving Leander in the bed alone.
But as her naked feet were whipping out,
He on the sudden slinged her so about,
That, mermaid-like, unto the floor she slid;
One half appeared, the other half was hid.
Thus near the bed she blushing stood upright,
And from her countenance behold ye might
A kind of twilight break, which through the hair,
As from an orient cloud, glimpsed here and there;
And round about the chamber this false morn
Brought forth the day before the day was born.
So Hero's ruddy cheek Hero betrayed,
And her all naked to his sight displayed:
Whence his admiring eyes more pleasure took
Than Dis, on heaps of gold fixing his look.
By this, Apollo's golden harp began
To sound forth music to the ocean;
Which watchful Hesperus no sooner heard,
But he the bright Day-bearing car prepared,
And ran before, as harbinger of light,
And with his flaring beams mocked ugly Night,
Till she, o'ercome with anguish, shame, and rage,
Danged down to hell her loathsome carriage.

JOHN MILTON

From *Paradise Lost*

[THE TEMPTATION OF EVE]

Pleasing was his shape,
And lovely, never since of serpent kind

Lovelier, not those that in Illyria changed
Hermione and Cadmus, or the god
In Epidaurus; nor to which transformed
Ammonian Jove, or Capitoline was seen,
He with Olympias, this with her who bore
Scipio the highth of Rome. With tract oblique
At first, as one who sought access, but feared
To interrupt, side-long he works his way.
As when a ship by skilful steersman wrought
Nigh river's mouth or foreland, where the wind
Veers oft, as oft so steers, and shifts her sail:
So varied he, and of his tortuous train
Curled many a wanton wreath in sight of Eve,
To lure her eye: she busied heard the sound
Of rustling leaves, but minded not, as used
To such disport before her through the field,
From every beast, more duteous at her call,
Than at Circean call the herd disguised.
He bolder now, uncalled before her stood:
But as in gaze admiring; oft he bowed
His turret crest, and sleek enamelled neck,
Fawning, and licked the ground whereon she trod.
His gentle dumb expression turned at length
The eye of Eve to mark his play: he glad
Of her attention gained, with serpent tongue
Organic, or impulse of vocal air,
His fraudulent temptation thus began.
    'Wonder not, sovereign mistress, if perhaps
Thou canst, who art sole wonder, much less arm
Thy looks, the Heaven of mildness, with disdain,
Displeased that I approach thee thus, and gaze
Insatiate, I thus single, nor have feared
Thy awful brow, more awful thus retired.
Fairest resemblance of thy Maker fair,
Thee all things living gaze on, all things thine
By gift, and thy celestial beauty adore
With ravishment beheld, there best beheld
Where universally admired: but here
In this enclosure wild, these beasts among,
Beholders rude, and shallow to discern
Half what in thee is fair, one man except,
Who sees thee? (and what is one?) who shouldst be seen
By angels numberless, thy daily train.'
    So glozed the tempter, and his proem tuned;
Into the heart of Eve his words made way,
Though at the voice much marvelling: at length
Not unamazed she thus in answer spake.

'What may this mean? Language of man pronounced
By tongue of brute, and human sense expressed?
The first at least of these I thought denied
To beasts, whom God on their creation day
Created mute to all articulate sound;
The latter I demur, for in their looks
Much reason, and in their actions oft appears.
Thee, serpent, subtlest beast of all the field
I knew, but not with human voice endued:
Redouble then this miracle, and say,
How cam'st thou speakable of mute, and how
To me so friendly grown above the rest
Of brutal kind, that daily are in sight?
Say, for such wonder claims attention due.'
     To whom the guileful Tempter thus replied.
'Empress of this fair world, resplendent Eve,
Easy to me it is to tell thee all
What thou commandst and right thou shouldst be obeyed:
I was at first as other beasts that graze
The trodden herb, of abject thoughts and low,
As was my food, nor aught but food discerned
Or sex, and apprehended nothing high:
Till on a day roving the field, I chanced
A goodly tree far distant to behold
Loaden with fruit of fairest colours mixed,
Ruddy and gold; I nearer drew to gaze:
When from the boughs a savoury odour blown,
Grateful to appetite, more pleased my sense
Than smell of sweetest fennel, or the teats
Of ewe or goat dropping with milk at even,
Unsucked of lamb or kid, that tend their play.
To satisfy the sharp desire I had
Of tasting those fair apples, I resolved
Not to defer: hunger and thirst at once,
Powerful persuaders, quickened at the scent
Of that alluring fruit, urged me so keen.
˙About the mossy trunk I wound me soon,
For high from ground the branches would require
Thy utmost reach, or Adam's: round the tree
All other beasts that saw, with like desire
Longing and envying stood, but could not reach.
Amid the tree now got, where plenty hung
Tempting so nigh, to pluck and eat my fill
I spared not, for such pleasure till that hour
At feed or fountain never had I found.
Sated at length, ere long I might perceive
Strange alteration in me, to degree

Of reason in my inward powers, and speech
Wanted not long, though to this shape retained.
Thenceforth to speculations high or deep
I turned my thoughts, and with capacious mind
Considered all things visible in Heaven,
Or earth, or middle, all things fair and good:
But all that fair and good in thy divine
Semblance, and in thy beauty's heavenly ray
United I beheld: no fair to thine
Equivalent or second, which compelled
Me thus, though importune perhaps, to come
And gaze, and worship thee of right declared
Sovereign of creatures, universal dame.'
    So talked the spirited sly snake: and Eve
Yet more amazed unwary thus replied.
    'Serpent, thy overpraising leaves in doubt
The virtue of that fruit, in thee first proved:
But say, where grows the tree, from hence how far?
For many are the trees of God that grow
In Paradise, and various, yet unknown
To us, in such abundance lies our choice,
As leaves a greater store of fruit untouched,
Still hanging incorruptible, till men
Grow up to their provision, and more hands
Help to disburden nature of her bearth.'
    To whom the wily adder, blithe and glad.
'Empress, the way is ready, and not long,
Beyond a row of myrtles, on a flat,
Fast by a fountain, one small thicket past
Of blowing myrrh and balm: if thou accept
My conduct, I can bring thee thither soon.'
    'Lead then,' said Eve. He leading swiftly rolled
In tangles, and made intricate seem straight,
To mischief swift. Hope elevates, and joy
Brightens his crest, as when a wandering fire
Compact of unctuous vapour, which the night
Condenses, and the cold environs round,
Kindled through agitation to a flame,
Which oft, they say, some evil spirit attends,
Hovering and blazing with delusive light,
Misleads th'amazed night-wanderer from his way
To bogs and mires, and oft through pond or pool,
There swallowed up and lost, from succour far.
So glistered the dire snake, and into fraud
Led Eve our credulous mother, to the tree
Of prohibition, root of all our woe:
Which when she saw, thus to her guide she spake.

'Serpent, we might have spared our coming hither,
Fruitless to me, though fruit be here to excess,
The credit of whose virtue rests with thee,
Wondrous indeed, if cause of such effects.
But of this tree we may not taste nor touch:
God so commanded, and left that command
Sole daughter of his voice; the rest, we live
Law to ourselves, our reason is our law.'
  To whom the tempter guilefully replied.
'Indeed? Hath God then said that of the fruit
Of all these garden trees ye shall not eat,
Yet lords declared of all in earth or air?'
  To whom thus Eve yet sinless. 'Of the fruit
Of each tree in the garden we may eat,
But of the fruit of this fair tree amidst
The garden, God hath said, "Ye shall not eat
Thereof, nor shall ye touch it, lest ye die." '
  She scarce had said, though brief, when now more bold,
The tempter, but with show of zeal and love
To man, and indignation at his wrong,
New part puts on, and as to passion moved,
Fluctuates disturbed, yet comely, and in act
Raised, as of some greater matter to begin.
As when of old some orator renowned
In Athens or free Rome, where eloquence
Flourished, since mute, to some great cause addressed,
Stood in himself collected, while each part,
Motion, each act won audience ere the tongue,
Sometimes in highth began, as no delay
Of preface brooking, through his zeal of right.
So standing, moving, or to highth upgrown
The tempter all impassioned thus began.
  'O sacred, wise and wisdom-giving plant,
Mother of science, now I feel thy power
Within me clear, not only to discern
Things in their causes, but to trace the ways
Of highest agents, deemed however wise.
Queen of this universe, do not believe
Those rigid threats of death: ye shall not die;
How should ye? By the fruit? it gives you life
To knowledge: by the threatner? look on me,
Me who have touched and tasted, yet both live,
And life more perfect have attained than fate
Meant me, by venturing higher than my lot.
Shall that be shut to man, which to the beast
Is open? Or will God incense his ire
For such a petty trespass, and not praise

39

Rather your dauntless virtue, whom the pain
Of death denounced, whatever thing death be,
Deterred not from achieving what might lead
To happier life, knowledge of good and evil;
Of good, how just? Of evil, if what is evil
Be real, why not known, since easier shunned?
God therefore cannot hurt ye, and be just;
Not just, not God; not feared then, nor obeyed:
Your fear itself of death removes the fear.
Why then was this forbid? Why but to awe,
Why but to keep ye low and ignorant,
His worshippers: he knows that in the day
Ye eat thereof, your eyes shall seem so clear,
Yet are but dim, shall perfectly be then
Opened and cleared, and ye shall be as gods,
Knowing both good and evil, as they know.
That ye should be as gods, since I as man,
Internal man, is but proportion meet,
I of brute human, ye of human gods.
So shall ye die perhaps, by putting off
Human, to put on gods: death to be wished,
Though threatened, which no worse than this can bring.
And what are gods that man may not become
As they, participating godlike food?
The gods are first, and that advantage use
On our belief, that all from them proceeds;
I question it, for this fair earth I see,
Warmed by the sun, producing every kind,
Them nothing. if they all things, who enclosed
Knowledge of good and evil in this tree,
That whoso eats thereof forthwith attains
Wisdom without their leave? And wherein lies
Th'offence, that man should thus attain to know?
What can your knowledge hurt him, or this tree
Impart against his will if all be his?
Or is it envy, and can envy dwell
In heavenly breasts? These, these, and many more
Causes import your need of this fair fruit.
Goddess humane, reach then, and freely taste.'
    He ended, and his words replete with guile
Into her heart too easy entrance won:
Fixed on the fruit she gazed, which to behold
Might tempt alone, and in her ears the sound
Yet rung of his persuasive words, impregned
With reason, to her seeming, and with truth;
Meanwhile the hour of noon drew on, and waked
An eager appetite, raised by the smell

So savoury of that fruit, which with desire,
Inclinable now grown to touch or taste,
Solicited her longing eye; yet first
Pausing awhile, thus to herself she mused.
  'Great are thy virtues, doubtless, best of fruits,
Though kept from man, and worthy to be admired,
Whose taste, too long forborn, at first assay
Gave elocution to the mute, and taught
The tongue not made for speech to speak thy praise:
Thy praise he also who forbids thy use,
Conceals not from us, naming thee the Tree
Of Knowledge, knowledge both of good and evil;
Forbids us then to taste, but his forbidding
Commends thee more, while it infers the good
By thee communicated, and our want:
For good unknown, sure is not had, or had
And yet unknown, is as not had at all.
In plain then, what forbids he but to know,
Forbids us good, forbids us to be wise?
Such prohibitions bind not. But if death
Binds us with after-bands, what profits then
Our inward freedom? In the day we eat
Of this fair fruit, our doom is, we shall die.
How dies the serpent? He hath eaten and lives,
And knows, and speaks, and reasons, and discerns,
Irrational till then. For us alone
Was death invented? Or to us denied
This intellectual food, for beasts reserved?
For beasts it seems: yet that one beast which first
Hath tasted, envies not, but brings with joy
The good befallen him, author unsuspect,
Friendly to man, far from deceit or guile.
What fear I then, rather what know to fear
Under this ignorance of good and evil,
Of God or death, of law or penalty?
Here grows the cure of all, this fruit divine,
Fair to the eye, inviting to the taste,
Of virtue to make wise: what hinders then
To reach, and feed at once both body and mind?'
  So saying, her rash hand in evil hour,
Forth reaching to the fruit, she plucked, she eat:
Earth felt the wound, and Nature from her seat
Sighing through all her works gave signs of woe,
That all was lost. Back to the thicket slunk
The guilty serpent, and well might, for Eve
Intent now wholly on her taste, naught else
Regarded, such delight till then, as seemed,

In fruit she never tasted, whether true
Or fancied so, through expectation high
Of knowledge, nor was godhead from her thought.
Greedily she ingorged without restraint,
And knew not eating death.

SIR JOHN SUCKLING

A Ballad upon a Wedding

I tell thee Dick where I have been,
Where I the rarest things have seen;
   O things without compare!
Such sights again cannot be found
In any place on English ground,
   Be it at wake, or fair.

At Charing-Cross, hard by the way
Where we (thou know'st) do sell our hay,
   There is a house with stairs;
And there did I see coming down
Such folk as are not in our town,
   Vorty, at least, in pairs.

Amongst the rest, one pest'lent fine,
(His beard no bigger though than thine)
   Walked on before the rest:
Our landlord looks like nothing to him:
The King (God bless him), 'twould undo him,
   Should he go still so drest.

At Course-a-Park, without all doubt,
He should have just been taken out
   By all the maids i' th' town;
Though lusty Roger there had been,
Or little George upon the Green,
   Or Vincent of the Crown.

But wot you what? the youth was going
To make an end of all his wooing;
   The parson for him staid;
Yet by his leave (for all his haste)
He did not so much wish all past,
   (Perchance) as did the maid.

The maid (and thereby hangs a tale)
For such a maid no Whitsun-ale
   Could ever yet produce:
No grape that's kindly ripe, could be
So round, so plump, so soft as she,
   Nor half so full of juice.

Her finger was so small, the ring
Would not stay on, which they did bring,
   It was too wide a peck;
And to say truth (for out it must)
It looked like a great collar (just)
   About our young colt's neck.

Her feet beneath her petticoat,
Like little mice stole in and out,
   As if they feared the light:
But oh! she dances such a way
No sun upon an Easter day
   Is half so fine a sight.

He would have kissed her once or twice,
But she would not, she was so nice,
   She would not do't in sight,
And then she looked as who should say
I will do what I list today;
   And you shall do't at night.

Her cheeks so rare a white was on,
No dazy makes comparison,
   (Who sees them is undone)
For streaks of red were mingled there,
Such as are on a Katherine pear,
   (The side that's next the sun).

Her lips were red, and one was thin,
Compared to that was next her chin;
   (Some bee had stung it newly).
But (Dick) her eyes so guard her face;
I durst no more upon them gaze,
   Than on the sun in July.

Her mouth so small when she does speak,
Thou'dst swear her teeth her words did break,
   That they might passage get,
But she so handled still the matter,
They came as good as ours, or better,
   And are not spent a whit.

If wishing should be any sin,
The parson himself had guilty bin;
   (She looked that day so purely)
And did the youth so oft the feat
At night, as some did in conceit,
   It would have spoiled him, surely.

Just in the nick the cook knocked thrice,
And all the waiters in a trice
   His summons did obey,
Each serving man with dish in hand,
Marched boldly up, like our Trained Band,
   Presented, and away.

When all the meat was on the table,
What man of knife, or teeth, was able
   To stay to be intreated?
And this the very reason was,
Before the parson could say Grace,
   The company was seated.

The bus'ness of the kitchin's great,
For it is fit that men should eat;
   Nor was it there denied:
Passion o' me! How I run on!
There's that that would be thought upon,
   (I trow) besides the bride.

Now hats fly off, and youths carouse;
Healths first go round, and then the house,
   The bride's came thick and thick;
And when 'twas named another's health,
Perhaps he made it hers by stealth.
   (And who could help it, Dick?)

O' th' sudden up they rise and dance;
Then sit again and sigh, and glance:
   Then dance again and kiss:
Thus sev'ral ways the time did pass,
Till ev'ry woman wished her place,
   And ev'ry man wished his.

By this time all were stol'n aside
To counsel and undress the bride;
   But that he must not know:

But yet 'twas thought he guessed her mind,
And did not mean to stay behind
   Above an hour or so.

When in he came (Dick) there she lay
Like new-fall'n snow melting away
   ('Twas time I trow to part).
Kisses were now the only stay,
Which soon she gave, as who would say,
   'Good boy! with all my heart.'

But just as heav'ns would have to cross it,
In came the bridesmaids with the posset:
   The bridegroom eat in spight;
For had he left the women to't
It would have cost two hours to do't
   Which were too much that night.

At length the candles out and out,
All that they had not done, they do't;
   What that is, who can tell?
But I believe it was no more
Than thou and I have done before
   With Bridget, and with Nell.

JOHN DRYDEN

Theodore and Honoria

Of all the cities in Romanian lands,
The chief and most renowned Ravenna stands;
Adorned in ancient times with arms and arts,
And rich inhabitants with generous hearts.
But Theodore the brave, above the rest
With gifts of fortune and of nature blessed,
The foremost place for wealth and honour held,
And all in feats of chivalry excelled.
  This noble youth to madness loved a dame
Of high degree, Honoria was her name.
Fair as the fairest but of haughty mind,
And fiercer than became so soft a kind;
Proud of her birth (for equal she had none);
The rest she scorned, but hated him alone.
His gifts, his constant courtship, nothing gained;

45

For she, the more he loved, the more disdained.
He lived with all the pomp he could devise,
At tilts and tournaments obtained the prize,
But found no favour in his lady's eyes.
Relentless as a rock, the lofty maid
Turned all to poison that he did or said.
Nor pray'rs nor tears nor offered vows could move;
The work went backward; and the more he strove
T' advance his suit, the farther from her love.
    Wearied at length, and wanting remedy,
He doubted oft and oft resolved to die.
But pride stood ready to prevent the blow,
For who would die to gratify a foe?
His generous mind disdained so mean a fate;
That passed, his next endeavour was to hate.
But vainer that relief than all the rest,
The less he hoped, with more desire possessed;
Love stood the siege and would not yield his breast.
Change was the next, but change deceived his care,
He sought a fairer but found none so fair.
He would have worn her out by slow degrees,
As men by fasting starve th' untamed disease;
But present love required a present ease.
Looking, he feeds alone his famished eyes,
Feeds ling'ring death, but, looking not, he dies.
Yet still he chose the longest way to fate,
Wasting at once his life, and his estate.
His friends beheld and pitied him in vain,
For what advice can ease a lover's pain!
Absence, the best expedient they could find,
Might save the fortune if not cure the mind:
This means they long proposed but little gained,
Yet after much pursuit at length obtained.
Hard, you may think it was, to give consent,
But struggling with his own desires he went:
With large expense, and with a pompous train
Provided, as to visit France or Spain,
Or for some distant voyage o'er the main.
But love had clipped his wings and cut him short,
Confined within the purlieus of his court.
Three miles he went, nor farther could retreat;
His travels ended at his country-seat.
To Chassis' pleasing plains he took his way,
There pitched his tents and there resolved to stay.
    The Spring was in the prime; the neighb'ring grove
Supplied with birds, the choristers of love;
Music unbought, that ministered delight

To morning-walks, and lulled his cares by night.
There he discharged his friends, but not th' expense
Of frequent treats and proud magnificence.
He lived as kings retire, though more at large,
From public business, yet with equal charge;
With house and heart still open to receive;
As well content as love would give him leave.
He would have lived more free, but many a guest,
Who could forsake the friend, pursued the feast.
   It happed one morning, as his fancy led,
Before his usual hour he left his bed
To walk within a lonely lawn, that stood
On ev'ry side surrounded by the wood.
Alone he walked to please his pensive mind,
And sought the deepest solitude to find.
'Twas in a grove of spreading pines he strayed;
The winds within the quiv'ring branches played,
And dancing-trees a mournful music made.
The place itself was suiting to his care,
Uncouth and savage as the cruel fair.
He wandered on unknowing where he went,
Lost in the wood and all on love intent.
The day already half his race had run,
And summoned him to due repast at noon,
But love could feel no hunger but his own.
While list'ning to the murm'ring leaves he stood,
More than a mile immersed within the wood,
At once the wind was laid; the whisp'ring sound
Was dumb; a rising earthquake rocked the ground;
With deeper brown the grove was overspread;
A sudden horror seized his giddy head,
And his ears tinkled, and his colour fled.
Nature was in alarm; some danger nigh
Seemed threatened, though unseen to mortal eye.
Unused to fear, he summoned all his soul
And stood collected in himself and whole;
Not long: for soon a whirlwind rose around,
And from afar he heard a screaming sound
As of a dame distressed, who cried for aid
And filled with loud laments the secret shade.
A thicket close beside the grove there stood
With briars and brambles choked, and dwarfish
   wood;
From thence the noise, which now approaching near
With more distinguished notes invades his ear.
He raised his head and saw a beauteous maid,
With hair dishevelled, issuing through the shade;

Stripped of her clothes, and e'en those parts revealed
Which modest nature keeps from sight concealed.
Her face, her hands, her naked limbs were torn
With passing through the brakes and prickly thorn;
Two mastiffs, gaunt and grim, her flight pursued
And oft their fastened fangs in blood imbrued;
Oft they came up and pinched her tender side,
'Mercy, O mercy, heav'n,' she ran and cried;
When heav'n was named they loosed their hold again;
Then sprung she forth, they followed her amain.
Not far behind, a knight of swarthy face,
High on a coal-black steed pursued the chase;
With flashing flames his ardent eyes were filled,
And in his hands a naked sword he held.
He cheered the dogs to follow her who fled,
And vowed revenge on her devoted head.
    As Theodore was born of noble kind,
The brutal action roused his manly mind.
Moved with unworthy usage of the maid,
He, though unarmed, resolved to give her aid.
A sapling pine he wrenched from out the ground,
The readiest weapon that his fury found.
Thus furnished for offence, he crossed the way
Betwixt the graceless villain and his prey.
The knight came thund'ring on, but from afar
Thus in imperious tone forbade the war:
'Cease, Theodore, to proffer vain relief,
Nor stop the vengeance of so just a grief;
But give me leave to seize my destined prey,
And let eternal justice take the way.
I but revenge my fate; disdained, betrayed,
And suff'ring death for this ungrateful maid.'
He said, at once dismounting from the steed;
For now the hell-hounds with superior speed
Had reached the dame, and fast'ning on her side,
The ground with issuing streams of purple dyed.
Stood Theodore surprised in deadly fright,
With chatt'ring teeth and bristling hair upright;
Yet armed with inborn worth, 'Whate'er,' said he,
'Thou art, who know'st me better than I thee;
Or prove thy rightful cause, or be defied.'
The spectre, fiercely staring, thus replied:
'Know, Theodore, thy ancestry I claim,
And Guido Cavalcanti was my name.
One common sire our fathers did beget,
My name and story some remember yet.
Thee, then a boy, within my arms I laid,

48

When for my sins I loved this haughty maid;
Not less adored in life, nor served by me,
Than proud Honoria now is loved by thee.
What did I not her stubborn heart to gain?
But all my vows were answered with disdain;
She scorned my sorrows and despised my pain.
Long time I dragged my days in fruitless care;
Then loathing life, and plunged in deep despair,
To finish my unhappy life, I fell
On this sharp sword, and now am damned in hell.
Short was her joy; for soon th' insulting maid
By heav'n's decree in the cold grave was laid,
And as in unrepenting sin she died,
Doomed to the same bad place, is punished for her
    pride;
Because she deemed I well deserved to die,
And made a merit of her cruelty.
There, then, we met; both tried and both were cast,
And this irrevocable sentence passed;
That she whom I so long pursued in vain,
Should suffer from my hands a ling'ring pain.
Renewed to life that she might daily die,
I daily doomed to follow, she to fly;
No more a lover but a mortal foe,
I seek her life (for love is none below).
As often as my dogs with better speed
Arrest her flight, is she to death decreed;
Then with this fatal sword on which I died,
I pierce her opened back or tender side,
And tear that hardened heart from out her breast,
Which, with her entrails, makes my hungry hounds a feast.
Nor lies she long but, as her fates ordain,
Springs up to life and, fresh to second pain,
Is saved today, tomorrow to be slain.'
This, versed in death, th' infernal knight relates,
And then for proof fulfilled their common fates;
Her heart and bowels through her back he drew,
And fed the hounds that helped him to pursue.
Stern looked the fiend, as frustrate of his will,
Not half sufficed and greedy yet to kill.
And now the soul expiring through the wound,
Had left the body breathless on the ground,
When thus the grisly spectre spoke again:
'Behold the fruit of ill-rewarded pain.
As many months as I sustained her hate,
So many years is she condemned by fate
To daily death; and ev'ry several place

Conscious of her disdain and my disgrace
Must witness her just punishment; and be
A scene of triumph and revenge to me.
As in this grove I took my last farewell,
As on this very spot of earth I fell,
As Friday saw me die, so she my prey
Becomes ev'n here on this revolving day.'
Thus while he spoke, the virgin from the ground
Upstarted fresh, already closed the wound,
And unconcerned for all she felt before
Precipitates her flight along the shore.
The hell-hounds, as ungorged with flesh and blood,
Pursue their prey and seek their wonted food;
The fiend remounts his courser, mends his pace,
And all the vision vanished from the place.
    Long stood the noble youth oppressed with awe,
And stupid at the wond'rous things he saw
Surpassing common faith, transgressing nature's law.
He would have been asleep and wished to wake,
But dreams, he knew, no long impression make,
Though strong at first. If vision, to what end,
But such as must his future state portend?
His love the damsel, and himself the fiend.
But yet reflecting that it could not be
From heav'n, which cannot impious acts decree,
Resolved within himself to shun the snare
Which hell for his destruction did prepare;
And as his better genius should direct
From an ill cause to draw a good effect.
Inspired from heav'n he homeward took his way,
Nor palled his new design with long delay;
But of his train a trusty servant sent
To call his friends together at his tent.
They came, and usual salutations paid,
With words premeditated thus he said:
'What you have often counselled, to remove
My vain pursuit of unregarded love;
By thrift my sinking fortune to repair,
Though late, yet is at last become my care.
My heart shall be my own; my vast expense
Reduced to bounds by timely providence.
This only I require; invite for me
Honoria, with her father's family,
Her friends and mine; the cause I shall display,
On Friday next, for that's th' appointed day.'
    Well pleased were all his friends, the task was light;
The father, mother, daughter they invite;

Hardly the dame was drawn to this repast,
But yet resolved, because it was the last.
The day was come; the guests invited came,
And, with the rest, th' inexorable dame.
A feast prepared with riotous expense,
Much cost, more care, and most magnificence.
The place ordained was in that haunted grove
Where the revenging ghost pursued his love.
The tables in a proud pavilion spread,
With flow'rs below, and tissue overhead.
The rest in rank; Honoria chief in place,
Was artfully contrived to set her face
To front the thicket and behold the chase.
The feast was served; the time so well forecast
That just when the dessert and fruits were placed
The fiend's alarm began; the hollow sound
Sung in the leaves, the forest shook around;
Air blackened; rolled the thunder; groaned the ground.
Nor long before the loud laments arise
Of one distressed, and mastiffs' mingled cries;
And first the dame came rushing through the wood,
And next the famished hounds that sought their food
And griped her flanks and oft essayed their jaws in blood.
Last came the felon on the sable steed,
Armed with his naked sword, and urged his dogs to speed.
She ran and cried; her flight directly bent
(A guest unbidden) to the fatal tent,
The scene of death and place ordained for punishment.
Loud was the noise, aghast was every guest,
The women shrieked, the men forsook the feast;
The hounds at nearer distance hoarsely bayed;
The hunter close pursued the visionary maid;
She rent the heav'n with loud laments, imploring aid.
The gallants, to protect the lady's right,
Their falchions brandished at the grisly sprite;
High on his stirrups, he provoked the fight.
Then on the crowd he cast a furious look,
And withered all their strength before he strook.
'Back on your lives; let be,' said he, 'my prey,
And let my vengeance take the destined way.
Vain are your arms, and vainer your defence,
Against th' eternal doom of providence.
Mine is th' ungrateful maid by heav'n designed:
Mercy she would not give, nor mercy shall she find.'
At this the former tale again he told
With thund'ring tone, and dreadful to behold.
Sunk were their hearts with horror of the crime,

Nor needed to be warned a second time,
But bore each other back; some knew the face,
And all had heard the much lamented case
Of him who fell for love, and this the fatal place.
And now th' infernal minister advanced,
Seized the due victim, and with fury lanced
Her back, and piercing through her inmost heart
Drew backward, as before, th' offending part.
The reeking entrails next he tore away,
And to his meagre mastiffs made a prey.
The pale assistants on each other stared
With gaping mouths for issuing words prepared;
The still-born sounds upon the palate hung,
And died imperfect on the falt'ring tongue.
The fright was general; but the female band
(A helpless train) in more confusion stand;
With horror shudd'ring, on a heap they run,
Sick at the sight of hateful justice done;
For conscience rung th' alarm, and made the case their own.
So spread upon a lake with upward eye
A plump of fowl behold their foe on high;
They close their trembling troop, and all attend
On whom the sowsing eagle will descend.
But most the proud Honoria feared th' event,
And thought to her alone the vision sent.
Her guilt presents to her distracted mind
Heav'n's justice, Theodore's revengeful kind,
And the same fate to the same sin assigned;
Already sees herself the monster's prey,
And feels her heart and entrails torn away.
'Twas a mute scene of sorrow, mixed with fear.
Still on the table lay th' unfinished cheer,
The knight and hungry mastiffs stood around,
The mangled dame lay breathless on the ground;
When on a sudden reinspired with breath,
Again she rose, again to suffer death;
Nor stayed the hell-hounds, nor the hunter stayed,
But followed as before the flying maid.
Th' avenger took from earth th' avenging sword
And, mounting light as air, his sable steed he spurred.
The clouds dispelled, the sky resumed her light,
And nature stood recovered of her fright.
   But fear, the last of ills, remained behind,
And horror heavy sat on ev'ry mind.
Nor Theodore encouraged more his feast,
But sternly looked, as hatching in his breast
Some deep design, which when Honoria viewed,

The fresh impulse her former fright renewed.
She thought herself the trembling dame who fled,
And him the grisly ghost that spurred th' infernal steed;
The more dismayed, for when the guests withdrew,
Their courteous host, saluting all the crew,
Regardless passed her o'er, nor graced with kind adieu.
That sting enfixed within her haughty mind,
The downfall of her empire she divined;
And her proud heart with secret sorrow pined.
Home as they went, the sad discourse renewed
Of the relentless dame to death pursued,
And of the sight obscene so lately viewed.
None durst arraign the righteous doom she bore,
Ev'n they who pitied most yet blamed her more.
The parallel they needed not to name,
But in the dead they damned the living dame.
At ev'ry little noise she looked behind,
For still the knight was present to her mind;
And anxious oft she started on the way
And thought the horseman-ghost came thund'ring for his prey.
Returned, she took her bed with little rest,
But in short slumbers dreamt the funeral feast;
Awaked, she turned her side, and slept again,
The same black vapours mounted in her brain,
And the same dreams returned with double pain.
Now forced to wake because afraid to sleep,
Her blood all fevered, with a furious leap
She sprung from bed, distracted in her mind,
And feared at every step a twitching sprite behind.
Darkling and desp'rate with a stagg'ring pace,
Of death afraid and conscious of disgrace;
Fear, pride, remorse, at once her heart assailed,
Pride put remorse to flight but fear prevailed.
Friday, the fatal day, when next it came,
Her soul forethought the fiend would change his game,
And her pursue; or Theodore be slain,
And two ghosts join their packs to hunt her o'er the plain.
This dreadful image so possessed her mind,
That desp'rate any succour else to find,
She ceased all farther hope; and now began
To make reflection on th' unhappy man.
Rich, brave, and young, who past expression loved,
Proof to disdain, and not to be removed.
Of all the men respected and admired,
Of all the dames, except herself, desired.
Why not of her? preferred above the rest
By him with knightly deeds and open love professed?

So had another been, where he his vows addressed.
This quelled her pride, yet other doubts remained,
That once disdaining she might be disdained.
The fear was just, but greater fear prevailed;
Fear of her life by hellish hounds assailed.
He took a low'ring leave; but who can tell
What outward hate might inward love conceal?
Her sex's arts she knew, and why not then
Might deep dissembling have a place in men?
Here hope began to dawn; resolved to try,
She fixed on this her utmost remedy;
Death was behind but hard it was to die.
'Twas time enough at last on death to call,
The precipice in sight; a shrub was all
That kindly stood betwixt to break the fatal fall.
One maid she had, beloved above the rest;
Secure of her, the secret she confessed;
And now the cheerful light her fears dispelled.
She with no winding turns the truth concealed
But put the woman off and stood revealed;
With faults confessed, commissioned her to go,
If pity yet had place, and reconcile her foe.
The welcome message made, was soon received;
'Twas what he wished and hoped but scarce believed;
Fate seemed a fair occasion to present,
He knew the sex, and feared she might repent
Should he delay the moment of consent.
There yet remained to gain her friends (a care
The modesty of maidens well might spare),
But she with such a zeal the cause embraced
(As women where they will are all in haste),
That father, mother, and the kin beside,
Were overborne by fury of the tide.
With full consent of all, she changed her state,
Resistless in her love as in her hate.
   By her example warned, the rest beware;
More easy, less imperious, were the fair;
And that one hunting which the devil designed
For one fair female, lost him half the kind.

JONATHAN SWIFT

Phillis or The Progress of Love

Desponding Phillis was endued
With ev'ry talent of a prude:
She trembled when a man drew near;
Salute her, and she turned her ear;
If o'er against her you were placed,
She durst not look above your waist;
She'd rather take you to her bed
Than let you see her dress her head;
In church you heard her thro' the crowd
Repeat the Absolution loud;
In church, secure behind her fan
She durst behold that monster, Man:
There practised how to place her head,
And bit her lips to make them red:
Or on the mat devoutly kneeling
Would lift her eyes up to the ceiling,
And heave her bosom unaware
For neighb'ring beaux to see it bare.
   At length a lucky lover came,
And found admittance to the dame.
Suppose all parties now agreed,
The writings drawn, the lawyer fee'd,
The vicar and the ring bespoke:
Guess, how could such a match be broke?
See then what mortals place their bliss in!
Next morn betimes the bride was missin',
The mother screamed, the father chid,
Where can this idle wench be hid?
No news of Phil. The bridegroom came,
And thought his bride had skulked for shame,
Because her father used to say
The girl had such a bashful way.
   Now, John the butler must be sent
To learn the road that Phillis went;·
The groom was wished to saddle Crop;
For John must neither light nor stop,
But find her whereso'er she fled,
And bring her back, alive or dead.
See here again the Dev'l to do;
For truly John was missing too:
The horse and pillion both were gone!
Phillis, it seems, was fled with John.
Old Madam who went up to find

What papers Phil had left behind,
A letter on the toilet sees,
'To my much honoured father, these':
('Tis always done, romances tell us,
When daughters run away with fellows)
Filled with the choicest commonplaces,
By others used in the like cases.
That, long ago a fortune-teller
Exactly said what now befell her,
And in a glass had made her see
A serving-man of low degree:
It was her fate; must be forgiven;
For marriages are made in Heaven:
His pardon begged, but to be plain,
She'd do't if'twere to do again.
Thank God, 'twas neither shame nor sin,
For John was come of honest kin:
Love never thinks of rich and poor,
She'd beg with John from door to door:
Forgive her, if it be a crime,
She'll never do't another time,
She ne'er before in all her life
Once disobeyed him, maid nor wife.
One argument she summed up all in,
The thing was done and past recallin':
And therefore hoped she should recover
His favour, when his passion's over.
She valued not what others thought her;
And was – His most obedient daughter.
    Fair maidens all attend the Muse
Who now the wand'ring pair pursues:
Away their rode in homely sort
They journey long, their money short;
The loving couple well bemired,
The horse and both the riders tired:
Their victuals bad, their lodging worse,
Phil cried, and John began to curse;
Phil wished that she had strained a limb
When first she ventured out with him:
John wished, that he had broke a leg
When first for her he quitted Peg.
    But what adventures more befell 'em
The Muse has now not time to tell 'em.
How Johnny wheedled, threatened, fawned,
Till Phillis all her trinkets pawned:
How oft she broke her marriage vows
In kindness to maintain her spouse,

Till swains unwholesome spoiled the trade,
For now the surgeon must be paid;
To whom those perquisites are gone
In Christian justice due to John.
    When food and raiment now grew scarce
Fate put a period to the farce;
And with exact poetic justice:
For John is landlord, Phillis hostess;
They keep at Staines the old Blue Boar,
Are cat and dog, and rogue and whore.

ALEXANDER POPE

The Rape of the Lock

CANTO I

What dire offence from am'rous causes springs,
What mighty contests rise from trivial things,
I sing – This verse to Caryl, Muse! is due:
This, ev'n Belinda may vouchsafe to view:
Slight is the subject, but not so the praise,
If she inspire, and he approve my lays.
    Say what strange motive, Goddess! could compel
A well-bred lord t' assault a gentle belle?
O say what stranger cause, yet unexplor'd,
Could make a gentle belle reject a lord?
In tasks so bold, can little men engage,
And in soft bosoms, dwells such mighty rage?
    Sol through white curtains shot a tim'rous ray,
And ope'd those eyes that must eclipse the day:
Now lap-dogs give themselves the rousing shake,
And sleepless lovers, just at twelve, awake:
Thrice rung the bell, the slipper knocked the ground,
And the press'd watch return'd a silver sound.
Belinda still her downy pillow pressed,
Her guardian sylph prolonged the balmy rest . . .
    . . .

CANTO II

Not with more glories, in th' ethereal plain,
The sun first rises o'er the purpled main,
Than, issuing forth, the rival of his beams

Launched on the bosom of the silver Thames.
Fair nymphs, and well-dressed youths around her shone,
But ev'ry eye was fixed on her alone.
On her white breast a sparkling cross she wore,
Which Jews might kiss, and infidels adore.
Her lively looks a sprightly mind disclose,
Quick as her eyes, and as unfixed as those:
Favours to none, to all she smiles extends;
Oft she rejects, but never once offends.
Bright as the sun, her eyes the gazers strike,
And, like the sun, they shine on all alike.
Yet graceful ease, and sweetness void of pride,
Might hide her faults, if belles had faults to hide:
If to her share some female errors fall,
Look on her face, and you'll forget 'em all.
   This nymph, to the destruction of mankind,
Nourished two locks, which graceful hung behind
In equal curls, and well conspired to deck
With shining ringlets the smooth iv'ry neck.
Love in these labyrinths his slaves detains,
And mighty hearts are held in slender chains.
With hairy springes we the birds betray,
Slight lines of hair surprise the finny prey,
Fair tresses man's imperial race ensnare,
And beauty draws us with a single hair.
   Th' advent'rous Baron the bright locks admired;
He saw, he wished, and to the prize aspired.
Resolved to win, he meditates the way,
By force to ravish, or by fraud betray;
For when success a lover's toil attends,
Few ask, if fraud or force attained his ends.
   For this, ere Phoebus rose, he had implored
Propitious Heav'n, and ev'ry pow'r adored,
But chiefly Love – to Love an altar built,
Of twelve vast French romances, neatly gilt.
There lay three garters, half a pair of gloves,
And all the trophies of his former loves;
With tender billet-doux he lights the pyre,
And breathes three am'rous sighs to raise the fire.
Then prostrate falls, and begs with ardent eyes
Soon to obtain, and long possess the prize:
The pow'rs gave ear, and granted half his pray'r,
The rest, the winds dispersed in empty air.
   But now secure the painted vessel glides,
The sun-beams trembling on the floating tides:
While melting music steals upon the sky,
And softened sounds along the waters die;

Smooth flow the waves, the zephyrs gently play,
Belinda smiled, and all the world was gay.
All but the sylph – with careful thoughts opprest,
Th' impending woe sat heavy on his breast.
He summons straight his denizens of air;
The lucid squadrons round the sails repair;
Soft o'er the shrouds aërial whispers breathe,
That seemed but zephyrs to the train beneath.
Some to the sun their insect-wings unfold,
Waft on the breeze, or sink in clouds of gold;
Transparent forms, too fine for mortal sight,
Their fluid bodies half dissolved in light.
Loose to the wind their airy garments flew,
Thin glitt'ring textures of the filmy dew,
Dipped in the richest tincture of the skies,
Where light disports in ever-mingling dyes;
While ev'ry beam new transient colours flings,
Colours that change whene'er they wave their wings.
Amid the circle, on the gilded mast,
Superior by the head, was Ariel placed;
His purple pinions op'ning to the sun,
He raised his azure wand, and thus begun.
    'Ye sylphs and sylphids, to your chief give ear,
Fays, fairies, genii, elves, and demons hear!
Ye know the spheres and various tasks assigned
By laws eternal to th' aërial kind.
Some in the fields of purest ether play,
And bask and whiten in the blaze of day.
Some guide the course of wand'ring orbs on high,
Or roll the planets through the boundless sky.
Some less refined, beneath the moon's pale light
Pursue the stars that shoot athwart the night,
Or suck the mists in grosser air below,
Or dip their pinions in the painted bow,
Or brew fierce tempests on the wintry main,
Or o'er the glebe distil the kindly rain.
Others on earth o'er human race preside,
Watch all their ways, and all their actions guide:
Of these the chief the care of nations own,
And guard with arms divine the British throne.
    'Our humbler province is to tend the fair,
Not a less pleasing, tho' less glorious care;
To save the powder from too rude a gale,
Nor let th' imprisoned essences exhale;
To draw fresh colours from the vernal flow'rs;
To steal from rainbows, e'er they drop in show'rs
A brighter wash; to curl their waving hairs,

Assist their blushes, and inspire their airs;
Nay oft, in dreams, invention we bestow,
To change a flounce, or add a furbelow.
    'This day, black omens threat the brightest fair
That e'er deserved a watchful spirit's care;
Some dire disaster, or by force, or slight;
But what, or where, the fates have wrapped in night.
Whether the nymph shall break Diana's law,
Or some frail China jar receive a flaw;
Or stain her honour, or her new brocade;
Forget her pray'rs, or miss a masquerade;
Or lose her heart, or necklace, at a ball;
Or whether Heav'n has doomed that Shock must fall.
Haste then, ye spirits! to your charge repair:
The flutt'ring fan be Zephyretta's care;
The drops to thee, Brillante, we consign;
And, Momentilla, let the watch be thine;
Do thou, Crispissa, tend her fav'rite lock;
Ariel himself shall be the guard of Shock.
    'To fifty chosen sylphs, of special note,
We trust th' important charge, the petticoat:
Oft have we known that seven-fold fence to fail,
Tho' stiff with hoops, and armed with ribs of whale;
Form a strong line about the silver bound,
And guard the wide circumference around.
    'Whatever spirit, careless of his charge,
His post neglects, or leaves the fair at large,
Shall feel sharp vengeance soon o'ertake his sins,
Be stopped in vials, or transfixed with pins;
Or plunged in lakes of bitter washes lie,
Or wedged whole ages in a bodkin's eye:
Gums and pomatums shall his flight restrain,
While, clogged, he beats his silken wings in vain;
Or alum styptics with contracting pow'r
Shrink his thin essence like a rivel'd flow'r:
Or, as Ixion fixed, the wretch shall feel
The giddy motion of the whirling mill,
In fumes of burning chocolate shall glow,
And tremble at the sea that froths below!'
    He spoke; the spirits from the sails descend;
Some, orb in orb, around the nymph extend;
Some thrid the mazy ringlets of her hair;
Some hang upon the pendants of her ear;
With beating hearts the dire event they wait,
Anxious, and trembling for the birth of Fate.

CANTO III

Close by those meads, for ever crowned with flow'rs,
Where Thames with pride surveys his rising tow'rs,
There stands a structure of majestic frame,
Which from the neighb'ring Hampton takes its name.
Here Britain's statesmen oft the fall foredoom
Of foreign tyrants, and of nymphs at home;
Here thou, great Anna! whom three realms obey,
Dost sometimes counsel take – and sometimes tea.

   Hither the heroes and the nymphs resort,
To taste awhile the pleasures of a Court;
In various talk th' instructive hours they past,
Who gave the ball, or paid the visit last;
One speaks the glory of the British queen,
And one describes a charming Indian screen;
A third interprets motions, looks, and eyes;
At ev'ry word a reputation dies.
Snuff, or the fan, supply each pause of chat,
With singing, laughing, ogling, *and all that*.

   Meanwhile, declining from the noon of day,
The sun obliquely shoots his burning ray;
The hungry judges soon the sentence sign,
And wretches hang that jury-men may dine;
The merchant from th' Exchange returns in peace,
And the long labours of the toilet cease.
Belinda now, whom thirst of fame invites,
Burns to encounter two advent'rous knights,
At Ombre singly to decide their doom;
And swells her breast with conquests yet to come.
Straight the three bands prepare in arms to join,
Each band the number of the sacred Nine.
Soon as she spreads her hand, th' aërial guard
Descend, and sit on each important card:
First Ariel perch'd upon a Matadore,
Then each according to the rank they bore;
For sylphs, yet mindful of their ancient race,
Are, as when women, wond'rous fond of place.

   Behold, four kings in majesty revered,
With hoary whiskers and a forky beard;
And four fair queens whose hands sustain a flow'r,
Th' expressive emblem of their softer pow'r;
Four knaves in garbs succinct, a trusty band,
Caps on their heads, and halberts in their hand;
And particoloured troops, a shining train,
Draw forth to combat on the velvet plain.
   The skilful nymph reviews her force with care:

'Let Spades be trumps!' she said, and trumps they were.
  Now move to war her sable Matadores,
In show like leaders of the swarthy Moors.
Spadillo first, unconquerable Lord!
Led off two captive trumps, and swept the board.
As many more Manillo forced to yield,
And marched a victor from the verdant field.
Him Basto followed, but his fate more hard
Gained but one trump and one plebeian card.
With his broad sabre next, a chief in years,
The hoary Majesty of Spades appears,
Puts forth one manly leg, to sight revealed,
The rest, his many-coloured robe concealed.
The rebel knave, who dares his prince engage,
Proves the just victim of his royal rage.
Ev'n mighty Pam, that kings and queens o'er-threw
And mowed down armies in the fights of Loo,
Sad chance of war! now destitute of aid,
Falls undistinguished by the victor Spade!
  Thus far both armies to Belinda yield;
Now to the Baron fate inclines the field.
His warlike amazon her host invades,
Th' imperial consort of the crown of Spades.
The Club's black tyrant first her victim died,
Spite of his haughty mien, and barb'rous pride:
What boots the regal circle on his head,
His giant limbs, in state unwieldy spread,
That long behind he trails his pompous robe,
And, of all monarchs, only grasps the globe?
  The Baron now his Diamonds pours apace;
Th' embroidered King who shows but half his face,
And his refulgent Queen, with pow'rs combined,
Of broken troops an easy conquest find.
Clubs, Diamonds, Hearts, in wild disorder seen,
With throngs promiscuous strow the level green.
Thus when dispersed a routed army runs,
Of Asia's troops, and Afric's sable sons,
With like confusion different nations fly,
Of various habit and of various dye;
The pierced battalions disunited fall,
In heaps on heaps; one fate o'erwhelms them all.
  The Knave of Diamonds tries his wily arts,
And wins (oh shameful chance!) the Queen of Hearts.
At this, the blood the virgin's cheek forsook,
A livid paleness spreads o'er all her look;
She sees, and trembles at th' approaching ill,
Just in the jaws of ruin, and Codille.

And now, (as oft in some distempered State)
On one nice trick depends the gen'ral fate:
An Ace of Hearts steps forth: the King unseen
Lurked in her hand, and mourned his captive Queen:
He springs to vengeance with an eager pace,
And falls like thunder on the prostrate Ace.
The nymph, exulting, fills with shouts the sky;
The walls, the woods, and long canals reply.
    O thoughtless mortals! ever blind to fate,
Too soon dejected, and too soon elate.
Sudden these honours shall be snatched away,
And cursed for ever this victorious day.
    For lo! the board with cups and spoons is crowned,
The berries crackle, and the mill turns round;
On shining altars of Japan they raise
The silver lamp; the fiery spirits blaze:
From silver spouts the grateful liquors glide,
While China's earth receives the smoking tide:
At once they gratify their scent and taste,
And frequent cups prolong the rich repast.
Straight hover round the fair her airy band;
Some, as she sipped, the fuming liquor fanned,
Some o'er her lap their careful plumes displayed,
Trembling, and conscious of the rich brocade.
Coffee (which makes the politician wise,
And see through all things with his half-shut eyes)
Sent up in vapours to the Baron's brain
New stratagems, the radiant lock to gain.
Ah cease, rash youth! desist ere 'tis too late,
Fear the just gods, and think of Scylla's fate!
Changed to a bird, and sent to flit in air,
She dearly pays for Nisus' injured hair!
    But when to mischief mortals bend their will,
How soon they find fit instruments of ill!
Just then, Clarissa drew with tempting grace
A two-edged weapon from her shining case:
So ladies in romance assist their knight,
Present the spear, and arm him for the fight.
He takes the gift with rev'rence, and extends
The little engine on his fingers' ends;
This just behind Belinda's neck he spread,
As o'er the fragrant steams she bends her head.
Swift to the lock a thousand sprites repair,
A thousand wings, by turns, blow back the hair;
And thrice they twitched the diamond in her ear;
Thrice she looked back, and thrice the foe drew near.
Just in that instant, anxious Ariel sought

The close recesses of the virgin's thought;
As on the nosegay in her breast reclined,
He watched th' ideas rising in her mind,
Sudden he viewed, in spite of all her art,
An earthly lover lurking at her heart.
Amazed, confused, he found his pow'r expired,
Resigned to fate, and with a sigh retired.

The Peer now spreads the glitt'ring forfex wide,
T' enclose the lock; now joins it, to divide.
Ev'n then, before the fatal engine closed,
A wretched sylph too fondly interposed;
Fate urged the sheers, and cut the sylph in twain,
(But airy substance soon unites again)
The meeting points the sacred hair dissever
From the fair head, for ever, and for ever!

Then flashed the living lightning from her eyes,
And screams of horror rend th' affrighted skies.
Not louder shrieks to pitying heav'n are cast,
When husbands, or when lap-dogs breathe their last;
Or when rich China vessels, fall'n from high,
In glitt'ring dust and painted fragments lie!

'Let wreaths of triumph now my temples twine,
(The victor cried) the glorious prize is mine!
While fish in streams, or birds delight in air,
Or in a coach-and-six the British fair,
As long as Atalantis shall be read,
Or the small pillow grace a lady's bed,
While visits shall be paid on solemn days,
When num'rous wax-lights in bright order blaze,
While nymphs take treats, or assignations give,
So long my honour, name, and praise shall live!'

What time would spare, from steel receives its date,
And monuments, like men, submit to fate!
Steel could the labour of the gods destroy,
And strike to dust th' imperial tow'rs of Troy;
Steel could the works of mortal pride confound,
And hew triumphal arches to the ground.
What wonder then, fair nymph! thy hairs should feel
The conqu'ring force of unresisted steel?

CANTO IV

But anxious cares the pensive nymph oppressed,
And secret passions laboured in her breast.
Not youthful kings in battle seized alive,
Not scornful virgins who their charms survive,

Not ardent lovers robbed of all their bliss,
Not ancient ladies when refused a kiss,
Not tyrants fierce that unrepenting die,
Not Cynthia when her manteau's pinned awry,
E'er felt such rage, resentment, and despair,
As thou, sad virgin! for thy ravished hair.

Belinda burns with more than mortal ire,
And fierce Thalestris fans the rising fire.
'O wretched maid!' she spread her hands, and cried,
(While Hampton's echoes 'Wretched maid!' replied)
'Was it for this you took such constant care
The bodkin, comb, and essence to prepare?
For this your locks in paper durance bound?
For this with tort'ring irons wreathed around?
For this with fillets strained your tender head?
And bravely bore the double loads of lead?
Gods! shall the ravisher display your hair,
While the fops envy, and the ladies stare?
Honour forbid! at whose unrivalled shrine
Ease, pleasure, virtue, all our sex resign.
Methinks already I your tears survey,
Already hear the horrid things they say,
Already see you a degraded toast,
And all your honour in a whisper lost!
How shall I, then, your helpless fame defend?
'Twill then be infamy to seem your friend!
And shall this prize, th' inestimable prize,
Exposed through crystal to the gazing eyes,
And heightened by the diamond's circling rays,
On that rapacious hand for ever blaze?
Sooner shall grass in Hyde-park Circus grow,
And wits take lodgings in the sound of Bow;
Sooner let earth, air, sea, to Chaos fall,
Men, monkeys, lap-dogs, parrots, perish all!'
  She said; then raging to Sir Plume repairs,
And bids her Beau demand the precious hairs;
(Sir Plume of amber snuff-box justly vain,
And the nice conduct of a clouded cane)
With earnest eyes, and round unthinking face,
He first the snuff-box opened, then the case,
And thus broke out – 'My Lord, why, what the devil!
Z—ds! damn the lock! 'fore Gad, you must be civil!
Plague on 't! 'tis past a jest – nay, prithee, pox!
Give her the hair' – he spoke, and rapped his box.
  'It grieves me much' (replied the Peer again)
'Who speaks so well should ever speak in vain.

But by this lock, this sacred lock I swear,
(Which never more shall join its parted hair;
Which never more its honours shall renew,
Clipped from the lovely head where late it grew)
That while my nostrils draw the vital air,
This hand, which won it, shall for ever wear.'
He spoke, and speaking, in proud triumph spread
The long-contended honours of her head.

. . .

Then see! the nymph in beauteous grief appears,
Her eyes half-languishing, half-drowned in tears;
On her heaved bosom hung her drooping head,
Which, with a sigh, she raised; and thus she said.
   'For ever cursed be this detested day,
Which snatched my best, my fav'rite curl away!
Happy! ah ten times happy had I been,
If Hampton-Court these eyes had never seen!
Yet am not I the first mistaken maid,
By love of Courts to num'rous ills betrayed.
Oh had I rather un-admired remained
In some lone isle, or distant Northern land;
Where the gilt chariot never marks the way,
Where none learn Ombre, none e'er taste Bohea!
There kept my charms concealed from mortal eye,
Like roses, that in deserts bloom and die.
What moved my mind with youthful lords to roam?
O had I stayed, and said my pray'rs at home!
'Twas this, the morning omens seemed to tell:
Thrice from my trembling hand the patch-box fell;
The tott'ring China shook without a wind,
Nay Poll sat mute, and Shock was most unkind!
A sylph too warned me of the threats of fate,
In mystic visions, now believed too late!
See the poor remnants of these slighted hairs!
My hands shall rend what ev'n thy rapine spares:
These in two sable ringlets taught to break,
Once gave new beauties to the snowy neck;
The sister-lock now sits uncouth, alone,
And in its fellow's fate foresees its own;
Uncurled it hangs, the fatal sheers demands,
And tempts, once more, thy sacrilegious hands.
O hadst thou, cruel! been content to seize
Hairs less in sight, or any hairs but these!'

CANTO V

She said: the pitying audience melt in tears,
But Fate and Jove had stopped the Baron's ears.
In vain Thalestris with reproach assails,
For who can move when fair Belinda fails?

. . .

'To arms, to arms!' the fierce virago cries,
And swift as lightning to the combat flies.
All side in parties, and begin th' attack;
Fans clap, silks russle, and tough whalebones crack;
Heroes' and heroines' shouts confusedly rise,
And bass and treble voices strike the skies.
No common weapons in their hands are found,
Like gods they fight, nor dread a mortal wound.
    So when bold Homer makes the Gods engage,
And heav'nly breasts with human passions rage;
'Gainst Pallas, Mars; Latona, Hermes arms,
And all Olympus rings with loud alarms:
Jove's thunder roars, heav'n trembles all around,
Blue Neptune storms, the bellowing deeps resound:
Earth shakes her nodding tow'rs, the ground gives way,
And the pale ghosts start at the flash of day!

. . .

Propped on their bodkin spears, the Sprites survey
The growing combat, or assist the fray.
    While through the press enraged Thalestris flies,
And scatters death around from both her eyes,
A beau and witling perished in the throng,
One died in metaphor, and one in song.
'O cruel nymph! a living death I bear,'
Cried Dapperwit, and sunk beside his chair.
A mournful glance Sir Fopling upwards cast,
'Those eyes are made so killing' – was his last.
Thus on Maeander's flow'ry margin lies
Th' expiring swan, and as he sings he dies.
    When bold Sir Plume had drawn Clarissa down,
Chloe stepped in, and killed him with a frown;
She smiled to see the doughty hero slain,
But at her smile, the beau revived again.
    Now Jove suspends his golden scales in air,
Weighs the men's wits against the lady's hair;
The doubtful beam long nods from side to side;
At length the wits mount up, the hairs subside.
    See, fierce Belinda on the Baron flies,
With more than usual lightning in her eyes:
Nor feared the chief th' unequal fight to try,

Who sought no more than on his foe to die.
But this bold lord, with manly strength endued,
She with one finger and a thumb subdued:
Just where the breath of life his nostrils drew,
A charge of snuff the wily virgin threw;
The gnomes direct, to ev'ry atom just,
The pungent grains of titillating dust;
Sudden, with starting tears each eye o'erflows,
And the high dome re-echoes to his nose.
  'Now meet thy fate!' incensed Belinda cried,
And drew a deadly bodkin from her side,
(The same, his ancient personage to deck,
Her great great grandsire wore about his neck,
In three seal-rings; which after, melted down,
Formed a vast buckle for his widow's gown:
Her infant grandame's whistle next it grew,
The bells she jingled, and the whistle blew;
Then in a bodkin graced her mother's hairs,
Which long she wore, and now Belinda wears.)
  'Boast not my fall,' (he cried) 'insulting foe!
Thou by some other shalt be laid as low.
Nor think, to die dejects my lofty mind;
All that I dread is leaving you behind!
Rather than so, ah let me still survive,
And burn in Cupid's flames – but burn alive.'
  'Restore the lock!' she cries; and all around
'Restore the lock!' the vaulted roofs rebound.
Not fierce Othello in so loud a strain
Roared for the handkerchief that caused his pain.
But see how oft ambitious aims are crossed,
And chiefs contend 'til all the prize is lost!
The lock, obtained with guilt, and kept with pain,
In ev'ry place is sought, but sought in vain:
With such a prize no mortal must be blest,
So Heav'n decrees! with Heav'n who can contest?
  Some thought it mounted to the lunar sphere,
Since all things lost on earth are treasured there.
There heroes' wits are kept in pond'rous vases,
And beaux' in snuff-boxes and tweezer-cases.
There broken vows, and death-bed alms are found,
And lovers' hearts with ends of ribband bound,
The courtier's promises, and sick man's pray'rs,
The smiles of harlots, and the tears of heirs,
Cages for gnats, and chains to yoke a flea,
Dried butterflies, and tomes of casuistry.
  But trust the Muse – she saw it upward rise,
Tho' marked by none but quick, poetic eyes:

THOMAS GRAY

(So Rome's great founder to the heav'ns withdrew,
To Proculus alone confessed in view)
A sudden star, it shot through liquid air,
And drew behind a radiant trail of hair.
Not Berenice's locks first rose so bright,
The heav'ns bespangling with dishevelled light.
The sylphs behold it kindling as it flies,
And pleased pursue its progress through the skies.

   This the *Beau monde* shall from the Mall survey,
And hail with music its propitious ray;
This the blessed lover shall for Venus take,
And send up vows from Rosamonda's lake;
This Partridge soon shall view in cloudless skies,
When next he looks through Galileo's eyes;
And hence th' egregious wizard shall foredoom
The fate of Louis, and the fall of Rome.

   Then cease, bright nymph! to mourn thy ravished hair,
Which adds new glory to the shining sphere!
Not all the tresses that fair head can boast,
Shall draw such envy as the lock you lost.
For, after all the murders of your eye,
When, after millions slain, yourself shall die;
When those fair suns shall set, as set they must,
And all those tresses shall be laid in dust,
This lock, the Muse shall consecrate to fame,
And 'midst the stars inscribe Belinda's name.

THOMAS GRAY

On a Favourite Cat, Drowned in a Tub of Gold Fishes

'Twas on a lofty vase's side,
Where China's gayest art had dyed
   The azure flowers that blow;
Demurest of the tabby kind,
The pensive Selima reclined,
   Gazed on the lake below.

Her conscious tail her joy declared;
The fair round face, the snowy beard,
   The velvet of her paws,
Her coat, that with the tortoise vies,
Her ears of jet, and emerald eyes,
   She saw; and purred applause.

Still had she gazed; but 'midst the tide
Two angel forms were seen to glide,

The genii of the stream;
Their scaly armour's Tyrian hue
Thro' richest purple to the view
   Betrayed a golden gleam.

The hapless nymph with wonder saw:
A whisker first and then a claw,
   With many an ardent wish,
She stretched in vain to reach the prize.
What female heart can gold despise?
   What cat's averse to fish?

Presumptuous maid! with looks intent
Again she stretched, again she bent,
   Nor knew the gulf between.
(Malignant Fate sat by, and smiled.)
The slipp'ry verge her feet beguiled,
   She tumbled headlong in.

Eight times emerging from the flood
She mewed to ev'ry wat'ry god,
   Some speedy aid to send.
No dolphin came, no nereid stirred:
Nor cruel Tom, nor Susan heard.
   A fav'rite has no friend!

From hence, ye beauties undeceived,
Know, one false step is ne'er retrieved,
   And be with caution bold.
Not all that tempts your wand'ring eyes
And heedless hearts, is lawful prize;
   Nor all that glisters, gold.

WILLIAM COWPER

The Diverting History of John Gilpin

John Gilpin was a citizen
   Of credit and renown,
A train-band captain eke was he
   Of famous London town.

John Gilpin's spouse said to her dear:
   'Though wedded we have been

These twice ten tedious years, yet we
  No holiday have seen.

'Tomorrow is our wedding-day,
  And we will then repair
Unto the Bell at Edmonton
  All in a chaise and pair.

'My sister, and my sister's child,
  Myself, and children three,
Will fill the chaise; so you must ride
  On horseback after we.'

He soon replied: 'I do admire
  Of womankind but one,
And you are she, my dearest dear,
  Therefore it shall be done.

'I am a linen-draper bold,
  As all the world doth know,
And my good friend the calender
  Will lend his horse to go.'

Quoth Mrs Gilpin: 'That's well said;
  And, for that wine is dear,
We will be furnished with our own,
  Which is both bright and clear.'

John Gilpin kissed his loving wife;
  O'erjoyed was he to find
That, though on pleasure she was bent,
  She had a frugal mind.

The morning came, the chaise was brought,
  But yet was not allowed
To drive up to the door, lest all
  Should say that she was proud.

So three doors off the chaise was stayed,
  Where they did all get in;
Six precious souls, and all agog
  To dash through thick and thin!

Smack went the whip, round went the wheels,
  Were never folk so glad;
The stones did rattle underneath,
  As if Cheapside were mad.

John Gilpin, at his horse's side,
   Seized fast the flowing mane,
And up he got, in haste to ride,
   But soon came down again;

For saddle-tree scarce reached had he,
   His journey to begin,
When, turning round his head, he saw
   Three customers come in.

So down he came; for loss of time,
   Although it grieved him sore,
Yet loss of pence, full well he knew,
   Would trouble him much more.

'Twas long before the customers
   Were suited to their mind,
When Betty screaming came downstairs:
   'The wine is left behind!'

'Good lack!' quoth he, 'yet bring it me,
   My leathern belt likewise,
In which I bear my trusty sword
   When I do exercise.'

Now Mistress Gilpin (careful soul!)
   Had two stone bottles found,
To hold the liquor that she loved,
   And keep it safe and sound.

Each bottle had a curling ear,
   Through which the belt he drew,
And hung a bottle on each side,
   To make his balance true.

Then, over all, that he might be
   Equipped from top to toe,
His long red cloak, well brushed and neat,
   He manfully did throw.

Now see him mounted once again
   Upon his nimble steed,
Full slowly pacing o'er the stones,
   With caution and good heed!

But finding soon a smoother road
   Beneath his well-shod feet,

The snorting beast began to trot,
  Which galled him in his seat.

So, 'Fair and softly,' John he cried,
  But John he cried in vain;
That trot became a gallop soon,
  In spite of curb and rein.

So stooping down, as needs he must
  Who cannot sit upright,
He grasped the mane with both his hands,
  And eke with all his might.

His horse, who never in that sort
  Had handled been before,
What thing upon his back had got
  Did wonder more and more.

Away went Gilpin, neck or nought;
  Away went hat and wig;
He little dreamt, when he set out,
  Of running such a rig!

The wind did blow, the cloak did fly,
  Like streamer long and gay,
Till, loop and button failing both,
  At last it flew away.

Then might all people well discern
  The bottles he had slung;
A bottle swinging at each side;
  As hath been said or sung.

The dogs did bark, the children screamed,
  Up flew the windows all;
And every soul cried out: 'Well done!'
  As loud as he could bawl.

Away went Gilpin – who but he?
  His fame soon spread around:
'He carries weight!' 'He rides a race!'
  ''Tis for a thousand pound!'

And still, as fast as he drew near,
  'Twas wonderful to view
How in a trice the turnpike men
  Their gates wide open threw.

And now, as he went bowing down
  His reeking head full low,
The bottles twain behind his back
  Were shattered at a blow.

Down ran the wine into the road,
  Most piteous to be seen,
Which made his horse's flanks to smoke
  As they had basted been.

But still he seemed to carry weight,
  With leathern girdle braced;
For all might see the bottle-necks
  Still dangling at his waist.

Thus all through merry Islington
  These gambols he did play,
And till he came unto the Wash
  Of Edmonton so gay.

And there he threw the Wash about
  On both sides of the way,
Just like unto a trundling mop,
  Or a wild goose at play.

At Edmonton his loving wife
  From the balcony spied,
Her tender husband, wondering much
  To see how he did ride.

'Stop, stop, John Gilpin! Here's the house!'
  They all at once did cry;
'The dinner waits, and we are tired';
  Said Gilpin: 'So am I!'

But yet his horse was not a whit
  Inclined to tarry there!
For why? his owner had a house
  Full ten miles off, at Ware.

So like an arrow swift he flew,
  Shot by an archer strong;
So did he fly – which brings me to
  The middle of my song.

Away went Gilpin, out of breath,
  And sore against his will,

Till at his friend the calender's
  His horse at last stood still.

The calender, amazed to see
  His neighbour in such trim,
Laid down his pipe, flew to the gate,
  And thus accosted him:

'What news? what news? your tidings tell;
  Tell me you must and shall –
Say why bare-headed you are come,
  Or why you come at all?'

Now Gilpin had a pleasant wit,
  And loved a timely joke;
And thus unto the calender
  In merry guise he spoke:

'I came because your horse would come;
  And, if I well forbode,
My hat and wig will soon be here –
  They are upon the road.'

The calender, right glad to find
  His friend in merry pin,
Returned him not a single word,
  But to the house went in;

Whence straight he came with hat and wig;
  A wig that flowed behind,
A hat not much the worse for wear,
  Each comely in its kind.

He held them up, and, in his turn,
  Thus showed his ready wit:
'My head is twice as big as yours,
  They therefore needs must fit.

'But let me scrape the dirt away,
  That hangs upon your face;
And stop and eat, for well you may
  Be in a hungry case.'

Said John: 'It is my wedding-day,
  And all the world would stare,
If wife should dine at Edmonton
  And I should dine at Ware.'

So, turning to his horse, he said:
  'I am in haste to dine;
'Twas for your pleasure you came here,
  You shall go back for mine.'

Ah, luckless speech, and bootless boast!
  For which he paid full dear;
For, while he spake, a braying ass
  Did sing most loud and clear;

Whereat his horse did snort, as he
  Had heard a lion roar,
And galloped off with all his might,
  As he had done before.

Away went Gilpin, and away
  Went Gilpin's hat and wig!
He lost them sooner than at first;
  For why? – they were too big!

Now, Mistress Gilpin, when she saw
  Her husband posting down
Into the country far away,
  She pulled out half-a-crown;

And thus unto the youth she said,
  That drove them to the Bell:
'This shall be yours when you bring back
  My husband safe and well.'

The youth did ride, and soon did meet
  John coming back amain,
Whom in a trice he tried to stop,
  By catching at his rein;

But, not performing what he meant,
  And gladly would have done,
The frighted steed he frighted more,
  And made him faster run.

Away went Gilpin, and away
  Went post-boy at his heels!
The post-boy's horse right glad to miss
  The lumbering of the wheels.

Six gentlemen upon the road,
  Thus seeing Gilpin fly,

With post-boy scampering in the rear,
   They raised the hue and cry:

'Stop thief! stop thief! a highwayman!'
   Not one of them was mute;
And all and each that passed that way
   Did join in the pursuit.

And now the turnpike gates again
   Flew open in short space;
The toll-men thinking, as before,
   That Gilpin rode a race.

And so he did, and won it too!
   For he got first to town;
Nor stopped till where he had got up
   He did again get down.

Now let us sing: Long live the king,
   And Gilpin long live he!
And, when he next doth ride abroad,
   May I be there to see!

GEORGE CRABBE

Peter Grimes

Old Peter Grimes made fishing his employ,
His wife he cabined with him and his boy,
And seemed that life laborious to enjoy:
To town came quiet Peter with his fish,
And had of all a civil word and wish.
He left his trade upon the Sabbath-day,
And took young Peter in his hand to pray:
But soon the stubborn boy from care broke loose,
At first refused, then added his abuse:
His father's love he scorned, his power defied,
But being drunk, wept sorely when he died.
   Yes! then he wept, and to his mind there came
Much of his conduct, and he felt the shame;
How he had oft the good old man reviled,
And never paid the duty of a child;
How, when the father in his Bible read,
He in contempt and anger left the shed:

'It is the word of life,' the parent cried;
'This is the life itself,' the boy replied;
And while old Peter in amazement stood,
Gave the hot spirit to his boiling blood:
How he, with oath and furious speech, began
To prove his freedom and assert the man;
And when the parent checked his impious rage,
How he had cursed the tyranny of age;
Nay, once had dealt the sacrilegious blow
On his bare head, and laid his parent low;
The father groaned: 'If thou art old,' said he,
'And hast a son, thou wilt remember me:
Thy mother left me in a happy time,
Thou killedst not her – Heav'n spares the double crime.'
   On an inn-settle, in his maudlin grief,
This he revolved, and drank for his relief.
   Now lived the youth in freedom, but debarred
From constant pleasure, and he thought it hard;
Hard that he could not every wish obey,
But must awhile relinquish ale and play;
Hard! that he could not to his cards attend,
But must acquire the money he would spend.
   With greedy eye he looked on all he saw,
He knew not justice, and he laughed at law.
On all he marked, he stretched his ready hand;
He fished by water and he filched by land:
Oft in the night has Peter dropped his oar,
Fled from his boat, and sought for prey on shore;
   Oft up the hedge-row glided, on his back
Bearing the orchard's produce in a sack,
Or farm-yard load, tugged fiercely from the stack;
And as these wrongs to greater numbers rose,
The more he looked on all men as his foes.
   He built a mud-walled hovel, where he kept
His various wealth, and there he oft-times slept;
But no success could please his cruel soul,
He wished for one to trouble and control;
He wanted some obedient boy to stand
And bear the blow of his outrageous hand;
And hoped to find in some propitious hour
A feeling creature subject to his power.
   Peter had heard there were in London then –
Still have they being! – workhouse-clearing men,
Who, undisturbed by feelings just or kind,
Would parish-boys to needy tradesmen bind:
They in their want a trifling sum would take,
And toiling slaves of piteous orphans make.

Such Peter sought, and when a lad was found,
The sum was dealt him, and the slave was bound.
Some few in town observed in Peter's trap
A boy, with jacket blue and woollen cap;
But none inquired how Peter used the rope,
Or what the bruise that made the stripling stoop;
None could the ridges on his back behold,
None sought him shiv'ring in the winter's cold;
None put the question: 'Peter dost thou give
The boy his food? What, man! the lad must live.
Consider, Peter, let the child have bread,
He'll serve thee better if he's stroked and fed.'
None reasoned thus – and some, on hearing cries,
Said calmly, 'Grimes is at his exercise.'
    Pinned, beaten, cold, pinched, threatened, and abused –
His efforts punished and his food refused –
Awake tormented – soon aroused from sleep –
Struck if he wept, and yet compelled to weep,
The trembling boy dropped down and strove to pray,
Received a blow, and trembling turned away,
Or sobbed and hid his piteous face; while he,
The savage master, grinned in horrid glee:
He'd now the power he ever loved to show,
A feeling being subject to his blow.
    Thus lived the lad, in hunger, peril, pain,
His tears despised, his supplications vain:
Compelled by fear to lie, by need to steal,
His bed uneasy and unblessed his meal,
For three sad years the boy his tortures bore,
And then his pains and trials were no more.
    'How died he, Peter?' when the people said,
He growled: 'I found him lifeless in his bed';
Then tried for softer tone, and sighed, 'Poor Sam is dead.'
Yet murmurs were there, and some questions asked
How he was fed, how punished, and how tasked?
Much they suspected, but they little proved,
And Peter passed untroubled and unmoved.
    Another boy with equal ease was found,
The money granted, and the victim bound;
And what his fate? One night it chanced he fell
From the boat's mast and perished in her well,
Where fish were living kept, and where the boy
(So reasoned men) could not himself destroy:
    'Yes! so it was,' said Peter, 'in his play,
(For he was idle both by night and day)
He climbed the main-mast and then fell below';
Then showed his corpse, and pointed to the blow:

'What said the jury?' They were long in doubt,
But sturdy Peter faced the matter out:
So they dismissed him, saying at the time,
'Keep fast your hatchway when you've boys who climb.'
This hit the conscience, and he coloured more
Than for the closest questions put before.

 Thus all his fears the verdict set aside,
And at the slave-shop Peter still applied.

 Then came a boy, of manners soft and mild –
Our seamen's wives with grief beheld the child;
All thought (the poor themselves) that he was one
Of gentle blood, some noble sinner's son,
Who had, belike, deceived some humble maid,
Whom he had first seduced and then betrayed:
However this, he seemed a gracious lad,
In grief submissive, and with patience sad.

 Passive he laboured, till his slender frame
Bent with his loads, and he at length was lame:
Strange that a frame so weak could bear so long
The grossest insult and the foulest wrong;
But there were causes – in the town they gave
Fire, food, and comfort, to the gentle slave;
And though stern Peter, with a cruel hand,
And knotted rope, enforced the rude command,
Yet he considered what he'd lately felt,
And his vile blows with selfish pity dealt.

 One day such draughts the cruel fisher made,
He could not vend them in his borough-trade,
But sailed for London-mart: the boy was ill,
But ever humbled to his master's will;
And on the river, where they smoothly sailed,
He strove with terror and awhile prevailed;
But new to danger on the angry sea,
He clung affrighten'd to his master's knee:
The boat grew leaky and the wind was strong,
Rough was the passage and the time was long;
His liquor failed, and Peter's wrath arose;
No more is known – the rest we must suppose,
Or learn of Peter: Peter says, he 'spied
The stripling's danger and for harbour tried;
Meantime the fish, and then th' apprentice died.'

 The pitying women raised a clamour round,
And weeping said, 'Thou hast thy 'prentice drowned.'

 Now the stern man was summoned to the hall,
To tell his tale before the burghers all:
He gave th' account; professed the lad he loved.
And kept his brazen features all unmoved.

The mayor himself with tone severe replied:
'Henceforth with thee shall never boy abide;
Hire thee a freeman, whom thou durst not beat,
But who, in thy despite, will sleep and eat:
Free thou art now! Again shouldst thou appear,
Thou'lt find thy sentence, like thy soul, severe.'
    Alas! for Peter not a helping hand,
So was he hated, could he now command;
Alone he rowed his boat, alone he cast
His nets beside, or made his anchor fast;
To hold a rope or hear a curse was none.
He toiled and railed; he groaned and swore alone.
    Thus by himself compelled to live each day,
To wait for certain hours the tide's delay;
At the same times the same dull views to see,
The bounding marsh-bank and the blighted tree;
The water only, when the tides were high,
When low, the mud half covered and half dry;
The sun-burnt tar that blisters on the planks,
And bank-side stakes in their uneven ranks;
Heaps of entangled weeds that slowly float,
As the tide rolls by the impeded boat.
    When tides were neap, and, in the sultry day,
Through the tall bounding mud-banks made their way,
Which on each side rose swelling, and below
The dark warm flood ran silently and slow;
There anchoring, Peter chose from man to hide,
There hang his head, and view the lazy tide
In its hot slimy channel slowly glide;
Where the small eels that left the deeper way
For the warm shore, within the shallows play;
Where gaping mussels, left upon the mud,
Slope their slow passage to the fallen flood;
Here dull and hopeless he'd lie down and trace
How sidelong crabs had scrawled their crooked race,
Or sadly listen to the tuneless cry
Of fishing gull or clanging golden-eye;
What time the sea-birds to the marsh would come,
And the loud bittern, from the bull-rush home,
Gave from the salt ditch side the bellowing boom:
He nursed the feelings these dull scenes produce,
And loved to stop beside the opening sluice;
Where the small stream, confined in narrow bound,
Ran with a dull, unvaried, sadd'ning sound;
Where all, presented to the eye or ear,
Oppressed the soul with misery, grief, and fear.
    Besides these objects, there were places three,

Which Peter seemed with certain dread to see;
When he drew near them he would turn from each,
And loudly whistle till he passed the reach.

A change of scene to him brought no relief;
In town, 'twas plain, men took him for a thief:
The sailors' wives would stop him in the street,
And say, 'Now, Peter, thou'st no boy to beat':
Infants at play when they perceived him, ran,
Warning each other, 'That's the wicked man':
He growled an oath, and in an angry tone
Cursed the whole place and wished to be alone.

Alone he was, the same dull scenes in view,
And still more gloomy in his sight they grew:
Though man he hated, yet employed alone
At bootless labour, he would swear and groan,
Cursing the shoals that glided by the spot,
And gulls that caught them when his arts could not.

Cold nervous tremblings shook his sturdy frame,
And strange disease – he couldn't say the name;
Wild were his dreams, and oft he rose in fright,
Waked by his views of horrors in the night,
Horrors that would the sternest minds amaze,
Horrors that demons might be proud to raise:
And though he felt forsaken, grieved at heart,
To think he lived from all mankind apart;
Yet, if a man approached, in terrors he would start.

A winter passed since Peter saw the town,
And summer-lodgers were again come down;
These, idly curious, with their glasses spied
The ships in bay as anchored for the tide,
The river's craft, the bustle of the quay,
And sea-port views, which landmen love to see.

One, up the river, had a man and boat
Seen day by day, now anchored, now afloat;
Fisher he seemed, yet used no net nor hook;
Of sea-fowl swimming by no heed he took,
But on the gliding waves still fixed his lazy look:
At certain stations he would view the stream,
As if he stood bewildered in a dream,
Or that some power had chained him for a time,
To feel a curse or meditate on crime.

This known, some curious, some in pity went,
And others questioned: 'Wretch, dost thou repent?'
He heard, he trembled, and in fear resigned
His boat: new terror filled his restless mind;
Furious he grew, and up the country ran,
And there they seized him – a distempered man:

Him we received, and to a parish-bed,
Followed and cursed, the groaning man was led.
    Here when they saw him, whom they used to shun,
A lost, lone man, so harassed and undone;
Our gentle females, ever prompt to feel,
Perceived compassion on their anger steal;
His crimes they could not from their memories blot,
But they were grieved, and trembled at his lot.
    A priest too came, to whom his words are told;
And all the signs they shuddered to behold.
    'Look! look!' they cried; 'his limbs with horror shake,
And as he grinds his teeth, what noise they make!
How glare his angry eyes, and yet he's not awake:
See! what cold drops upon his forehead stand,
And how he clenches that broad bony hand.'
    The priest attending, found he spoke at times
As one alluding to his fears and crimes;
'It was the fall,' he muttered, 'I can show
The manner how; I never struck a blow':
And then aloud – 'Unhand me, free my chain;
On oath, he fell – it struck him to the brain:
Why ask my father? That old man will swear
Against my life; besides, he wasn't there:
What, all agreed? Am I to die today?
My Lord, in mercy give me time to pray.'
    Then, as they watched him, calmer he became,
And grew so weak he couldn't move his frame,
But murmuring spake, while they could see and hear
The start of terror and the groan of fear;
See the large dew-beads on his forehead rise,
And the cold death-drop glaze his sunken eyes;
Nor yet he died, but with unwonted force
Seemed with some fancied being to discourse:
He knew us not, or with accustomed art
He hid the knowledge, yet exposed his heart;
'Twas part confession and the rest defence,
A madman's tale, with gleams of waking sense.
    'I'll tell you all,' he said, 'the very day
When the old man first placed them in my way:
My father's spirit – he who always tried
To give me trouble, when he lived and died –
When he was gone he could not be content
To see my days in painful labour spent,
But would appoint his meetings, and he made
Me watch at these, and so neglect my trade.
    ''Twas one hot noon, all silent, still serene,
No living being had I lately seen:

I paddled up and down and dipped my net,
But (such his pleasure) I could nothing get –
A father's pleasure, when his toil was done,
To plague and torture thus an only son!
And so I sat and looked upon the stream,
How it ran on, and felt as in a dream:
But dream it was not: No! I fixed my eyes
On the mid stream and saw the spirits rise:
I saw my father on the water stand,
And hold a thin pale boy in either hand;
And there they glided ghastly on the top
Of the salt flood, and never touched a drop:
I would have struck them, but they knew th' intent,
And smiled upon the oar, and down they went.
    'Now, from that day, whenever I began
To dip my net, there stood the hard old man –
He and those boys: I humbled me and prayed
They would be gone; they heeded not, but stayed:
Nor could I turn, nor would the boat go by,
But, gazing on the spirits, there was I:
They bade me leap to death, but I was loth to die:
And every day, as sure as day arose,
Would these three spirits meet me ere the close;
To hear and mark them daily was my doom,
And "Come," they said, with weak, sad voices, "come."
To row away, with all my strength I tried,
But there were they, hard by me in the tide,
The three unbodied forms – and "Come," still "come," they cried.
    'Fathers should pity, but this old man shook
His hoary locks, and froze me by a look:
Thrice, when I struck them, through the water came
A hollow groan, that weakened all my frame:
"Father!" said I, "have mercy": he replied,
I know not what – the angry spirit lied –
"Didst thou not draw thy knife?" said he: 'Twas true,
But I had pity and my arm withdrew:
He cried for mercy, which I kindly gave,
But he has no compassion in his grave.
    'There were three places, where they ever rose –
The whole long river has not such as those –
Places accursed, where, if a man remain,
He'll see the things which strike him to the brain;
And there they made me on my paddle lean,
And look at them for hours; accursed scene!
When they would glide to that smooth eddy-space,
Then bid me leap and join them in the place;
And at my groans each little villain sprite

Enjoyed my pains and vanished in delight.
  'In one fierce summer-day, when my poor brain
Was burning hot, and cruel was my pain,
Then came this father-foe, and there he stood
With his two boys again upon the flood:
There was more mischief in their eyes, more glee
In their pale faces when they glared at me;
Still they did force me on the oar to rest,
And when they saw me fainting and oppressed,
He, with his hand, the old man, scooped the flood,
And there came flame about him mixed with blood;
He bade me stoop and look upon the place,
Then flung the hot-red liquor in my face;
Burning it blazed, and then I roared for pain,
I thought the demons would have turned my brain.
  'Still there they stood, and forced me to behold
A place of horrors – they can not be told;
Where the flood opened, there I heard the shriek
Of tortured guilt – no earthly tongue can speak:
"All days alike! for ever!" did they say,
"And unremitted torments every day" –
Yes, so they said.' But here he ceased and gazed
On all around, affrightened and amazed;
And still he tried to speak, and looked in dread
Of frightened females gathering round his bed;
Then dropped exhausted and appeared at rest,
Till the strong foe the vital powers possessed:
Then with an inward, broken voice he cried,
'Again they come!' and muttered as he died.

ROBERT BURNS

Tam O'Shanter

When chapman billies leave the street,	*pedlar fellows*
And drouthy neebors neebors meet,	*thirsty*
As market-days are wearing late,	
An' folk begin to tak the gate,	*road*
While we sit bousing at the nappy,	*ale*
An' getting fou and unco happy,	*drunk; very*
We think na on the lang Scots miles,	
The mosses, waters, slaps, and styles,	
That lie between us and our hame,	
Whare sits our sulky sullen dame,	

Gathering her brows like gathering storm,
Nursing her wrath to keep it warm.
    This truth fand honest Tam o' Shanter,
As he frae Ayr ae night did canter –
(Auld Ayr, wham ne'er a town surpasses
For honest men and bonie lasses).
    O Tam! hadst thou but been sae wise
As ta'en thy ain wife Kate's advice!
She tauld thee weel thou was a skellum;   *rogue*
A blethering, blustering, drunken blellum,   *babbler*
That frae November till October,
Ae market-day thou was nae sober;
That ilka melder wi' the miller   *every; meal-*
Thou sat as lang as thou had siller;   *grinding*
That ev'ry naig was ca'd a shoe on,   *nag that was shod*
The smith and thee gat roaring fou on;
That at the Lord's house, even on Sunday,
Thou drank wi' Kirkton Jean till Monday.
She prophesied that, late or soon,
Thou would be found deep drowned in Doon;
Or catched wi' warlocks in the mirk
By Alloway's auld haunted kirk.
    Ah, gentle dames! it gars me greet   *makes me weep*
To think how monie counsels sweet,
How monie lengthened sage advices,
The husband frae the wife despises!
    But to our tale: Ae market night,
Tam had got planted unco right,
Fast by an ingle, bleezing finely,
Wi' reaming swats, that drank divinely;   *frothing ale*
And at his elbow, Souter Johnie,   *Cobbler*
His ancient, trusty, drouthy cronie;
Tam lo'ed him like a very brither;
They had been fou for weeks thegither.
The night drave on wi' sangs and clatter,
And aye the ale was growing better:
The landlady and Tam grew gracious,
Wi' secret favours, sweet, and precious;
The souter tauld his queerest stories;
The landlord's laugh was ready chorus;
The storm without might rair and rustle,
Tam did na mind the storm a whistle.
    Care, mad to see a man sae happy,
E'en drowned himsel amang the nappy.
As bees flee hame wi' lades o' treasure,
The minutes winged their way wi' pleasure;
Kings may be blest, but Tam was glorious,

O'er a' the ills o' life victorious!
  But pleasures are like poppies spread:
You seize the flow'r, its bloom is shed;
Or like the snow falls in the river,
A moment white – then melts for ever;
Or like the borealis race,
That flit ere you can point their place;
Or like the rainbow's lovely form
Evanishing amid the storm.
Nae man can tether time or tide;
The hour approaches Tam maun ride:
That hour, o' night's black arch the key-stane,
That dreary hour Tam mounts his beast in;
And sic a night he taks the road in,
As ne'er poor sinner was abroad in.
  The wind blew as 'twad blawn its last;
The rattling showers rose on the blast;
The speedy gleams the darkness swallowed;
Loud, deep, and lang, the thunder bellowed:
That night, a child might understand,
The Deil had business on his hand.
  Weel mounted on his gray mare, Meg,
A better never lifted leg,
Tam skelpit on thro' dub and mire,   *dashed; puddle*
Despising wind, and rain, and fire;
Whiles holding fast his guid blue bonnet;
Whiles crooning o'er some auld Scots sonnet;
Whiles glow'ring round wi' prudent cares,
Lest bogles catch him unawares:
Kirk-Alloway was drawing nigh,
Whare ghaists and houlets nightly cry.
  By this time he was cross the ford,
Whare in the snaw the chapman smoored;   *smothered*
And past the birks and meikle stane,   *birches; big*
Whare drunken Charlie brak's neck-bane;
And thro' the whins, and by the cairn,
Whare hunters fand the murdered bairn;
And near the thorn, aboon the well,
Whare Mungo's mither hanged hersel.
Before him Doon pours all his floods;
The doubling storm roars thro' the woods;
The lightnings flash from pole to pole;
Near and more near the thunders roll:
When, glimmering thro' the groaning trees,
Kirk-Alloway seemed in a bleeze,
Thro' ilka bore the beams were glancing,   *every chink*
And loud resounded mirth and dancing.

Inspiring bold John Barleycorn,
What dangers thou canst make us scorn!
Wi' tippenny, we fear nae evil;   *ale*
Wi' usquabae, we'll face the Devil!   *whisky*
The swats sae reamed in Tammie's noddle,
Fair play, he cared na deils a boddle.   *farthing*
But Maggie stood right sair astonished,
Till, by the heel and hand admonished,
She ventured forward on the light;
And, vow! Tam saw an unco sight!
   Warlocks and witches in a dance:
Nae cotillon brent new frae France,   *brand*
But hornpipes, jigs, strathspeys, and reels,
Put life and mettle in their heels.
A winnock-bunker in the east,   *window-seat*
There sat Auld Nick, in shape o' beast;
A touzie tyke, black, grim, and large,   *shaggy dog*
To gie them music was his charge:
He screwed the pipes and gart them skirl,
Till roof and rafters a' did dirl.   *ring*
Coffins stood round like open presses,
That shawed the dead in their last dresses;
And by some devilish cantraip sleight   *eerie*
Each in its cauld hand held a light:
By which heroic Tam was able
To note upon the haly table,
A murderer's banes in gibbet-airns;   *irons*
Twa span-lang, wee, unchristened bairns;
A thief new-cutted frae a rape –   *rope*
Wi' his last gasp his gab did gape;
Five tomahawks, wi' bluid red-rusted;
Five scymitars, wi' murder crusted;
A garter, which a babe had strangled;
A knife, a father's throat had mangled,
Whom his ain son o' life bereft –
The gray hairs yet stack to the heft;   *haft*
Wi' mair of horrible and awefu',
Which even to name wad be unlawfu'.
   As Tammie glowered, amazed, and curious,
The mirth and fun grew fast and furious:
The piper loud and louder blew;
The dancers quick and quicker flew;
They reeled, they set, they crossed, they cleekit,
Till ilka carlin swat and reekit,   *witch*
And coost her duddies to the wark,   *rags*
And linkit at it in her sark!   *tripped; shirt*
   Now Tam, O Tam! had thae been queans,

A' plump and strapping in their teens;
Their sarks, instead o' creeshie flannen,   *greasy*
Been snaw-white seventeen hunder linen!
Thir breeks o' mine, my only pair,   *these*
That ance were plush, o' guid blue hair,
I wad hae gi'en them off my hurdies,   *buttocks*
For ae blink o' the bonnie burdies!   *lasses*
    But withered beldams, auld and droll,
Rigwoodie hags wad spean a foal.   *lean; wean*
Louping and flinging on a crummock,   *leaping; stick*
I wonder didna turn thy stomach!
    But Tam kend what was what fu' brawlie:
There was ae winsome wench and wawlie,   *choice*
That night enlisted in the core,   *company*
Lang after kend on Carrick shore
(For monie a beast to dead she shot,
And perished monie a bonie boat,
And shook baith meikle corn and bear,   *barley*
And kept the country-side in fear).
Her cutty sark, o' Paisley harn,   *short shift; cloth*
That while a lassie she had worn,
In longitude tho' sorely scanty,
It was her best, and she was vauntie. –   *vain*
Ah! little kend thy reverend grannie
That sark she coft for her wee Nannie   *bought*
Wi' twa pund Scots ('twas a' her riches)
Wad ever graced a dance of witches!
    But here my Muse her wing maun cour;   *stoop*
Sic flights are far beyond her pow'r:
To sing how Nannie lap and flang   *kicked*
(A souple jad she was, and strang),
And how Tam stood, like ane bewitched,
And thought his very een enriched;
Even Satan glowered, and fidged fu' fain,   *fidgeted delightedly*
And hotched and blew wi' might and main: *jerked*
Till first ae caper, syne anither,
Tam tint his reason a' thegither,   *lost*
And roars out, 'Weel done, Cutty-sark!'
And in an instant all was dark!
And scarcely had he Maggie rallied,
When out the hellish legion sallied.
    As bees bizz out wi' angry fyke   *fret*
When plundering herds assail their byke;   *shepherds; hive*
As open pussie's mortal foes   *the hare's*
When pop! she starts before their nose;
As eager runs the market-crowd,
When 'Catch the thief!' resounds aloud:

So Maggie runs; the witches follow,
Wi' monie an eldritch skriech and hollo.   *unearthly*
  Ah, Tam! ah, Tam! thou'll get thy fairin'!   *deserts*
In hell they'll roast thee like a herrin'!
In vain thy Kate awaits thy comin'!
Kate soon will be a woefu' woman!
Now do thy speedy utmost, Meg,
And win the key-stane of the brig:
There at them thou thy tail may toss,
A running stream they darena cross!
But ere the key-stane she could make,
The fient a tail she had to shake;   *devil*
For Nannie, far before the rest,
Hard upon noble Maggie prest,
And flew at Tam wi' furious ettle;   *intent*
But little wist she Maggie's mettle!
Ae spring brought off her master hale,
But left behind her ain grey tail:
The carlin claught her by the rump,   *clutched*
And left poor Maggie scarce a stump.
  Now, wha this tale o' truth shall read,
Ilk man and mother's son, take heed;
Whene'er to drink you are inclin'd,
Or cutty-sarks run in your mind,
Think! ye may buy the joys o'er dear:
Remember Tam o' Shanter's mare.

WILLIAM ROBERT SPENCER

Beth Gêlert, or The Grave of the Greyhound

The spearmen heard the bugle sound,
And cheerly smiled the morn;
And many a brach, and many a hound,
Obeyed Llewelyn's horn.

And still he blew a louder blast,
And gave a lustier cheer:
'Come, Gêlert, come, wer't never last
Llewelyn's horn to hear.

'Oh where does faithful Gêlert roam,
The flower of all his race;
So true, so brave, a lamb at home,
A lion in the chase?'

'Twas only at Llewelyn's board
The faithful Gêlert fed;
He watched, he served, he cheered his lord,
And sentinelled his bed.

In sooth he was a peerless hound,
The gift of royal John;
But now no Gêlert could be found,
And all the chase rode on.

And now, as o'er the rocks and dells
The gallant chidings rise,
All Snowdon's craggy chaos yells
The many-mingled cries.

That day Llewelyn little loved
The chase of hart and hare;
And scant and small the booty proved,
For Gêlert was not there.

Unpleased Llewelyn homeward hied,
When near the portal seat
His truant Gêlert he espied,
Bounding his lord to greet.

But when he gained his castle door
Aghast the chieftain stood;
The hound all o'er was smeared with gore,
His lips, his fangs, ran blood.

Llewelyn gazed with fierce surprise;
Unused such looks to meet,
His favourite checked his joyful guise,
And crouched, and licked his feet.

Onward in haste Llewelyn passed,
And on went Gêlert too;
And still, where'er his eyes he cast,
Fresh blood-gouts shocked his view.

O'erturned his infant's bed he found,
With blood-stained covert rent;
And all around the walls and ground
With recent blood besprent.

He called his child – no voice replied –
He searched with terror wild;

Blood, blood he found on every side,
But nowhere found his child.

'Hell hound! my child's by thee devoured,'
The frantic father cried;
And to the hilt his vengeful sword
He plunged in Gêlert's side.

His suppliant looks, as prone he fell,
No pity could impart;
But still his Gêlert's dying yell
Passed heavy o'er his heart.

Aroused by Gêlert's dying yell,
Some slumberer wakened nigh:
What words the parent's joy could tell
To hear his infant's cry!

Concealed beneath a tumbled heap
His hurried search had missed,
All glowing from his rosy sleep,
The cherub boy he kissed.

Nor scathe had he, nor harm, nor dread,
But, the same couch beneath,
Lay a gaunt wolf, all torn and dead,
Tremendous still in death.

Ah, what was then Llewelyn's pain!
For now the truth was clear;
His gallant hound the wolf had slain,
To save Llewelyn's heir.

Vain, vain was all Llewelyn's woe:
'Best of thy kind, adieu!
The frantic blow, which laid thee low,
This heart shall ever rue.'

And now a gallant tomb they raise,
With costly sculpture decked;
And marbles storied with his praise
Poor Gêlert's bones protect.

There never could the spearman pass,
Or forester, unmoved;
There, oft the tear-besprinkled grass
Llewelyn's sorrow proved.

And there he hung his horn and spear,
And there, as evening fell,
In fancy's ear he oft would hear
Poor Gêlert's dying yell.

And till great Snowdon's rocks grow old,
And cease the storm to brave,
The consecrated spot shall hold
The name of 'Gêlert's grave'.

SIR WALTER SCOTT

Lochinvar

O, young Lochinvar is come out of the west,
Through all the wide Border his steed was the best;
And save his good broadsword he weapons had none,
He rode all unarmed, and he rode all alone.
So faithful in love, and so dauntless in war,
There never was knight like the young Lochinvar.

He stayed not for brake, and he stopped not for stone,
He swam the Esk river where ford there was none;
But ere he alighted at Netherby gate,
The bride had consented, the gallant came late:
For a laggard in love, and a dastard in war,
Was to wed the fair Ellen of brave Lochinvar.

So boldly he entered the Netherby Hall,
Among bridesmen, and kinsmen, and brothers, and all:
Then spoke the bride's father, his hand on his sword
(For the poor craven bridegroom said never a word),
'O come ye in peace here, or come ye in war,
Or to dance at our bridal, young Lord Lochinvar?'

'I long wooed your daughter, my suit you denied –
Love swells like the Solway, but ebbs like its tide –
And now am I come, with this lost love of mine,
To lead but one measure, drink one cup of wine.
There are maidens in Scotland more lovely by far,
That would gladly be bride to the young Lochinvar.'

The bride kissed the goblet: the knight took it up,

He quaffed off the wine, and he threw down the cup.
She looked down to blush, and she looked up to sigh,
With a smile on her lips, and a tear in her eye.
He took her soft hand, ere her mother could bar –
'Now tread we a measure!' said young Lochinvar.

So stately his form, and so lovely her face,
That never a hall such a galliard did grace;
While her mother did fret, and her father did fume,
And the bridegroom stood dangling his bonnet and plume;
And the bride-maidens whispered, ''Twere better by far,
To have matched our fair cousin with young Lochinvar.'

One touch to her hand, and one word in her ear,
When they reached the hall door, and the charger stood near;
So light to the croupe the fair lady he swung,
So light to the saddle before her he sprung!
'She is won! we are gone, over bank, bush, and scaur;
They'll have fleet steeds that follow,' quoth young Lochinvar.

There was mounting 'mong Graemes of the Netherby clan;
Forsters, Fenwicks, and Musgraves, they rode and they ran:
There was racing and chasing on Cannobie Lee,
But the lost bride of Netherby ne'er did they see.
So daring in love, and so dauntless in war,
Have ye e'er heard of gallant like young Lochinvar?

SAMUEL TAYLOR COLERIDGE

The Rime of the Ancient Mariner

PART I

It is an ancient Mariner
And he stoppeth one of three.
'By thy long grey beard and glittering eye,
Now wherefore stopp'st thou me?

An ancient Mariner meeteth three Gallants bidden to a wedding-feast, and detaineth one.

'The Bridegroom's doors are opened wide,
And I am next of kin;
The guests are met, the feast is set:
May'st hear the merry din.'

He holds him with his skinny hand,
'There was a ship,' quoth he.

'Hold off! unhand me, grey-beard loon!'
Eftsoons his hand dropped he.

He holds him with his glittering eye –
The Wedding-Guest stood still,
And listens like a three years' child:
The Mariner hath his will.

The Wedding-Guest is spellbound by the eye of the old seafaring man, and constrained to hear his tale.

The Wedding-Guest sat on a stone:
He cannot choose but hear;
And thus spake on that ancient man,
The bright-eyed Mariner.

'The ship was cheered, the harbour cleared,
Merrily did we drop
Below the kirk, below the hill,
Below the lighthouse top.

The Mariner tells how the ship sailed southward with a good wind and fair weather, till it reached the Line.

'The Sun came up upon the left,
Out of the sea came he!
And he shone bright, and on the right
Went down into the sea.

'Higher and higher every day,
Till over the mast at noon – '
The Wedding-Guest here beat his breast,
For he heard the loud bassoon.

The bride hath paced into the hall,
Red as a rose is she;
Nodding their heads before her goes
The merry minstrelsy.

The Wedding-Guest heareth the bridal music; but the Mariner continueth his tale.

The Wedding-Guest he beat his breast,
Yet he cannot choose but hear;
And thus spake on that ancient man,
The bright-eyed Mariner.

'And now the STORM-BLAST came, and he
Was tyrannous and strong:
He struck with his o'ertaking wings,
And chased us south along.

The ship driven by a storm toward the South Pole.

'With sloping masts and dipping prow,
As who pursued with yell and blow
Still treads the shadow of his foe,

And forward bends his head,
The ship drove fast, loud roared the blast,
And southward aye we fled.

'And now there came both mist and snow,
And it grew wondrous cold:
And ice, mast-high, came floating by,
As green as emerald.

'And through the drifts the snowy clifts
Did send a dismal sheen:
Nor shapes of men nor beasts we ken –
The ice was all between.

*The land of ice, and of fearful
sounds, where no living thing
was to be seen.*

'The ice was here, the ice was there,
The ice was all around:
It cracked and growled, and roared and howled,
Like noises in a swound!

'At length did cross an Albatross,
Thorough the fog it came;
As if it had been a Christian soul,
We hailed it in God's name.

*Till a great sea-bird, called the
Albatross, came through the
snow-fog, and was received
with great joy and hospitality.*

'It ate the food it ne'er had eat,
And round and round it flew.
The ice did split with a thunder-fit;
The helmsman steered us through!

'And a good south wind sprung up behind;
The Albatross did follow,
And every day, for food or play,
Came to the mariners' hollo!

*And lo! the Albatross proveth a
bird of good omen, and
followeth the ship as it returned
northward through fog and
floating ice.*

'In mist or cloud, on mast or shroud,
It perched for vespers nine;
Whiles all the night, through fog-smoke white,
Glimmered the white Moon-shine.'

'God save thee, ancient Mariner!
From the fiends, that plague thee thus! –
Why look'st thou so?' – 'With my cross-bow
I shot the ALBATROSS.'

*The ancient Mariner
inhospitably killeth the pious
bird of good omen.*

PART II

'The Sun now rose upon the right:
Out of the sea came he,
Still hid in mist, and on the left
Went down into the sea.

'And the good south wind still blew behind,
But no sweet bird did follow,
Nor any day for food or play
Came to the mariners' hollo!

'And I had done a hellish thing,
And it would work 'em woe:
For all averred, I had killed the bird
That made the breeze to blow.
Ah wretch! said they, the bird to slay,
That made the breeze to blow!

His shipmates cry out against the ancient Mariner, for killing the bird of good luck.

'Nor dim nor red, like God's own head,
The glorious Sun uprist:
Then all averred, I had killed the bird
That brought the fog and mist.
'Twas right, said they, such birds to slay,
That bring the fog and mist.

But when the fog cleared off, they justify the same, and thus make themselves accomplices in the crime.

'The fair breeze blew, the white foam flew,
The furrow followed free;
We were the first that ever burst
Into that silent sea.

The fair breeze continues; the ship enters the Pacific Ocean, and sails northward, even till it reaches the Line.

'Down dropped the breeze, the sails dropped down,
'Twas sad as sad could be;
And we did speak only to break
The silence of the sea!

The ship hath been suddenly becalmed.

'All in a hot and copper sky,
The bloody Sun, at noon,
Right up above the mast did stand,
No bigger than the Moon.

'Day after day, day after day,
We stuck, nor breath nor motion;
As idle as a painted ship
Upon a painted ocean.

'Water, water, everywhere,
And all the boards did shrink;
Water, water, everywhere,
Nor any drop to drink.

And the Albatross begins to be avenged.

'The very deep did rot: O Christ!
That ever this should be!
Yea, slimy things did crawl with legs
Upon the slimy sea.

'About, about, in reel and rout
The death-fires danced at night;
The water, like a witch's oils,
Burnt green, and blue and white.

'And some in dreams assurèd were
Of the Spirit that plagued us so;
Nine fathom deep he had followed us
From the land of mist and snow.

A Spirit had followed them; one of the invisible inhabitants of this planet neither departed souls nor angels; concerning whom the learned Jew Josephus, and the Platonic Constantinopolitan, Michael Psellus, may be consulted. They are very numerous, and there is no climate or element without one or more.

'And every tongue, through utter drought,
Was withered at the root;
We could not speak, no more than if
We had been choked with soot.

'Ah! well a-day! What evil looks
Had I from old and young!
Instead of the cross, the Albatross
About my neck was hung.'

The shipmates in their sore distress, would fain throw the whole guilt on the ancient Mariner: in sign whereof they hang the dead seabird round his neck.

PART III

'There passed a weary time. Each throat
Was parched, and glazed each eye.
A weary time! a weary time!
How glazed each weary eye,
When looking westward, I beheld
A something in the sky.

The ancient Mariner beholdeth a sign in the element afar off.

'At first it seemed a little speck,
And then it seemed a mist;
It moved and moved, and took at last
A certain shape, I wist.

'A speck, a mist, a shape, I wist!
And still it neared and neared:

As if it dodged a water-sprite,
It plunged and tacked and veered.

'With throats unslaked, with black lips baked,
We could nor laugh nor wail;
Through utter drought all dumb we stood!
I bit my arm, I sucked the blood,
And cried, A sail! a sail!

At its nearer approach, it
seemeth him to be a ship; and at
a dear ransom he freeth his
speech from the bonds of thirst.

'With throats unslaked, with black lips baked,
Agape they heard me call:
Gramercy! they for joy did grin,
And all at once their breath drew in,
As they were drinking all.

A flash of joy;

' "See! see!" (I cried) "she tacks no more!
Hither to work us weal;
Without a breeze, without a tide,
She steadies with upright keel!"

And horror follows. For can it
be a ship that comes onward
without wind or tide?

'The western wave was all a-flame.
The day was well nigh done!
Almost upon the western wave
Rested the broad bright Sun;
When that strange shape drove suddenly
Betwixt us and the Sun.

'And straight the Sun was flecked with bars,
(Heaven's Mother send us grace!)
As if through a dungeon-grate he peered
With broad and burning face.

It seemeth him but the skeleton
of a ship.

'Alas! (thought I, and my heart beat loud)
How fast she nears and nears!
Are those *her* sails that glance in the Sun,
Like restless gossameres?

'Are those *her* ribs through which the Sun
Did peer, as through a grate?
And is that Woman all her crew?
Is that a DEATH? and are there two?
Is DEATH that woman's mate?

And its ribs are seen as bars on
the face of the setting Sun. The
Spectre-Woman and her
Death-mate, and no other on
board the skeleton ship.

'*Her* lips were red, *her* looks were free,
Her locks were yellow as gold:
Her skin was as white as leprosy,
The Night-mare LIFE-IN-DEATH was she,
Who thicks man's blood with cold.

Like vessel, like crew! Death
and Life-in-Death have diced
for the ship's crew, and she
(the latter) winneth the ancient
Mariner.

'The naked hulk alongside came,
And the twain were casting dice;
"The game is done! I've won! I've won!"
Quoth she, and whistles thrice.

'The Sun's rim dips; the stars rush out: *No twilight within the courts of*
At one stride comes the dark;   *the Sun.*
With far-heard whisper, o'er the sea,
Off shot the spectre-bark.

'We listened and looked sideways up!   *At the rising of the Moon,*
Fear at my heart, as at a cup,
My life-blood seemed to sip!
The stars were dim, and thick the night,
The steersman's face by his lamp gleamed white;
From the sails the dew did drip –
Till clomb above the eastern bar
The hornèd Moon, with one bright star
Within the nether tip.

'One after one, by the star-dogged Moon,   *One after another,*
Too quick for groan or sigh,
Each turned his face with a ghastly pang,
And cursed me with his eye.

'Four times fifty living men,   *His shipmates drop down dead.*
(And I heard nor sign nor groan)
With heavy thump, a lifeless lump,
They dropped down one by one.

'The souls did from their bodies fly –   *But Life-in-Death begins her*
They fled to bliss or woe!   *work on the ancient Mariner.*
And every soul, it passed me by,
Like the whizz of my cross-bow!'

PART IV

'I fear thee, ancient Mariner!   *The Wedding-Guest feareth*
I fear thy skinny hand!   *that a Spirit is talking to him;*
And thou art long, and lank, and brown,
As is the ribbed sea-sand.

'I fear thee and thy glittering eye,
And thy skinny hand, so brown.' –
'Fear not, fear not, thou Wedding-Guest!   *But the ancient Mariner*
This body dropt not down.   *assureth him of his bodily life,*

'Alone, alone, all, all alone,
Alone on a wide wide sea!
And never a saint took pity on
My soul in agony.

*and proceedeth to relate his
horrible penance.*

'The many men, so beautiful!
And they all dead did lie:
And a thousand thousand slimy things
Lived on; and so did I.

*He despiseth the creatures of the
calm,*

'I looked upon the rotting sea,
And drew my eyes away;
I looked upon the rotting deck,
And there the dead men lay.

*And envieth that they should
live, and so many lie dead.*

'I looked to Heaven, and tried to pray;
But or ever a prayer had gusht,
A wicked whisper came, and made
My heart as dry as dust.

'I closed my lids, and kept them close,
And the balls like pulses beat;
For the sky and the sea, and the sea and the sky
Lay like a load on my weary eye,
And the dead were at my feet.

'The cold sweat melted from their limbs,
Nor rot nor reek did they:
The look with which they looked on me
Had never passed away.

*But the curse liveth for him in
the eye of the dead men.*

'An orphan's curse would drag to hell
A spirit from on high;
But oh! more horrible than that
Is the curse in a dead man's eye!
Seven days, seven nights, I saw that curse,
And yet I could not die.

'The moving Moon went up the sky,
And nowhere did abide:
Softly she was going up,
And a star or two beside –

*In his loneliness and fixedness he
yearneth towards the journeying
Moon, and the stars that still
sojourn, yet still move onward;
and everywhere the blue sky*

'Her beams bemocked the sultry main,
Like April hoar-frost spread;
But where the ship's huge shadow lay,
The charmèd water burnt alway
A still and awful red.

*belongs to them, and is their
appointed rest, and their native
country and their own natural
homes, which they enter
unannounced, as lords that are
certainly expected and yet there is
a silent joy at their arrival.*

'Beyond the shadow of the ship,
I watched the water-snakes:
They moved in tracks of shining white,
And when they reared, the elfish light
Fell off in hoary flakes.

By the light of the Moon he beholdeth God's creatures of the great calm.

'Within the shadow of the ship
I watched their rich attire:
Blue, glossy green, and velvet black,
They coiled and swam; and every track
Was a flash of golden fire.

'O happy living things! no tongue
Their beauty might declare:
A spring of love gushed from my heart,
And I blessed them unaware:
Sure my kind Saint took pity on me,
And I blessed them unaware.

Their beauty and their happiness.

He blesseth them in his heart.

'The self-same moment I could pray;
And from my neck so free
The Albatross fell off, and sank
Like lead into the sea.'

The spell begins to break.

PART V

'Oh sleep! it is a gentle thing,
Beloved from pole to pole!
To Mary Queen the praise be given!
She sent the gentle sleep from Heaven,
That slid into my soul.

'The silly buckets on the deck,
That had so long remained,
I dreamt that they were filled with dew;
And when I awoke, it rained.

By grace of the holy Mother, the ancient Mariner is refreshed with rain.

'My lips were wet, my throat was cold,
My garments all were dank;
Sure I had drunken in my dreams,
And still my body drank.

'I moved, and could not feel my limbs:
I was so light – almost
I thought that I had died in sleep,
And was a blessèd ghost.

'And soon I heard a roaring wind:
It did not come anear;
But with its sound it shook the sails,
That were so thin and sere.

*He heareth sounds and seeth
strange sights and commotions
in the sky and the element.*

'The upper air burst into life!
And a hundred fire-flags sheen,
To and fro they were hurried about!
And to and fro, and in and out,
The wan stars danced between.

'And the coming wind did roar more loud,
And the sails did sigh like sedge;
And the rain poured down from one black cloud;
The Moon was at its edge.

'The thick black cloud was cleft, and still
The Moon was at its side:
Like waters shot from some high crag,
The lightning fell with never a jag,
A river steep and wide.

'The loud wind never reached the ship,
Yet now the ship moved on!
Beneath the lightning and the Moon
The dead men gave a groan.

*The bodies of the ship's crew
are inspired and the ship moves
on;*

'They groaned, they stirred, they all uprose,
Nor spake, nor moved their eyes;
It had been strange, even in a dream,
To have seen those dead men rise.

'The helmsman steered, the ship moved on;
Yet never a breeze up-blew;
The mariners all 'gan work the ropes,
Where they were wont to do;
They raised their limbs like lifeless tools –
We were a ghastly crew.

'The body of my brother's son
Stood by me, knee to knee:
The body and I pulled at one rope,
But he said nought to me.'

'I fear thee, ancient Mariner!'
'Be calm, thou Wedding-Guest!
'Twas not those souls that fled in pain,

*But not by the souls of the
men, nor by daemons of earth
or middle air, but by a blessed*

Which to their corses came again,
But a troop of spirits blest:

*troop of angelic spirits, sent
down by the invocation of the
guardian saint.*

'For when it dawned – they dropped their
      arms,
And clustered round the mast;
Sweet sounds rose slowly through their
      mouths,
And from their bodies passed.

'Around, around, flew each sweet sound,
Then darted to the Sun;
Slowly the sounds came back again,
Now mixed, now one by one.

'Sometimes a–dropping from the sky
I heard the sky–lark sing;
Sometimes all little birds that are,
How they seemed to fill the sea and air
With their sweet jargoning!

'And now 'twas like all instruments,
Now like a lonely flute;
And now it is an angel's song,
That makes the heavens be mute.

'It ceased; yet still the sails made on
A pleasant noise till noon,
A noise like of a hidden brook
In the leafy month of June,
That to the sleeping woods all night
Singeth a quiet tune.

'Till noon we quietly sailed on,
Yet never a breeze did breathe:
Slowly and smoothly went the ship,
Moved onward from beneath.

'Under the keel nine fathom deep,
From the land of mist and snow,
The spirit slid: and it was he
That made the ship to go.
The sails at noon left off their tune,
And the ship stood still also.

*The lonesome Spirit from the
South Pole carries on the ship
as far as the Line, in obedience
to the angelic troop, but still
requireth vengeance.*

'The Sun, right up above the mast,
Had fixed her to the ocean:

But in a minute she 'gan stir,
With a short uneasy motion –
Backwards and forwards half her length
With a short uneasy motion.

'Then like a pawing horse let go,
She made a sudden bound:
It flung the blood into my head,
And I fell down in a swound.

'How long in that same fit I lay,
I have not to declare;
But ere my living life returned,
I heard and in my soul discerned
Two voices in the air.

' "Is it he?" quoth one, "Is this the man?
By him who died on cross,
With his cruel bow he laid full low
The harmless Albatross.

' "The spirit who bideth by himself
In the land of mist and snow,
He loved the bird that loved the man
Who shot him with his bow."

'The other was a softer voice,
As soft as honey-dew:
Quoth he, "The man hath penance done,
And penance more will do." '

The Polar Spirit's fellow-daemons, the invisible inhabitants of the element, take part in his wrong; and two of them relate, one to the other, that penance long and heavy for the ancient Mariner hath been accorded to the Polar Spirit who returneth southward.

PART VI

FIRST VOICE

' "But tell me, tell me! speak again,
Thy soft response renewing –
What makes that ship drive on so fast?
What is the ocean doing?"

SECOND VOICE

' "Still as a slave before his lord,
The ocean hath no blast;
His great bright eye most silently
Up to the Moon is cast –

' "If he may know which way to go;
For she guides him smooth or grim.
See, brother, see! how graciously
She looketh down on him."

FIRST VOICE

' "But why drives on that ship so fast,
Without or wave or wind?"

*The Mariner hath been cast
into a trance; for the angelic
power causeth the vessel to
drive northward faster than
human life could endure.*

SECOND VOICE

' "The air is cut away before,
And closes from behind.

' "Fly, brother, fly! more high, more high!
Or we shall be belated:
For slow and slow that ship will go,
When the Mariner's trance is abated."

'I woke, and we were sailing on
As in a gentle weather:
'Twas night, calm night, the moon was high;
The dead men stood together.

*The supernatural motion is
retarded; the Mariner awakes,
and his penance begins anew.*

'All stood together on the deck,
For a charnel–dungeon fitter:
All fixed on me their stony eyes,
That in the Moon did glitter.

'The pang, the curse, with which they died,
Had never passed away:
I could not draw my eyes from theirs,
Nor turn them up to pray.

'And now this spell was snapped: once more
I viewed the ocean green,
And looked far forth, yet little saw
Of what had else been seen –

The curse is finally expiated.

'Like one, that on a lonesome road
Doth walk in fear and dread,
And having once turned round walks on,
And turns no more his head;
Because he knows, a frightful fiend
Doth close behind him tread.

'But soon there breathed a wind on me,
Nor sound nor motion made:
Its path was not upon the sea,
In ripple or in shade.

'It raised my hair, it fanned my cheek
Like a meadow-gale of spring –
It mingled strangely with my fears,
Yet it felt like a welcoming.

'Swiftly, swiftly flew the ship,
Yet she sailed softly too:
Sweetly, sweetly blew the breeze –
On me alone it blew.

'Oh! dream of joy! is this indeed
The light-house top I see?
Is this the hill? is this the kirk?
Is this mine own countree?

And the ancient Mariner beholdeth his native country.

'We drifted o'er the harbour-bar,
And I with sobs did pray –
O let me be awake, my God!
Or let me sleep alway.

'The harbour-bay was clear as glass,
So smoothly it was strewn!
And on the bay the moonlight lay,
And the shadow of the Moon.

'The rock shone bright, the kirk no less,
That stands above the rock:
The moonlight steeped in silentness
The steady weathercock.

'And the bay was white with silent light,
Till rising from the same,
Full many shapes, that shadows were,
In crimson colours came.

The angelic spirits leave the dead bodies,

'A little distance from the prow
Those crimson shadows were:
I turned my eyes upon the deck –
Oh, Christ! what saw I there!

And appear in their own forms of light.

'Each corse lay flat, lifeless and flat,
And, by the holy rood!

A man all light, a seraph-man,
On every corse there stood.

'This seraph-band, each waved his hand:
It was a heavenly sight!
They stood as signals to the land,
Each one a lovely light;

'This seraph-band, each waved his hand,
No voice did they impart –
No voice; but oh! the silence sank
Like music on my heart.

'But soon I heard the dash of oars,
I heard the Pilot's cheer;
My head was turned perforce away
And I saw a boat appear.

'The Pilot and the Pilot's boy,
I heard them coming fast:
Dear Lord in Heaven! it was a joy
The dead men could not blast.

'I saw a third – I heard his voice:
It is the Hermit good!
He singeth loud his godly hymns
That he makes in the wood.
He'll shrieve my soul, he'll wash away
The Albatross's blood.'

PART VII

'This Hermit good lives in that wood   *The Hermit of the Wood,*
Which slopes down to the sea.
How loudly his sweet voice he rears!
He loves to talk with marineres
That come from a far countree.

'He kneels at morn, and noon, and eve –
He hath a cushion plump:
It is the moss that wholly hides
The rotted old oak-stump.

'The skiff-boat neared: I heard them talk,
"Why, this is strange, I trow!
Where are those lights so many and fair,
That signal made but now?"

' "Strange, by my faith!" the Hermit said –   *Approacheth the ship with*
"And they answered not our cheer!   *wonder.*
The planks looked warped! and see those
        sails,
How thin they are and sere!
I never saw aught like to them,
Unless perchance it were

' "Brown skeletons of leaves that lag
My forest-brook along;
When the ivy-tod is heavy with snow,
And the owlet whoops to the wolf below,
That eats the she-wolf's young."

' "Dear Lord! it hath a fiendish look – "
(The Pilot made reply)
"I am a-feared" – "Push on, push on!"
Said the Hermit cheerily.

'The boat came closer to the ship,
But I nor spake nor stirred;
The boat came close beneath the ship,
And straight a sound was heard.

'Under the water it rumbled on,   *The ship suddenly sinketh.*
Still louder and more dread:
It reached the ship, it split the bay;
The ship went down like lead.

'Stunned by that loud and dreadful sound,
Which sky and ocean smote,
Like one that hath been seven days drowned
My body lay afloat;
But swift as dreams, myself I found
Within the Pilot's boat.

The ancient Mariner is saved in the Pilot's boat.

'Upon the whirl, where sank the ship,
The boat spun round and round;
And all was still, save that the hill
Was telling of the sound.

'I moved my lips – the Pilot shrieked
And fell down in a fit;
The holy Hermit raised his eyes,
And prayed where he did sit.

'I took the oars: the Pilot's boy,
Who now doth crazy go,
Laughed loud and long, and all the while
His eyes went to and fro.
"Ha! Ha!" quoth he, "full plain I see,
The Devil knows how to row."

'And now, all in my own countree,
I stood on the firm land!
The Hermit stepped forth from the boat,
And scarcely he could stand.

' "O shrieve me, shrieve me, holy man!"
The Hermit crossed his brow.
"Say quick," quoth he, "I bid thee say –
What manner of man art thou?"

The ancient Mariner earnestly entreateth the Hermit to shrieve him; and the penance of life falls on him.

'Forthwith this frame of mine was wrenched
With a woeful agony,
Which forced me to begin my tale;
And then it left me free.

'Since then, at an uncertain hour,
That agony returns:
And till my ghastly tale is told,
This heart within me burns.

And ever and anon throughout his future life an agony constraineth him to travel from land to land;

'I pass, like night, from land to land;
I have strange power of speech;
That moment that his face I see,

I know the man that must hear me:
To him my tale I teach.

'What loud uproar bursts from that door!
The wedding-guests are there:
But in the garden-bower the bride
And bride-maids singing are:
And hark the little vesper bell,
Which biddeth me to prayer!

'O Wedding-Guest! this soul hath been
Alone on a wide wide sea:
So lonely 'twas, that God himself
Scarce seemèd there to be.

'O sweeter than the marriage-feast,
'Tis sweeter far to me,
To walk together to the kirk
With a goodly company! –

'To walk together to the kirk
And all together pray,
While each to his great Father bends,
Old men, and babes, and loving friends
And youths and maidens gay!

'Farewell, farewell! but this I tell
To thee, thou Wedding-Guest!
He prayeth well, who loveth well
Both man and bird and beast.

And to teach, by his own example, love and reverence to all things that God made and loveth.

'He prayeth best, who loveth best
All things both great and small;
For the dear God who loveth us,
He made and loveth all.'

The Mariner, whose eye is bright,
Whose beard with age is hoar,
Is gone: and now the Wedding-Guest
Turned from the bridegroom's door.

He went like one that hath been stunned,
And is of sense forlorn:
A sadder and a wiser man,
He rose the morrow morn.

ROBERT SOUTHEY

The Inchcape Rock

No stir in the air, no stir in the sea;
The ship was still as she could be;
Her sails from heaven received no motion,
Her keel was steady in the ocean.

Without either sign or sound of their shock
The waves flowed over the Inchcape Rock;
So little they rose so little they fell,
They did not move the Inchcape Bell.

The Abbot of Aberbrothok
Had placed that bell on the Inchcape Rock;
On a buoy in the storm it floated and swung,
And over the waves its warning rung.

When the Rock was hid by the surge's swell,
The mariners heard the warning bell;
And then they knew the perilous rock,
And blessed the Abbot of Aberbrothok.

The sun in heaven was shining gay,
All things were joyful on that day;
The sea-birds scream'd as they wheeled round,
And there was joyaunce in their sound.

The buoy of the Inchcape Bell was seen
A darker speck on the ocean green;
Sir Ralph the Rover walked his deck,
And he fixed his eye on the darker speck.

He felt the cheering power of spring,
It made him whistle, it made him sing;
His heart was mirthful to excess,
But the Rover's mirth was wickedness.

His eye was on the Inchcape Float;
Quoth he, 'My men, put out the boat,
And row me to the Inchcape Rock,
And I'll plague the Abbot of Aberbrothok.'

The boat is lowered, the boatmen row,
And to the Inchcape Rock they go;
Sir Ralph bent over from the boat,

And he cut the Bell from the Inchcape Float.

Down sunk the Bell with a gurgling sound,
The bubbles rose and burst around;
Quoth Sir Ralph, 'The next who comes to the Rock
Won't bless the Abbot of Aberbrothok.'

Sir Ralph the Rover sailed away,
He scoured the seas for many a day;
And now grown rich with plundered store,
He steers his course for Scotland's shore.

So thick a haze o'erspreads the sky
They cannot see the sun on high;
The wind hath blown a gale all day,
At evening it hath died away.

On the deck the Rover takes his stand,
So dark it is they see no land.
Quoth Sir Ralph, 'It will be lighter soon,
For there is the dawn of the rising Moon.'

'Can'st hear', said one, 'the breakers roar?
For methinks we should be near the shore.'
'Now, where we are I cannot tell,
But I wish we could hear the Inchcape Bell.'

They hear no sound, the swell is strong;
Though the wind hath fallen they drift along,
Till the vessel strikes with a shivering shock –
'Oh Christ! it is the Inchcape Rock!'

Sir Ralph the Rover tore his hair;
He cursed himself in his despair;
The waves rush in on every side,
The ship is sinking beneath the tide.

But even in his dying fear
One dreadful sound could the Rover hear,
A sound as if, with the Inchcape Bell,
The Devil below was ringing his knell.

GEORGE GORDON, LORD BYRON

From *Don Juan*

[JUAN AND HAIDÉE]

His eyes he opened, shut, again unclosed,
    For all was doubt and dizziness; he thought
He still was in the boat, and had but dozed,
    And felt again with his despair o'erwrought,
And wished it death in which he had reposed,
    And then once more his feelings back were brought,
And slowly by his swimming eyes was seen
A lovely female face of seventeen.

'Twas bending close o'er his, and the small mouth
    Seemed almost prying into his for breath;
And chafing him, the soft warm hand of youth
    Recalled his answering spirits back from death;
And, bathing his chill temples, tried to soothe
    Each pulse to animation, till beneath
Its gentle touch and trembling care, a sigh
To these kind efforts made a low reply.

Then was the cordial poured, and mantle flung
    Around his scarce-clad limbs; and the fair arm
Raised higher the faint head which o'er it hung;
    And her transparent cheek, all pure and warm,
Pillowed his death-like forehead; then she wrung
    His dewy curls, long drenched by every storm;
And watched with eagerness each throb that drew
A sigh from his heaved bosom, – and hers, too.

And lifting him with care into the cave,
    The gentle girl, and her attendant, – one
Young, yet her elder, and of brow less grave,
    And more robust of figure, – then begun
To kindle fire, and as the new flames gave
    Light to the rocks that roofed them, which the sun
Had never seen, the maid, or whatsoe'er
She was, appeared distinct, and tall, and fair.

. . .

I'll tell you who they were, this female pair,
    Lest they should seem princesses in disguise;
Besides, I hate all mystery, and that air
    Of clap-trap, which your recent poets prize;
And so, in short, the girls they really were

114

They shall appear before your curious eyes,
Mistress and maid; the first was only daughter
Of an old man, who lived upon the water.

A fisherman he had been in his youth,
    And still a sort of fisherman was he;
But other speculations were, in sooth,
    Added to his connection with the sea,
Perhaps not so respectable, in truth:
    A little smuggling, and some piracy,
Left him, at last, the sole of many masters
Of an ill-gotten million of piastres.

A fisher, therefore, was he, – though of men,
    Like Peter the Apostle, – and he fished
For wandering merchant-vessels, now and then,
    And sometimes caught as many as he wished;
The cargoes he confiscated, and gain
    He sought in the slave-market too, and dished
Full many a morsel for that Turkish trade,
By which, no doubt, a good deal may be made.

He was a Greek, and on his isle had built
    (One of the wild and smaller Cyclades)
A very handsome house from out his guilt,
    And there he lived exceedingly at ease;
Heaven knows what cash he got or blood he spilt,
    A sad old fellow was he, if you please;
But this I know, it was a spacious building,
Full of barbaric carving, paint, and gilding.

He had an only daughter, called Haidée,
    The greatest heiress of the Eastern Isles;
Besides, so very beautiful was she,
    Her dowry was as nothing to her smiles:
Still in her teens, and like a lovely tree
    She grew to womanhood, and between whiles
Rejected several suitors, just to learn
How to accept a better in his turn.

And walking out upon the beach, below
    The cliff, towards sunset, on that day she found,
Insensible, – not dead, but nearly so, –
    Don Juan, almost famished, and half drowned;
But being naked, she was shocked, you know,
    Yet deemed herself in common pity bound,
As far as in her lay, 'to take him in,
A stranger' dying, with so white a skin.

But taking him into her father's house
   Was not exactly the best way to save,
But like conveying to the cat the mouse,
   Or people in a trance into their grave;
Because the good old man had so much 'νους',
   Unlike the honest Arab thieves so brave,
He would have hospitably cured the stranger,
And sold him instantly when out of danger.

And therefore, with her maid, she thought it best
   (A virgin always on her maid relies)
To place him in the cave for present rest:
   And when, at last, he opened his black eyes,
Their charity increased about their guest;
   And their compassion grew to such a size,
It opened half the turnpike gates to heaven –
(St Paul says, 'tis the toll which must be given).

They made a fire, – but such a fire as they
   Upon the moment could contrive with such
Materials as were cast up round the bay, –
   Some broken planks, and oars, that to the touch
Were nearly tinder, since so long they lay
   A mast was almost crumbled to a crutch;
But, by God's grace, here wrecks were in such plenty,
That there was fuel to have furnished twenty.

He had a bed of furs, and a pelisse,
   For Haidée stripped her sables off to make
His couch; and, that he might be more at ease,
   And warm, in case by chance he should awake,
They also gave a petticoat apiece,
   She and her maid, – and promised by daybreak
To pay him a fresh visit, with a dish
For breakfast, of eggs, coffee, bread, and fish.

. . .

The morn broke, and found Juan slumbering still
   Fast in his cave, and nothing clashed upon
His rest; the rushing of the neighbouring rill,
   And the young beams of the excluded sun,
Troubled him not, and he might sleep his fill;
   And need he had of slumber yet, for none
Had suffered more – his hardships were comparative
To those related in my grand–dad's 'Narrative'.

Not so Haidée: she sadly tossed and tumbled,
   And started from her sleep, and, turning o'er,

Dreamed of a thousand wrecks, o'er which she stumbled,
  And handsome corpses strewed upon the shore;
And woke her maid so early that she grumbled,
  And called her father's old slaves up, who swore
In several oaths – Armenian, Turk, and Greek –
They knew not what to think of such a freak.

But up she got, and up she made them get,
  With some pretence about the sun, that makes
Sweet skies just when he rises, or is set;
  And 'tis, no doubt, a sight to see when breaks
Bright Phoebus, while the mountains still are wet
  With mist, and every bird with him awakes,
And night is flung off like a mourning suit
Worn for a husband, – or some other brute.

                . . .

And down the cliff the island virgin came,
  And near the cave her quick light footsteps drew,
While the sun smiled on her with his first flame,
  And the young Aurora kissed her lips with dew,
Taking her for a sister; just the same
  Mistake you would have made on seeing the two,
Although the mortal, quite as fresh and fair,
Had all the advantage, too, of not being air.

And when into the cavern Haidée stepped
  All timidly, yet rapidly, she saw
That like an infant Juan sweetly slept;
  And then she stopped, and stood as if in awe
(For sleep is awful), and on tiptoe crept
  And wrapt him closer, lest the air, too raw,
Should reach his blood; then o'er him still as death
Bent, with hushed lips, that drank his scarce-drawn breath.

And thus like to an angel o'er the dying
  Who die in righteousness, she leaned; and there
All tranquilly the shipwrecked boy was lying,
  As o'er him lay the calm and stirless air:
But Zoë the meantime some eggs was frying,
  Since, after all, no doubt the youthful pair
Must breakfast, and betimes – lest they should ask it,
She drew out her provision from the basket.

She knew that the best feelings must have victual,
  And that a shipwrecked youth would hungry be;
Besides, being less in love, she yawned a little,
  And felt her veins chilled by the neighbouring sea;

And so, she cooked their breakfast to a tittle;
   I can't say that she gave them any tea,
But there were eggs, fruit, coffee, bread, fish, honey,
With Scio wine, – and all for love, not money.

And Zoë, when the eggs were ready, and
   The coffee made, would fain have wakened Juan;
But Haidée stopped her with her quick small hand,
   And without word, a sign her finger drew on
Her lip, which Zoë needs must understand;
   And, the first breakfast spoilt, prepared a new one,
Because her mistress would not let her break
That sleep which seemed as it would ne'er awake.

For still he lay, and on his thin worn cheek
   A purple hectic played like dying day
On the snow-tops of distant hills; the streak
   Of sufferance yet upon his forehead lay,
Where the blue veins looked shadowy, shrunk, and weak;
   And his black curls were dewy with the spray,
Which weighed upon them yet, all damp and salt,
Mixed with the stony vapours of the vault.

And she bent o'er him, and he lay beneath,
   Hushed as the babe upon its mother's breast,
Drooped as the willow when no winds can breathe,
   Lulled like the depth of ocean when at rest,
Fair as the crowning rose of the whole wreath,
   Soft as the callow cygnet in its nest;
In short, he was a very pretty fellow,
Although his woes had turned him rather yellow.

He woke and gazed, and would have slept again,
   But the fair face which met his eyes forbade
Those eyes to close, though weariness and pain
   Had further sleep a further pleasure made;
For woman's face was never formed in vain
   For Juan, so that even when he prayed
He turned from grisly saints, and martyrs hairy,
To the sweet portraits of the Virgin Mary.

And thus upon his elbow he arose,
   And looked upon the lady, in whose cheek
The pale contended with the purple rose,
   As with an effort she began to speak;
Her eyes were eloquent, her words would pose,
   Although she told him, in good modern Greek,

With an Ionian accent, low and sweet,
That he was faint, and must not talk, but eat.

Now Juan could not understand a word,
   Being no Grecian; but he had an ear,
And her voice was the warble of a bird,
   So soft, so sweet, so delicately clear,
That finer, simpler music ne'er was heard;
   The sort of sound we echo with a tear,
Without knowing why – an overpowering tone,
Whence Melody descends as from a throne.

     . . .

And Juan, too, was helped out from his dream,
   Or sleep, or whatsoe'er it was, by feeling
A most prodigious appetite: the steam
   Of Zoë's cookery no doubt was stealing
Upon his senses, and the kindling beam
   Of the new fire, which Zoë kept up, kneeling,
To stir her viands, made him quite awake
And long for food, but chiefly a beef-steak.

But beef is rare within these oxless isles;
   Goat's flesh there is, no doubt, and kid, and mutton
And, when a holiday upon them smiles,
   A joint upon their barbarous spits they put on;
But this occurs but seldom, between whiles,
   For some of these are rocks with scarce a hut on,
Others are fair and fertile, among which
This, though not large, was one of the most rich.

     . . .

But to resume. The languid Juan raised
   His head upon his elbow, and he saw
A sight on which he had not lately gazed,
   As all his latter meals had been quite raw,
Three or four things, for which the Lord be praised,
   And, feeling still the famished vulture gnaw,
He fell upon whate'er was offered, like
A priest, a shark, an alderman, or pike.

He ate, and he was well supplied; and she,
   Who watched him like a mother, would have fed
Him past all bounds, because she smiled to see
   Such appetite in one she had deemed dead:
But Zoë, being older than Haidée,
   Knew (by tradition for she ne'er had read)
That famished people must be slowly nurst,
And fed by spoonfuls, else they always burst.

And so she took the liberty to state,
    Rather by deeds than words, because the case
Was urgent, that the gentleman, whose fate
    Had made her mistress quit her bed to trace
The sea-shore at this hour, must leave his plate,
    Unless he wished to die upon the place –
She snatched it, and refused another morsel,
Saying, he had gorged enough to make a horse ill.

Next they – he being naked, save a tattered
    Pair of scarce decent trousers – went to work,
And in the fire his recent rags they scattered,
    And dressed him, for the present, like a Turk,
Or Greek – that is, although it not much mattered,
    Omitting turban, slippers, pistols, dirk, –
They furnished him, entire, except some stitches,
With a clean shirt and very spacious breeches.

And then fair Haidée tried her tongue at speaking,
    But not a word could Juan comprehend,
Although he listened so that the young Greek in
    Her earnestness would ne'er have made an end;
And, as he interrupted not, went eking
    Her speech out to her protégé and friend,
Till pausing at the last her breath to take,
She saw he did not understand Romaic.

And then she had recourse to nods, and signs,
    And smiles, and sparkles of the speaking eye,
And read (the only book she could) the lines
    Of his fair face, and found, by sympathy,
The answer eloquent, where the soul shines
    And darts in one quick glance a long reply;
And thus in every word she saw exprest
A world of words, and things at which she guessed.

And now, by dint of fingers and of eyes,
    And words repeated after her, he took
A lesson in her tongue; but by surmise,
    No doubt, less of her language than her look:
As he who studies fervently the skies
    Turns oftener to the stars than to his book,
Thus Juan learned his alpha beta better
From Haidée's glance than any graven letter.

'Tis pleasing to be schooled in a strange tongue
    By female lips and eyes – that is, I mean,

When both the teacher and the taught are young,
   As was the case, at least, where I have been;
They smile so when one's right, and when one's wrong
   They smile still more, and then there intervene
Pressure of hands, perhaps even a chaste kiss; –
I learned the little that I know by this.

        . . .

Return we to Don Juan. He begun
   To hear new words, and to repeat them; but
Some feelings, universal as the sun,
   Were such as could not in his breast be shut
More than within the bosom of a nun:
   He was in love, – as you would be, no doubt,
With a young benefactress, – so was she,
Just in the way we very often see.

And every day by daybreak – rather early
   For Juan, who was somewhat fond of rest –
She came into the cave, but it was merely
   To see her bird reposing in his nest;
And she would softly stir his locks so curly,
   Without disturbing her yet slumbering guest,
Breathing all gently o'er his cheek and mouth,
As o'er a bed of roses the sweet south.

        . . .

When Juan woke he found some good things ready,
   A bath, a breakfast, and the finest eyes
That ever made a youthful heart less steady,
   Besides her maid's, as pretty for their size;
But I have spoken of all this already –
   And repetition's tiresome and unwise, –
Well – Juan, after bathing in the sea,
Came always back to coffee and Haidée.

Both were so young, and one so innocent,
   That bathing passed for nothing; Juan seemed
To her, as t'were, the kind of being sent,
   Of whom these two years she had nightly dreamed,
A something to be loved, a creature meant
   To be her happiness, and whom she deemed
To render happy; all who joy would win
Must share it – Happiness was born a twin.

It was such pleasure to behold him, such
   Enlargement of existence to partake
Nature with him, to thrill beneath his touch,
   To watch him slumbering, and to see him wake:

To live with him for ever were too much;
    But then the thought of parting made her quake;
He was her own, her ocean-treasure, cast
Like a rich wreck – her first love, and her last.

And thus a moon rolled on, and fair Haidée
    Paid daily visits to her boy, and took
Such plentiful precautions, that still he
    Remained unknown within his craggy nook;
At last her father's prows put out to sea,
    For certain merchantmen upon the look,
Not as of yore to carry off an Io,
But three Ragusan vessels, bound for Scio.

Then came her freedom, for she had no mother,
    So that, her father being at sea, she was
Free as a married woman, or such other
    Female, as where she likes may freely pass,
Without even the incumbrance of a brother,
    The freest she that ever gazed on glass;
I speak of Christian lands in this comparison,
Where wives, at least, are seldom kept in garrison.

Now she prolonged her visits and her talk
    (For they must talk), and he had learnt to say
So much as to propose to take a walk, –
    For little had he wandered since the day
On which, like a young flower snapped from the stalk,
    Drooping and dewy on the beach he lay, –
And thus they walked out in the afternoon,
And saw the sun set opposite the moon.

It was a wild and breaker-beaten coast,
    With cliffs above, and a broad sandy shore,
Guarded by shoals and rocks as by an host,
    With here and there a creek, whose aspect wore
A better welcome to the tempest-tost;
    And rarely ceased the haughty billow's roar,
Save on the dead long summer days, which make
The outstretched ocean glitter like a lake.

And the small ripple spilt upon the beach
    Scarcely o'erpassed the cream of your champagne,
When o'er the brim the sparkling bumpers reach,
    That spring-dew of the spirit! the heart's rain!
Few things surpass old wine; and they may preach
    Who please – the more because they preach in vain –

Let us have wine and women, mirth and laughter,
Sermons and soda-water the day after.

. . .

The coast – I think it was the coast that I
   Was just describing – Yes, it *was* the coast –
Lay at this period quiet as the sky,
   The sands untumbled, the blue waves untost,
And all was stillness, save the sea-bird's cry,
   And dolphin's leap, and little billow crost
By some low rock or shelve, that made it fret
Against the boundary it scarcely wet.

And forth they wandered, her sire being gone,
   As I have said, upon an expedition;
And mother, brother, guardian, she had none
   Save Zoë, who, although with due precision
She waited on her lady with the sun,
   Thought daily service was her only mission,
Bringing warm water, wreathing her long tresses,
And asking now and then for cast-off dresses.

It was the cooling hour, just when the rounded
   Red sun sinks down behind the azure hill,
Which then seems as if the whole earth it bounded,
   Circling all nature, hushed, and dim, and still,
With the far mountain-crescent half surrounded
   On one side, and the deep sea calm and chill
Upon the other, and the rosy sky
With one star sparkling through it like an eye.

And thus they wandered forth, and hand in hand,
   Over the shining pebbles and the shells,
Glided along the smooth and hardened sand,
   And in the worn and wild receptacles
Worked by the storms, yet worked as it were planned,
   In hollow halls, with sparry roofs and cells,
They turned to rest; and, each clasped by an arm,
Yielded to the deep twilight's purple charm.

They looked up to the sky, whose floating glow
   Spread like a rosy ocean, vast and bright;
They gazed upon the glittering sea below,
   Whence the broad moon rose circling into sight;
They heard the waves splash, and the wind so low,
   And saw each other's dark eyes darting light
Into each other – and, beholding this,
   Their lips drew near, and clung into a kiss;

A long, long kiss, a kiss of youth, and love,
　And beauty, all concentrating like rays
Into one focus, kindled from above;
　Such kisses as belong to early days,
Where heart, and soul, and sense, in concert move,
　And the blood's lava, and the pulse a blaze,
Each kiss a heart-quake, – for a kiss's strength,
I think, it must be reckoned by its length.

By length I mean duration; theirs endured
　Heaven knows how long – no doubt they never reckoned;
And if they had, they could not have secured
　The sum of their sensations to a second:
They had not spoken; but they felt allured,
　As if their souls and lips each other beckoned,
Which, being joined, like swarming bees they clung –
Their hearts the flowers from whence the honey sprung.

They were alone, but not alone as they
　Who shut in chambers think it loneliness;
The silent ocean, and the starlight bay,
　The twilight glow, which momently grew less,
The voiceless sands, and dropping caves, that lay
　Around them, made them to each other press,
As if there were no life beneath the sky
Save theirs, and that their life could never die.

They feared no eyes nor ears on that lone beach,
　They felt no terrors from the night; they were
All in all to each other: though their speech
　Was broken words, they *thought* a language there, –
And all the burning tongues the passions teach
　Found in one sigh the best interpreter
Of nature's oracle – first love – that all
Which Eve has left her daughters since her fall.

Haidée spoke not of scruples, asked no vows,
　Nor offered any; she had never heard
Of plight and promises to be a spouse,
　Or perils by a loving maid incurred;
She was all which pure ignorance allows,
　And flew to her young mate like a young bird;
And, never having dreamt of falsehood, she
Had not one word to say of constancy.

She loved, and was beloved – she adored,
　And she was worshipped; after nature's fashion,

Their intense souls, into each other poured,
    If souls could die, had perished in that passion, –
But by degrees their senses were restored,
    Again to be o'ercome, again to dash on;
And, beating 'gainst *his* bosom, Haidée's heart
Felt as if never more to beat apart.

Alas! they were so young, so beautiful,
    So lonely, loving, helpless, and the hour
Was that in which the heart is always full,
    And, having o'er itself no further power,
Prompts deeds eternity can not annul,
    But pays off moments in an endless shower
Of hell-fire – all prepared for people giving
Pleasure or pain to one another living.

Alas! for Juan and Haidée! they were
    So loving and so lovely – till then never,
Excepting our first parents, such a pair
    Had run the risk of being damned for ever:
And Haidée, being devout as well as fair,
    Had, doubtless, heard about the Stygian river,
And hell and purgatory – but forgot
Just in the very crisis she should not.

They look upon each other, and their eyes
    Gleam in the moonlight; and her white arm clasps
Round Juan's head, and his around her lies
    Half buried in the tresses which it grasps;
She sits upon his knee, and drinks his sighs,
    He hers, until they end in broken gasps;
And thus they form a group that's quite antique,
Half naked, loving, natural, and Greek.

And when those deep and burning moments passed,
    And Juan sunk to sleep within her arms,
She slept not, but all tenderly, though fast,
    Sustained his head upon her bosom's charms;
And now and then her eye to heaven is cast,
    And then on the pale cheek her breast now warms,
Pillowed on her o'erflowing heart, which pants
With all it granted, and with all it grants.

An infant when it gazes on a light,
    A child the moment when it drains the breast,
A devotee when soars the Host in sight,
    An Arab with a stranger for a guest,

A sailor when the prize has struck in fight,
  A miser filling his most hoarded chest,
Feel rapture; but not such true joy are reaping
As they who watch o'er what they love while sleeping.

For there it lies so tranquil, so beloved,
  All that it hath of life with us is living;
So gentle, stirless, helpless, and unmoved,
  And all unconscious of the joy 'tis giving;
All it hath felt, inflicted, passed, and proved,
  Hushed into depths beyond the watcher's diving;
There lies the thing we love with all its errors
And all its charms, like death without its terrors.

The lady watched her lover – and that hour
  Of love's, and night's, and ocean's solitude,
O'erflowed her soul with their united power;
  Amidst the barren sand and rocks so rude
She and her wave-worn love had made their bower,
  Where nought upon their passion could intrude,
And all the stars that crowded the blue space
Saw nothing happier than her glowing face.

RICHARD HARRIS BARHAM

The Jackdaw of Rheims

The jackdaw sat on the Cardinal's chair!
Bishop, and abbot, and prior were there;
  Many a monk, and many a friar,
  Many a knight, and many a squire,
With a great many more of lesser degree –
In sooth a goodly company;
And they served the Lord Primate on bended knee.
  Never, I ween,
  Was a prouder seen,
Read of in books, or dreamt of in dreams,
Than the Cardinal Lord Archbishop of Rheims!

  In and out
  Through the motley rout,
That little jackdaw kept hopping about;
  Here and there
  Like a dog in a fair,

Over comfits and cates,
   And dishes and plates,
Cowl and cope, and rochet and pall,
Mitre and crosier! he hopped upon all!
   With saucy air,
   He perched on the chair
Where, in state, the great Lord Cardinal sat
In the great Lord Cardinal's great red hat;
   And he peered in the face
   Of his Lordship's Grace,
With a satisfied look, as if he would say,
'We two are the greatest folks here today!'
   And the priests with awe,
   As such freaks they saw,
Said, 'The Devil must be in that little jackdaw!'

The feast was over, the board was cleared,
The flawns and the custards had all disappeared,
And six little singing-boys – dear little souls!
In nice clean faces, and nice white stoles,
   Came, in order due,
   Two by two,
Marching that grand refectory through.
A nice little boy held a golden ewer,
Embossed and filled with water, as pure
As any that flows between Rheims and Namur,
Which a nice little boy stood ready to catch
In a fine golden hand-basin made to match.
Two nice little boys, rather more grown,
Carried lavender water, and Eau de Cologne;
And a nice little boy had a nice cake of soap,
Worthy of washing the hands of the Pope.
   One little boy more
   A napkin bore,
Of the best white diaper, fringed with pink,
And a Cardinal's Hat marked in permanent ink.

The great Lord Cardinal turns at the sight
Of these nice little boys dressed all in white:
   From his finger he draws
   His costly turquoise;
And, not thinking at all about little jackdaws,
   Deposits it straight
   By the side of his plate,
While the nice little boys on his Eminence wait;
Till, when nobody's dreaming of any such thing,
That little jackdaw hops off with the ring!

There's a cry and a shout,
  And a deuce of a rout,
And nobody seems to know what they're about,
But the monks have their pockets all turned inside out.
  The friars are kneeling,
  And hunting and feeling
The carpet, the floor, and the walls, and the ceiling.
  The Cardinal drew
  Off each plum-coloured shoe,
And left his red stockings exposed to the view;
  He peeps and he feels
  In the toes and the heels;
They turn up the dishes, they turn up the plates,
They take up the poker and poke out the grates,
  – They turn up the rugs,
  They examine the mugs:
  But, no! – no such thing –
  They can't find THE RING!
And the Abbot declared that 'when nobody twigged it,
Some rascal or other had popped in and prigged it'.

The Cardinal rose with a dignified look,
He called for his candle, his bell, and his book.
  In holy anger and pious grief,
  He solemnly cursed that rascally thief.
  He cursed him at board, he cursed him in bed;
  From the sole of his foot to the crown of his head;
  He cursed him in sleeping, that every night
  He should dream of the devil, and wake in a fright;
  He cursed him in eating, he cursed him in drinking,
  He cursed him in coughing, in sneezing, in winking;
  He cursed him in sitting, in standing, in lying;
  He cursed him in walking, in riding, in flying;
  He cursed him in living, he cursed him in dying.
Never was heard such a terrible curse!
  But what gave rise
  To no little surprise,
Nobody seemed one penny the worse!

  The day was gone,
  The night came on,
The monks and the friars they searched till dawn;
  When the Sacristan saw,
  On crumpled claw,
Come limping a poor little lame jackdaw!
  No longer gay,
  As on yesterday;

RICHARD HARRIS BARHAM

His feathers all seemed to be turned the wrong way;
His pinions drooped, he could hardly stand,
His head was as bald as the palm of your hand;
    His eye so dim,
    So wasted each limb,
That, heedless of grammar, they all cried, 'THAT'S HIM' –
That's the scamp that has done this scandalous thing!
That's the thief that has got my Lord Cardinal's ring!'

    The poor little jackdaw,
    When the monks he saw,
Feebly gave vent to the ghost of a caw;
And turned his bald head, as much as to say,
'Pray, be so good as to walk this way!'
    Slower and slower
    He limped on before,
Till they came to the back of the belfry door,
    Where the first thing they saw,
    Midst the sticks and the straw,
Was the RING in the nest of that little jackdaw!

Then the great Lord Cardinal called for his book,
And off that terrible curse he took;
    The mute expression
    Served in lieu of confession,
And, being thus coupled with full restitution,
The jackdaw got plenary absolution.
    – When those words were heard,
    That poor little bird
Was so changed in a moment, 'twas really absurd.
    He grew sleek and fat;
    In addition to that,
A fresh crop of feathers came thick as a mat.
    His tail waggled more
    Even than before;
But no longer it wagged with an impudent air,
No longer he perched on the Cardinal's chair.

    He hopped now about
    With a gait devout;
At Matins, at Vespers, he never was out;
And, so far from any more pilfering deeds,
He always seemed telling the Confessor's beads.
If anyone lied, or if anyone swore,
Or slumbered in prayer-time and happened to snore,
    That good jackdaw
    Would give a great 'Caw!'

As much as to say, 'Don't do so any more!'
While many remarked, as his manners they saw,
That they 'never had known such a pious jackdaw!'
 He long lived the pride
 Of that countryside,
And at last in the odour of sanctity died;
 When, as words were too faint
 His merits to paint,
The Conclave determined to make him a Saint;
And on newly-made Saints and Popes, as you know,
It's the custom at Rome, new names to bestow,
So they canonized him by the name of Jim Crow!

JOHN KEATS

The Eve of St Agnes

St Agnes' Eve – Ah, bitter chill it was!
The owl, for all his feathers, was a-cold;
The hare limped trembling through the frozen grass,
And silent was the flock in woolly fold:
Numb were the Beadsman's fingers, while he told
His rosary, and while his frosted breath,
Like pious incense from a censer old,
Seemed taking flight for Heaven, without a death,
Past the sweet Virgin's picture, while his prayer he saith.

His prayer he saith, this patient, holy man;
Then takes his lamp, and riseth from his knees,
And back returneth, meagre, barefoot, wan,
Along the chapel aisle by slow degrees:
The sculptured dead, on each side, seem to freeze,
Emprisoned in black, purgatorial rails:
Knights, ladies, praying in dumb orat'ries,
He passeth by; and his weak spirit fails
To think how they may ache in icy hoods and mails.

Northward he turneth through a little door,
And scarce three steps, ere music's golden tongue
Flattered to tears this aged man and poor;
But no – already had his deathbell rung:
The joys of all his life were said and sung:
His was harsh penance on St Agnes' Eve:
Another way he went, and soon among

Rough ashes sat he for his soul's reprieve,
And all night kept awake, for sinners' sake to grieve.

That ancient Beadsman heard the prelude soft;
And so it chanced, for many a door was wide,
From hurry to and fro. Soon, up aloft,
The silver, snarling trumpets 'gan to chide:
The level chambers, ready with their pride,
Were glowing to receive a thousand guests:
The carved angels, ever eager-eyed,
Stared, where upon their heads the cornice rests,
With hair blown back and wings put cross-wise on their breasts.

At length burst in the argent revelry,
With plume, tiara, and all rich array,
Numerous as shadows haunting faerily
The brain, new stuffed, in youth, with triumphs gay
Of old romance. These let us wish away,
And turn, sole-thoughted, to one lady there,
Whose heart had brooded, all that wintry day,
On love, and winged St Agnes' saintly care,
As she had heard old dames full many times declare.

They told her how, upon St Agnes' Eve,
Young virgins might have visions of delight,
And soft adorings from their loves receive
Upon the honeyed middle of the night,
If ceremonies due they did aright;
As, supperless to bed they must retire,
And couch supine their beauties, lily white;
Nor look behind, nor sideways, but require
Of Heaven with upward eyes for all that they desire.

Full of this whim was thoughtful Madeline:
The music, yearning like a God in pain,
She scarcely heard: her maiden eyes divine,
Fixed on the floor, saw many a sweeping train
Pass by – she heeded not at all: in vain
Came many a tiptoe, amorous cavalier,
And back retired; not cooled by high disdain,
But she saw not: her heart was otherwhere:
She sighed for Agnes' dreams, the sweetest of the year.

She danced along with vague, regardless eyes,
Anxious her lips, her breathing quick and short:
The hallowed hour was near at hand: she sighs
Amid the timbrels, and the thronged resort

Of whisperers in anger, or in sport;
'Mid looks of love, defiance, hate, and scorn,
Hoodwinked with faery fancy; all amort,
Save to St Agnes and her lambs unshorn,
And all the bliss to be before to-morrow morn.

So, purposing each moment to retire,
She lingered still. Meantime, across the moors,
Had come young Porphyro, with heart on fire
For Madeline. Beside the portal doors,
Buttress'd from moonlight, stands he, and implores
All saints to give him sight of Madeline,
But for one moment in the tedious hours,
That he might gaze and worship all unseen;
Perchance speak, kneel, touch, kiss – in sooth such things have been.

He ventures in: let no buzzed whisper tell:
All eyes be muffled, or a hundred swords
Will storm his heart, Love's fev'rous citadel:
For him, those chambers held barbarian hordes,
Hyena foemen, and hot-blooded lords,
Whose very dogs would execrations howl
Against his lineage: not one breast affords
Him any mercy, in that mansion foul,
Save one old beldame, weak in body and in soul.

Ah, happy chance! the aged creature came,
Shuffling along with ivory-headed wand,
To where he stood, hid from the torch's flame,
Behind a broad hall-pillar, far beyond
The sound of merriment and chorus bland:
He startled her; but soon she knew his face,
And grasped his fingers in her palsied hand,
Saying, 'Mercy, Porphyro! hie thee from this place:
They are all here to-night, the whole blood-thirsty race!

'Get hence! get hence! there's dwarfish Hildebrand;
He had a fever late, and in the fit
He cursed thee and thine, both house and land:
Then there's that old Lord Maurice, not a whit
More tame for his gray hairs – Alas me! flit!
Flit like a ghost away.' – 'Ah, Gossip dear,
We're safe enough; here in this arm chair sit,
And tell me how' – 'Good saints! not here, not here;
Follow me, child, or else these stones will be thy bier.'

He followed through a lowly arched way,
Brushing the cobwebs with his lofty plume,

And as she muttered 'Well-a – well-a-day!'
He found him in a little moonlight room,
Pale, latticed, chill, and silent as a tomb.
'Now tell me where is Madeline,' said he,
'Oh tell me Angela, by the holy loom
Which none but secret sisterhood may see,
When they St Agnes' wool are weaving piously.'

'St Agnes! Ah! it is St Agnes' Eve –
Yet men will murder upon holy days:
Thou must hold water in a witch's sieve,
And be liege-lord of all the elves and fays,
To venture so: it fills me with amaze
To see thee, Porphyro! – St Agnes' Eve!
God's help! my lady fair the conjuror plays
This very night: good angels her deceive!
But let me laugh awhile, I've mickle time to grieve.'

Feebly she laugheth in the languid moon,
While Porphyro upon her face doth look,
Like puzzled urchin on an aged crone
Who keepeth closed a wond'rous riddle-book,
As spectacled she sits in chimney nook.
But soon his eyes grew brilliant, when she told
His lady's purpose; and he scarce could brook
Tears, at the thought of those enchantments cold,
And Madeline asleep in lap of legends old.

Sudden a thought came like a full-blown rose,
Flushing his brow, and in his pained heart
Made purple riot: then doth he propose
A stratagem, that makes the beldame start:
'A cruel man and impious thou art:
Sweet lady, let her pray, and sleep, and dream
Alone with her good angels, far apart
From wicked men like thee. Go, go! I deem
Thou canst not surely be the same that thou didst seem.'

'I will not harm her, by all saints I swear,'
Quoth Porphyro: 'O may I ne'er find grace
When my weak voice shall whisper its last prayer,
If one of her soft ringlets I displace,
Or look with ruffian passion in her face:
Good Angela, believe me by these tears;
Or I will, even in a moment's space,
Awake, with horrid shout, my foemen's ears,
And beard them, though they be more fanged than wolves and bears.'

'Ah! why wilt thou affright a feeble soul?
A poor, weak, palsy-stricken, churchyard thing,
Whose passing-bell may ere the midnight toll;
Whose prayers for thee, each morn and evening,
Were never missed.' Thus plaining, doth she bring
A gentler speech from burning Porphyro;
So woeful, and of such deep sorrowing,
That Angela gives promise she will do
Whatever he shall wish, betide her weal or woe.

Which was, to lead him, in close secrecy,
Even to Madeline's chamber, and there hide
Him in a closet, of such privacy
That he might see her beauty unespied,
And win perhaps that night a peerless bride,
While legioned faeries paced the coverlet,
And pale enchantment held her sleepy-eyed.
Never on such a night have lovers met,
Since Merlin paid his Demon all the monstrous debt.

'It shall be as thou wishest,' said the Dame:
'All cates and dainties shall be stored there
Quickly on this feast-night: by the tambour frame
Her own lute thou wilt see: no time to spare,
For I am slow and feeble, and scarce dare
On such a catering trust my dizzy head.
Wait here, my child, with patience; kneel in prayer
The while: Ah! thou must needs the lady wed,
Or may I never leave my grave among the dead.'

So saying she hobbled off with busy fear.
The lover's endless minutes slowly passed;
The dame returned, and whispered in his ear
To follow her; with aged eyes aghast
From fright of dim espial. Safe at last,
Through many a dusky gallery, they gain
The maiden's chamber, silken, hushed, and chaste;
Where Porphyro took covert, pleased amain.
His poor guide hurried back with agues in her brain.

Her faltering hand upon the balustrade,
Old Angela was feeling for the stair,
When Madeline, St Agnes' charmed maid,
Rose, like a missioned spirit, unaware:
With silver taper's light, and pious care,

She turned, and down the aged gossip led
To a safe level matting. Now prepare,
Young Porphyro, for gazing on that bed;
She comes, she comes again, like ring-dove frayed and fled.

Out went the taper as she hurried in;
Its little smoke, in pallid moonshine, died:
She closed the door, she panted, all akin
To spirits of the air, and visions wide:
No uttered syllable, or, woe betide!
But to her heart, her heart was voluble,
Paining with eloquence her balmy side;
As though a tongueless nightingale should swell
Her throat in vain, and die, heart-stifled, in her dell.

A casement high and triple-arched there was,
All garlanded with carven imag'ries
Of fruits, and flowers, and bunches of knot-grass,
And diamonded with panes of quaint device,
Innumerable of stains and splendid dyes,
As are the tiger-moth's deep-damasked wings;
And in the midst, 'mong thousand heraldries,
And twilight saints, and dim emblazonings,
A shielded scutcheon blushed with blood of queens and kings.

Full on this casement shone the wintry moon,
And threw warm gules on Madeline's fair breast,
As down she knelt for heaven's grace and boon;
Rose-bloom fell on her hands, together prest,
And on her silver cross soft amethyst,
And on her hair a glory, like a saint:
She seemed a splendid angel, newly drest,
Save wings, for heaven: – Porphyro grew faint:
She knelt, so pure a thing, so free from mortal taint.

Anon his heart revives: her vespers done,
Of all its wreathed pearls her hair she frees;
Unclasps her warmed jewels one by one;
Loosens her fragrant bodice; by degrees
Her rich attire creeps rustling to her knees:
Half-hidden like a mermaid in sea-weed,
Pensive awhile she dreams awake, and sees,
In fancy, fair St Agnes in her bed,
But dares not look behind, or all the charm is fled.

Soon, trembling in her soft and chilly nest,
In sort of wakeful swoon, perplexed she lay,

Until the poppied warmth of sleep oppressed
Her soothed limbs, and soul fatigued away;
Flown, like a thought, until the morrow-day;
Blissfully havened both from joy and pain;
Clasped like a missal where swart Paynims pray;
Blinded alike from sunshine and from rain,
As though a rose should shut, and be a bud again.

Stol'n to this paradise, and so entranced,
Porphyro gazed upon her empty dress,
And listened to her breathing, if it chanced
To wake into a slumberous tenderness;
Which when he heard, that minute did he bless,
And breathed himself: then from the closet crept,
Noiseless as fear in a wide wilderness,
And over the hushed carpet, silent stepped,
And 'tween the curtains peeped, where, lo! how fast she slept.

Then by the bed-side where the faded moon,
Made a dim, silver twilight, soft he set
A table, and, half anguished, threw thereon
A cloth of woven crimson, gold, and jet: –
O for some drowsy Morphean amulet!
The boisterous, midnight, festive clarion,
The kettle-drum, and far-heard clarinet,
Affray his ears, though but in dying tone: –
The hall door shuts again, and all the noise is gone.

And still she slept an azure-lidded sleep,
In blanched linen, smooth, and lavendered,
While he from forth the closet brought a heap
Of candied apple, quince, and plum, and gourd;
With jellies soother than the creamy curd,
And lucent syrups, tinct with cinnamon;
Manna and dates, in argosy transferred
From Fez; and spiced dainties, every one,
From silken Samarcand to cedared Lebanon.

These delicates he heaped with glowing hand
On golden dishes and in baskets bright
Of wreathed silver: sumptuous they stand
In the retired quiet of the night,
Filling the chilly room with perfume light. –
'And now, my love, my seraph fair, awake!
Thou art my heaven, and I thine eremite:
Open thine eyes for meek St Agnes' sake,
Or I shall drowse beside thee, so my soul doth ache.'

Thus whispering, his warm, unnerved arm
Sank in her pillow. Shaded was her dream
By the dusk curtains: 'twas a midnight charm
Impossible to melt as iced stream:
The lustrous salvers in the moonlight gleam:
Broad golden fringe upon the carpet lies:
It seemed he never, never could redeem
From such a stedfast spell his lady's eyes;
So mused awhile, entoiled in woofed phantasies.

Awakening up, he took her hollow lute, –
Tumultuous, – and, in chords that tenderest be,
He played an ancient ditty, long since mute,
In Provence called, 'La belle dame sans mercy':
Close to her ear touching the melody; –
Wherewith disturbed, she uttered a soft moan:
He ceased – she panted quick – and suddenly
Her blue affrayed eyes wide open shone:
Upon his knees he sank, pale as smooth-sculptured stone.

Her eyes were open, but she still beheld,
Now wide awake, the vision of her sleep.
There was a painful change, that nigh expelled
The blisses of her dream so pure and deep
At which fair Madeline began to weep,
And moan forth witless words with many a sigh;
While still her gaze on Porphyro would keep;
Who knelt, with joined hand, and piteous eye,
Fearing to move or speak, she looked so dreamingly.

'Ah, Porphyro!' said she, 'but even now
Thy voice was at sweet tremble in mine ear,
Made tuneable with every sweetest vow;
And those sad eyes were spiritual and clear:
How changed thou art! how pallid, chill, and drear!
Give me that voice again, my Porphyro,
Those looks immortal, those complainings dear!
Oh leave me not in this eternal woe,
For if thou diest, my Love, I know not where to go.'

Beyond a mortal man impassioned far
At these voluptuous accents, he arose,
Ethereal, flushed, and like a throbbing star
Seen mid the sapphire heaven's deep repose;
Into her dream he melted, as the rose
Blendeth its odour with the violet, –
Solution sweet: meantime the frost-wind blows

Like Love's alarum pattering the sharp sleet
Against the window-panes; St Agnes' moon hath set.

'Tis dark: quick pattereth the flaw-blown sleet:
'This is no dream, my bride, my Madeline!'
'Tis dark: the iced gusts still rave and beat:
'No dream, alas! alas! and woe is mine!
Porphyro will leave me here to fade and pine.
Cruel! what traitor could thee hither bring?
I curse not, for my heart is lost in thine,
Though thou forsakest a deceived thing;
A dove forlorn and lost with sick unpruned wing.'

'My Madeline! sweet dreamer! lovely bride!
Say, may I be for aye thy vassal blest?
Thy beauty's shield, heart-shaped and vermeil dyed?
Ah, silver shrine, here will I take my rest
After so many hours of toil and quest,
A famished pilgrim, – saved by miracle.
Though I have found, I will not rob thy nest
Saving of thy sweet self; if thou think'st well
To trust, fair Madeline, to no rude infidel.

'Hark! 'tis an elfin-storm from faery land,
Of haggard seeming, but a boon indeed:
Arise! arise! the morning is at hand;
The bloated wassaillers will never heed:
Let us away, my love, with happy speed;
There are no ears to hear, or eyes to see, –
Drowned all in Rhenish and the sleepy mead:
Awake! arise! my love, and fearless be,
For o'er the southern moors I have a home for thee.'

She hurried at his words, beset with fears,
For there were sleeping dragons all around,
At glaring watch, perhaps, with ready spears –
Down the wide stairs a darkling way they found.
In all the house was heard no human sound.
A chain-drooped lamp was flickering by each door;
The arras, rich with horseman, hawk, and hound,
Fluttered in the besieging wind's uproar;
And the long carpets rose along the gusty floor.

They glide, like phantoms, into the wide hall;
Like phantoms, to the iron porch they glide;
Where lay the Porter, in uneasy sprawl,
With a huge empty flagon by his side:

The wakeful bloodhound rose, and shook his hide,
But his sagacious eye an inmate owns:
By one, and one, the bolts full easy slide:
The chains lie silent on the footworn stones;
The key turns, and the door upon its hinges groans.

And they are gone: ay, ages long ago
These lovers fled away into the storm.
That night the Baron dreamt of many a woe,
And all his warrior-guests, with shade and form
Of witch, and demon, and large coffin-worm,
Were long be-nightmared. Angela the old
Died palsy-twitched, with meagre face deform;
The Beadsman, after thousand aves told,
For aye unsought for slept among his ashes cold.

THOMAS BABINGTON, LORD MACAULAY

Horatius

Lars Porsena of Clusium
  By the Nine Gods he swore
That the great house of Tarquin
  Should suffer wrong no more.
By the Nine Gods he swore it,
  And named a trysting day,
And bade his messengers ride forth,
East and west and south and north,
  To summon his array.

East and west and south and north
  The messengers ride fast,
And tower and town and cottage
  Have heard the trumpet's blast.
Shame on the false Etruscan
  Who lingers in his home,
When Porsena of Clusium
  Is on the march for Rome.

The horsemen and the footmen
  Are pouring in amain
From many a stately market-place;
  From many a fruitful plain;
From many a lonely hamlet,

Which, hid by beech and pine,
Like an eagle's nest, hangs on the crest
    Of purple Apennine.

            . . .

There be thirty chosen prophets,
    The wisest of the land,
Who always by Lars Porsena
    Both morn and evening stand:
Evening and morn the Thirty
    Have turned the verses o'er,
Traced from the right on linen white
    By mighty seers of yore.

And with one voice the Thirty
    Have their glad answer given:
'Go forth, go forth, Lars Porsena;
    Go forth, beloved of Heaven;
Go, and return in glory
    To Clusium's royal dome;
And hang round Nurscia's altars
    The golden shields of Rome.'

And now hath every city
    Sent up her tale of men;
The foot are fourscore thousand,
    The horse are thousands ten.
Before the gates of Sutrium
    Is met the great array.
A proud man was Lars Porsena
    Upon the trysting day.

            . . .

Now, from the rock Tarpeian,
    Could the wan burghers spy
The line of blazing villages
    Red in the midnight sky.
The Fathers of the City,
    They sat all night and day,
For every hour some horseman came
    With tidings of dismay.

            . . .

I wis, in all the Senate,
    There was no heart so bold,
But sore it ached, and fast it beat,
    When that ill news was told.
Forthwith up rose the Consul,
    Up rose the Fathers all;
In haste they girded up their gowns,
    And hied them to the wall.

They held a council standing
  Before the River-Gate;
Short time was there, ye well may guess,
  For musing or debate.
Out spake the Consul roundly:
  'The bridge must straight go down;
For, since Janiculum is lost,
  Nought else can save the town.'

Just then a scout came flying,
  All wild with haste and fear:
'To arms! to arms! Sir Consul;
  Lars Porsena is here.'
On the low hills to westward
  The Consul fixed his eye,
And saw the swarthy storm of dust
  Rise fast along the sky.

And nearer fast and nearer
  Doth the red whirlwind come;
And louder still and still more loud,
From underneath that rolling cloud,
Is heard the trumpet's war-note proud,
  The trampling, and the hum.
And plainly and more plainly
  Now through the gloom appears,
Far to left and far to right,
In broken gleams of dark-blue light,
The long array of helmets bright,
  The long array of spears.

            . . .

But the Consul's brow was sad,
  And the Consul's speech was low,
And darkly looked he at the wall,
  And darkly at the foe.
'Their van will be upon us
  Before the bridge goes down;
And if they once may win the bridge,
  What hope to save the town?'

Then out spake brave Horatius,
  The Captain of the gate:
'To every man upon this earth
  Death cometh soon or late.
And how can man die better
  Than facing fearful odds,
For the ashes of his father
  And the temples of his Gods.

            . . .

'Hew down the bridge, Sir Consul,
  With all the speed ye may;
I, with two more to help me,
  Will hold the foe in play.
In yon strait path a thousand
  May well be stopped by three.
Now who will stand on either hand,
  And keep the bridge with me?'

Then out spake Spurius Lartius;
  A Ramnian proud was he:
'Lo, I will stand at thy right hand,
  And keep the bridge with thee.'
And out spake strong Herminius;
  Of Titian blood was he:
'I will abide on thy left side,
  And keep the bridge with thee.'

'Horatius,' quoth the Consul,
  'As thou sayest, so let it be.'
And straight against that great array
  Forth went the dauntless Three.
For Romans in Rome's quarrel
  Spared neither land nor gold,
Nor son nor wife, nor limb nor life,
  In the brave days of old.

Then none was for a party;
  Then all were for the state;
Then the great man helped the poor,
  And the poor man loved the great:
Then lands were fairly portioned;
  Then spoils were fairly sold:
The Romans were like brothers
  In the brave days of old.

. . .

Now while the Three were tightening
  Their harness on their backs,
The Consul was the foremost man
  To take in hand an axe:
And Fathers mixed with Commons
  Seized hatchet, bar, and crow,
And smote upon the planks above,
  And loosed the props below.

Meanwhile the Tuscan army,
  Right glorious to behold,

Came flashing back the noonday light,
Rank behind rank, like surges bright
  Of a broad sea of gold.
Four hundred trumpets sounded
  A peal of warlike glee,
As that great host, with measured tread,
And spears advanced, and ensigns spread,
Rolled slowly towards the bridge's head,
  Where stood the dauntless Three.

The Three stood calm and silent
  And looked upon the foes,
And a great shout of laughter
  From all the vanguard rose:
And forth three chiefs came spurring
  Before that deep array;
To earth they sprang, their swords they drew,
And lifted high their shields, and flew
  To win the narrow way;

Aunus from green Tifernum,
  Lord of the Hill of Vines;
And Seius, whose eight hundred slaves
  Sicken in Ilva's mines;
And Picus, long to Clusium
  Vassal in peace and war,
Who led to fight his Umbrian powers
From that grey crag where, girt with towers,
The fortress of Nequinum lowers
  O'er the pale waves of Nar.

Stout Lartius hurled down Aunus
  Into the stream beneath:
Herminius struck at Seius,
  And clove him to the teeth:
At Picus brave Horatius
  Darted one fiery thrust;
And the proud Umbrian's gilded arms
  Clashed in the bloody dust.

Then Ocnus of Falerii
  Rushed on the Roman Three;
And Lausulus of Urgo,
  The rover of the sea;
And Aruns of Volsinium,
  Who slew the great wild boar,
The great wild boar that had his den

Amidst the reeds of Cosa's fen,
And wasted fields, and slaughtered men,
  Along Albinia's shore.

Herminius smote down Aruns:
  Lartius laid Ocnus low:
Right to the heart of Lausulus
  Horatius sent a blow.
'Lie there,' he cried, 'fell pirate!
  No more, aghast and pale,
From Ostia's walls the crowd shall mark
The track of thy destroying bark.
No more Campania's hinds shall fly
To woods and caverns when they spy
  Thy thrice accursed sail.'

But now no sound of laughter
  Was heard amongst the foes.
A wild and wrathful clamour
  From all the vanguard rose.
Six spears' lengths from the entrance
  Halted that deep array,
And for a space no man came forth
  To win the narrow way.

But hark! the cry is Astur:
  And lo! the ranks divide;
And the great Lord of Luna
  Comes with his stately stride.
Upon his ample shoulders
  Clangs loud the four-fold shield,
And in his hand he shakes the brand
  Which none but he can wield.

He smiled on those bold Romans
  A smile serene and high;
He eyed the flinching Tuscans,
  And scorn was in his eye.
Quoth he, 'The she-wolf's litter
  Stand savagely at bay:
But will ye dare to follow,
  If Astur clears the way?'

Then, whirling up his broadsword
  With both hands to the height,
He rushed against Horatius,
  And smote with all his might.

With shield and blade Horatius
  Right deftly turned the blow.
The blow, though turned, came yet too nigh;
It missed his helm, but gashed his thigh:
The Tuscans raised a joyful cry
  To see the red blood flow.

He reeled, and on Herminius
  He leaned one breathing-space;
Then, like a wild cat mad with wounds,
  Sprang right at Astur's face.
Through teeth, and skull, and helmet,
  So fierce a thrust he sped,
The good sword stood a hand-breadth out
  Behind the Tuscan's head.

And the great Lord of Luna
  Fell at that deadly stroke,
As falls on Mount Alvernus
  A thunder-smitten oak.
Far o'er the crashing forest
  The giant arms lie spread;
And the pale augurs, muttering low,
  Gaze on the blasted head.

On Astur's throat Horatius
  Right firmly pressed his heel,
And thrice and four times tugged amain,
  Ere he wrenched out the steel.
'And see,' he cried, 'the welcome,
  Fair guests, that waits you here!
What noble Lucumo comes next
  To taste our Roman cheer?'

But at his haughty challenge
  A sullen murmur ran,
Mingled of wrath, and shame, and dread,
  Along that glittering van.
There lacked not men of prowess,
  Nor men of lordly race;
For all Etruria's noblest
  Were round the fatal place.

But all Etruria's noblest
  Felt their hearts sink to see
On the earth the bloody corpses,
  In the path the dauntless Three:

And, from the ghastly entrance
  Where those bold Romans stood,
All shrank, like boys who unaware,
Ranging the woods to start a hare,
Come to the mouth of the dark lair
Where, growling low, a fierce old bear
  Lies amidst bones and blood.

Was none who would be foremost
  To lead such dire attack;
But those behind cried 'Forward!'
  And those before cried 'Back!'
And backward now and forward
  Wavers the deep array;
And on the tossing sea of steel,
To and fro the standards reel;
And the victorious trumpet-peal
  Dies fitfully away.

      . . .

But meanwhile axe and lever
  Have manfully been plied;
And now the bridge hangs tottering
  Above the boiling tide.
'Come back, come back, Horatius!'
  Loud cried the Fathers all.
'Back, Lartius! back, Herminius!
  Back, ere the ruin fall!'

Back darted Spurius Lartius;
  Herminius darted back:
And, as they passed, beneath their feet
  They felt the timbers crack.
But when they turned their faces,
  And on the farther shore
Saw brave Horatius stand alone,
  They would have crossed once more.

But with a crash like thunder
  Fell every loosened beam,
And, like a dam, the mighty wreck
  Lay right athwart the stream:
And a long shout of triumph
  Rose from the walls of Rome,
As to the highest turret-tops
  Was splashed the yellow foam.

And, like a horse unbroken
   When first he feels the rein,
The furious river struggled hard,
   And tossed his tawny mane;
And burst the curb, and bounded,
   Rejoicing to be free;
And whirling down, in fierce career,
Battlement, and plank, and pier,
   Rushed headlong to the sea.

Alone stood brave Horatius,
   But constant still in mind;
Thrice thirty thousand foes before,
   And the broad flood behind.
'Down with him!' cried false Sextus,
   With a smile on his pale face.
'Now yield thee,' cried Lars Porsena,
   'Now yield thee to our grace.'

Round turned he, as not deigning
   Those craven ranks to see;
Nought spake he to Lars Porsena,
   To Sextus nought spake he;
But he saw on Palatinus
   The white porch of his home;
And he spake to the noble river
   That rolls by the towers of Rome.

'Oh, Tiber! father Tiber!
   To whom the Romans pray,
A Roman's life, a Roman's arms,
   Take thou in charge this day!'
So he spake, and speaking sheathed
   The good sword by his side,
And with his harness on his back,
   Plunged headlong in the tide.

No sound of joy or sorrow
   Was heard from either bank;
But friends and foes in dumb surprise,
With parted lips and straining eyes,
   Stood gazing where he sank;
And when above the surges
   They saw his crest appear,
All Rome sent forth a rapturous cry,
And even the ranks of Tuscany
   Could scarce forbear to cheer.

But fiercely ran the current,
　　Swollen high by months of rain:
And fast his blood was flowing;
　　And he was sore in pain,
And heavy with his armour,
　　And spent with changing blows:
And oft they thought him sinking,
　　But still again he rose.

Never, I ween, did swimmer,
　　In such an evil case,
Struggle through such a raging flood
　　Safe to the landing place:
But his limbs were borne up bravely
　　By the brave heart within,
And our good father Tiber
　　Bare bravely up his chin.

　　　　　　. . .

And now he feels the bottom;
　　Now on dry earth he stands;
Now round him throng the Fathers
　　To press his gory hands;
And now with shouts and clapping,
　　And noise of weeping loud,
He enters through the River-Gate,
　　Borne by the joyous crowd.

They gave him of the corn-land,
　　That was of public right,
As much as two strong oxen
　　Could plough from morn till night;
And they made a molten image,
　　And set it up on high,
And there it stands unto this day
　　To witness if I lie.

It stands in the Comitium,
　　Plain for all folk to see;
Horatius in his harness,
　　Halting upon one knee:
And underneath is written,
　　In letters all of gold,
How valiantly he kept the bridge
　　In the brave days of old.

HENRY WADSWORTH LONGFELLOW

The Wreck of the Hesperus

It was the schooner Hesperus,
　That sailed the wintry sea;
And the skipper had taken his little daughter,
　To bear him company.

Blue were her eyes as the fairy-flax,
　Her cheeks like the dawn of day,
And her bosom white as the hawthorn buds
　That ope in the month of May.

The skipper he stood beside the helm,
　His pipe was in his mouth,
And he watched how the veering flaw did blow
　The smoke now west, now south.

Then up and spake an old sailor,
　Had sailed the Spanish Main,
'I pray thee, put into yonder port,
　For I fear a hurricane.

'Last night the moon had a golden ring,
　And tonight no moon we see!'
The skipper he blew a whiff from his pipe,
　And a scornful laugh laughed he.

Colder and louder blew the wind,
　A gale from the north-east,
The snow fell hissing in the brine,
　And the billows frothed like yeast.

Down came the storm, and smote amain
　The vessel in its strength;
She shuddered and paused, like a frighted steed,
　Then leaped her cable's length.

'Come hither! come hither! my little daughter,
　And do not tremble so;
For I can weather the roughest gale
　That ever wind did blow.'

He wrapped her warm in his seaman's coat
　Against the stinging blast;
He cut a rope from a broken spar,
　And bound her to the mast.

'O father! I hear the church bells ring,
   O say, what may it be?'
''Tis a fog-bell on a rock-bound coast!' –
   And he steered for the open sea.

'O father! I hear the sound of guns,
   O say, what may it be?'
'Some ship in distress, that cannot live
   In such an angry sea!'

'O father! I see a gleaming light,
   O say, what may it be?'
But the father answered never a word,
   A frozen corpse was he.

Lashed to the helm, all stiff and stark,
   With his face turned to the skies,
The lantern gleamed through the gleaming snow
   On his fixed and glassy eyes.

Then the maiden clasped her hands and prayed
   That savèd she might be;
And she thought of Christ, who stilled the wave
   On the Lake of Galilee.

And fast through the midnight dark and drear,
   Through the whistling sleet and snow,
Like a sheeted ghost the vessel swept
   Towards the reef of Norman's Woe.

And ever the fitful gusts between
   A sound came from the land;
It was the sound of the trampling surf
   On the rocks and the hard sea-sand.

The breakers were right beneath her bows,
   She drifted a dreary wreck,
And a whooping billow swept the crew
   Like icicles from her deck.

She struck where the white and fleecy waves
   Looked soft as carded wool,
But the cruel rocks they gored her side
   Like the horns of an angry bull.

Her rattling shrouds, all sheathed in ice,
   With the masts went by the board;
Like a vessel of glass she stove and sank –
   Ho! ho! the breakers roared!

At daybreak on the bleak sea-beach
   A fisherman stood aghast,
To see the form of a maiden fair
   Lashed close to a drifting mast.

The salt sea was frozen on her breast,
   The salt tears in her eyes;
And he saw her hair, like the brown sea-weed,
   On the billows fall and rise.

Such was the wreck of the Hesperus,
   In the midnight and the snow!
Christ save us all from a death like this,
   On the reef of Norman's Woe!

Paul Revere's Ride

Listen, my children, and you shall hear
Of the midnight ride of Paul Revere,
On the eighteenth of April, in Seventy-five;
Hardly a man is now alive
Who remembers that famous day and year.

He said to his friend, 'If the British march
By land or sea from the town tonight,
Hang a lantern aloft in the belfry arch
Of the North Church tower as a signal light –
One, if by land, and two, if by sea;
And I on the opposite shore will be,
Ready to ride and spread the alarm
Through every Middlesex village and farm,
For the country folk to be up and to arm.'

Then he said 'Good night!' and with muffled oar
Silently rowed to the Charlestown shore,
Just as the moon rose over the bay,
Where swinging wide at her moorings lay
The *Somerset*, British man-of-war;
A phantom ship, with each mast and spar
Across the moon like a prison bar,
And a huge black hulk, that was magnified
By its own reflection in the tide.

Meanwhile, his friend, through alley and street,
Wanders and watches with eager ears,
Till in the silence around him he hears
The muster of men at the barrack door,
The sound of arms, and the tramp of feet,
And the measured tread of the grenadiers
Marching down to their boats on the shore.

Then he climbed the tower of the Old North Church,
By the wooden stairs, with stealthy tread,
To the belfry chamber overhead,
And startled the pigeons from their perch
On the sombre rafters, that round him made
Masses and moving shapes of shade –
By the trembling ladder, steep and tall,
To the highest window in the wall,
Where he paused to listen and look down
A moment on the roofs of the town,
And the moonlight flowing over all.

Beneath, in the churchyard, lay the dead,
In their night-encampment on the hill,
Wrapped in silence so deep and still
That he could hear, like a sentinel's tread,
The watchful night-wind, as it went
Creeping along from tent to tent,
And seeming to whisper, 'All is well!'
A moment only he feels the spell
Of the place and the hour, and the secret dread
Of the lonely belfry and the dead;
For suddenly all his thoughts are bent
On a shadowy something far away,
Where the river widens to meet the bay –
A line of black that bends and floats
On the rising tide, like a bridge of boats.

Meanwhile, impatient to mount and ride,
Booted and spurred, with a heavy stride
On the opposite shore walked Paul Revere.
Now he patted his horse's side,
Now gazed at the landscape far and near,
Then, impetuous, stamped the earth,
And turned and tightened his saddle-girth;
But mostly he watched with eager search
The belfry-tower of the Old North Church,
As it rose above the graves on the hill,
Lonely and spectral and sombre and still.

And lo! as he looks, on the belfry's height
A glimmer, and then a gleam of light!
He springs to the saddle, the bridle he turns,
But lingers and gazes, till full on his sight
A second lamp in the belfry burns!

A hurry of hoofs in a village street,
A shape in the moonlight, a bulk in the dark,
And beneath, from the pebbles, in passing, a spark
Struck out by a steed flying fearless and fleet:
That was all! And yet, through the gloom and the light,
The fate of a nation was riding that night;
And the spark struck out by that steed, in his flight,
Kindled the land into flame with its heat.

He has left the village and mounted the steep,
And beneath him, tranquil and broad and deep,
Is the Mystic, meeting the ocean tides;
And under the alders, that skirt its edge,
Now soft on the sand, now loud on the ledge,
Is heard the tramp of his steed as he rides.

It was twelve by the village clock
When he crossed the bridge into Medford town.
He heard the crowing of the cock,
And the barking of the farmer's dog,
And felt the damp of the river fog,
That rises after the sun goes down.

It was one by the village clock,
When he galloped into Lexington.
He saw the gilded weathercock
Swim in the moonlight as he passed,
And the meeting-house windows, blank and bare,
Gaze at him with a spectral glare,
As if they already stood aghast
At the bloody work they would look upon.

It was two by the village clock,
When he came to the bridge in Concord town.
He heard the bleating of the flock,
And the twitter of birds among the trees,
And felt the breath of the morning breeze
Blowing over the meadows brown.
And one was safe and asleep in his bed
Who at the bridge would be first to fall,
Who that day would be lying dead,
Pierced by a British musket-ball.

You know the rest. In the books you have read,
How the British Regulars fired and fled,
How the farmers gave them ball for ball,
From behind each fence and farmyard wall;
Chasing the red-coats down the lane,
Then crossing the fields to emerge again
Under the trees at the turn of the road,
And only pausing to fire and load.

So through the night rode Paul Revere;
And so through the night went his cry of alarm
To every Middlesex village and farm –
A cry of defiance and not of fear,
A voice in the darkness, a knock at the door,
And a word that shall echo for evermore!
For, borne on a night-wind of the Past,
Through all our history, to the last,
In the hour of darkness and peril and need,
The people will waken and listen to hear
The hurrying hoof-beats of that steed,
And the midnight message of Paul Revere.

From *The Song of Hiawatha*

[HIAWATHA'S WOOING]

'As unto the bow the cord is,
So unto the man is woman,
Though she bends him, she obeys him,
Though she draws him, yet she follows,
Useless each without the other!'
    Thus the youthful Hiawatha
Said within himself and pondered,
Much perplexed by various feelings,
Listless, longing, hoping, fearing,
Dreaming still of Minnehaha,
Of the lovely Laughing Water,
In the land of the Dacotahs.

    'Wed a maiden of your people,'
Warning said the old Nokomis;
'Go not eastward, go not westward,
For a stranger, whom we know not!
Like a fire upon the hearthstone
Is a neighbour's homely daughter;
Like the starlight or the moonlight
Is the handsomest of strangers!'

Thus dissuading spake Nokomis,
And my Hiawatha answered
Only this: 'Dear old Nokomis,
Very pleasant is the firelight,
But I like the starlight better,
Better do I like the moonlight!'

Gravely then said old Nokomis:
'Bring not here an idle maiden,
Bring not here a useless woman,
Hands unskilful, feet unwilling;
Bring a wife with nimble fingers,
Heart and hand that move together,
Feet that run on willing errands!'

Smiling answered Hiawatha:
'In the land of the Dacotahs
Lives the Arrow-maker's daughter,
Minnehaha, Laughing Water,
Handsomest of all the women.
I will bring her to your wigwam,
She shall run upon your errands,
Be your starlight, moonlight, firelight,
Be the sunlight of my people!'

Still dissuading said Nokomis:
'Bring not to my lodge a stranger
From the land of the Dacotahs!
Very fierce are the Dacotahs,
Often is there war between us,
There are feuds yet unforgotten,
Wounds that ache and still may open!'

Laughing answered Hiawatha:
'For that reason, if no other,
Would I wed the fair Dacotah,
That our tribes might be united,
That old feuds might be forgotten,
And old wounds be healed for ever!'

Thus departed Haiwatha
To the land of the Dacotahs,
To the land of handsome women;
Striding over moor and meadow,
Through interminable forests,
Through uninterrupted silence.

With his moccasins of magic,
At each stride a mile he measured;
Yet the way seemed long before him,
And his heart outran his footsteps;
And he journeyed without resting,
Till he heard the cataract's laughter,

Heard the Falls of Minnehaha
Calling to him through the silence.
'Pleasant is the sound!' he murmured,
'Pleasant is the voice that calls me!'
   On the outskirts of the forest,
'Twixt the shadow and the sunshine,
Herds of fallow deer were feeding,
But they saw not Haiwatha;
To his bow he whispered, 'Fail not!'
To his arrow whispered, 'Swerve not!'
Sent it singing on its errand,
To the red heart of the roebuck;
Threw the deer across his shoulder,
And sped forward without pausing.
   At the doorway of his wigwam
Sat the ancient Arrow-maker,
In the land of the Dacotahs,
Making arrow-heads of jasper,
Arrow-heads of chalcedony.
At his side, in all her beauty,
Sat the lovely Minnehaha,
Sat his daughter, Laughing Water,
Plaiting mats of flags and rushes;
Of the past the old man's thoughts were,
And the maiden's of the future.
   He was thinking, as he sat there,
Of the days when with such arrows
He had struck the deer and bison,
On the Muskoday, the meadow;
Shot the wildgoose, flying southward,
On the wing, the clamorous Wawa;
Thinking of the great war-parties,
How they came to buy his arrows,
Could not fight without his arrows.
Ah, no more such noble warriors
Could be found on earth as they were!
Now the men were all like women,
Only used their tongues for weapons!
   She was thinking of a hunter,
From another tribe and country,
Young and tall and very handsome,
Who one morning in the Springtime
Came to buy her father's arrows,
Sat and rested in the wigwam,
Lingered long about the doorway,
Looking back as he departed.
She had heard her father praise him,

Praise his courage and his wisdom;
Would he come again for arrows
To the Falls of Minnehaha?
On the mat her hands lay idle,
And her eyes were very dreamy.
   Through their thoughts they heard a footstep,
Heard a rustling in the branches,
And with glowing cheek and forehead,
With the deer upon his shoulders,
Suddenly from out the woodlands
Haiwatha stood before them.
   Straight the ancient Arrow-maker
Looked up gravely from his labour,
Laid aside the unfinished arrow,
Bade him enter at the doorway,
Saying, as he rose to meet him,
'Hiawatha, you are welcome!'
   At the feet of Laughing Water
Hiawatha laid his burden,
Threw the red deer from his shoulders;
And the maiden looked up at him,
Looked up from her mat of rushes,
Said with gentle look and accent,
'You are welcome, Hiawatha!'
   Very spacious was the wigwam,
Made of deerskin dressed and whitened,
With the Gods of the Dacotahs
Drawn and painted on its curtains,
And so tall the doorway, hardly
Hiawatha stooped to enter,
Hardly touched his eagle-feathers
As he entered at the doorway.
   Then uprose the Laughing Water,
From the ground fair Minnehaha,
Laid aside her mat unfinished,
Brought forth food and set before them,
Water brought them from the brooklet,
Gave them food in earthen vessels,
Gave them drink in bowls of basswood,
Listened while the guest was speaking,
Listened while her father answered;
But not once her lips she opened,
Not a single word she uttered.
   Yes, as in a dream she listened
To the words of Hiawatha,
As he talked of old Nokomis,
Who had nursed him in his childhood,

As he told of his companions,
Chibiabos, the musician,
And the very strong man, Kwasind,
And of happiness and plenty
In the land of the Ojibways,
In the pleasant land and peaceful.
    'After many years of warfare,
Many years of strife and bloodshed,
There is peace between the Ojibways
And the tribe of the Dacotahs.'
Thus continued Hiawatha,
And then added, speaking slowly,
'That this peace may last for ever,
And our hands be clasped more closely,
And our hearts be more united,
Give me as my wife this maiden,
Minnehaha, Laughing Water,
Loveliest of Dacotah women!'
    And the ancient Arrow-maker
Paused a moment ere he answered,
Smoked a little while in silence,
Looked at Hiawatha proudly,
Fondly looked at Laughing Water,
And made answer very gravely:
'Yes, if Minnehaha wishes;
Let your heart speak, Minnehaha!'
    And the lovely Laughing Water
Seemed more lovely, as she stood there,
Neither willing nor reluctant,
As she went to Hiawatha,
Softly took the seat beside him,
While she said, and blushed to say it,
'I will follow you, my husband!'
    This was Hiawatha's wooing!
Thus it was he won the daughter
Of the ancient Arrow-maker,
In the land of the Dacotahs!
    From the wigwam he departed,
Leading with him Laughing Water;
Hand in hand they went together,
Through the woodland and the meadow,
Left the old man standing lonely
At the doorway of his wigwam,
Heard the Falls of Minnehaha
Calling to them from the distance,
Crying to them, from afar off,
'Fare thee well, O Minnehaha!'

And the ancient Arrow-maker
Turned again unto his labour,
Sat down by his sunny doorway,
Murmuring to himself, and saying:
'Thus it is our daughters leave us,
Those we love, and those who love us!
Just when they have learned to help us,
When we are old and lean upon them,
Comes a youth with flaunting feathers,
With his flute of reeds, a stranger
Wanders piping through the village,
Beckons to the fairest maiden,
And she follows where he leads her,
Leaving all things for the stranger!'
    Pleasant was the journey homeward,
Through the interminable forests,
Over meadow, over mountain,
Over river, hill, and hollow.
Short it seemed to Hiawatha,
Though they journeyed very slowly,
Though his pace he checked and slackened
To the steps of Laughing Water.
    Over wide and rushing rivers
In his arms he bore the maiden;
Light he thought her as a feather,
As the plume upon his head-gear;
Cleared the tangled pathway for her,
Bent aside the swaying branches,
Made at night a lodge of branches,
And a bed with boughs of hemlock,
And a fire before the doorway
With the dry cones of the pine-tree.
    All the travelling winds went with them,
O'er the meadow, through the forest;
All the stars of night looked at them,
Watched with sleepless eyes their slumber;
From his ambush in the oak-tree
Peeped the squirrel, Adjidaumo,
Watched with eager eyes the lovers;
And the rabbit, the Wabasso,
Scampered from the path before them,
Peering, peeping from his burrow,
Sat erect upon his haunches,
Watched with curious eyes the lovers.
    Pleasant was the journey homeward!
All the birds sang loud and sweetly
Songs of happiness and heart's-ease;

Sang the bluebird, the Owaissa,
'Happy are you, Hiawatha,
Having such a wife to love you!'
Sang the robin, the Opechee,
'Happy are you, Laughing Water,
Having such a noble husband!'
  From the sky the sun benignant
Looked upon them through the branches,
Saying to them, 'O my children,
Love is sunshine, hate is shadow,
Life is checkered shade and sunshine,
Rule by love, O Hiawatha!'
  From the sky the moon looked at them,
Filled the lodge with mystic splendours,
Whispered to them, 'O my children,
Day is restless, night is quiet,
Man imperious, woman feeble;
Half is mine, although I follow;
Rule by patience, Laughing Water!'
  Thus it was they journeyed homeward;
Thus it was that Hiawatha
To the lodge of old Nokomis
Brought the moonlight, starlight, firelight,
Brought the sunshine of his people,
Minnehaha, Laughing Water,
Handsomest of all the women
In the land of the Dacotahs,
In the land of handsome women.

JOHN GREENLEAF WHITTIER

Barbara Frietchie

Up from the meadows rich with corn,
Clear in the cool September morn,
The clustered spires of Frederick stand
Green-walled by the hills of Maryland.
Round about them orchards sweep,
Apple and peach tree fruited deep,
Fair as the garden of the Lord
To the eyes of the famished rebel horde,
On that pleasant morn of the early fall
When Lee marched over the mountain-wall;

Over the mountains winding down,
Horse and foot, into Frederick town.

Forty flags with their silver stars,
Forty flags with their crimson bars,
Flapped in the morning wind: the sun
Of noon looked down, and saw not one.
Up rose old Barbara Frietchie then,
Bowed with her fourscore years and ten;
Bravest of all in Frederick town
She took up the flag the men hauled down;
In her attic window the staff she set,
To show that one heart was loyal yet.

Up the street came the rebel tread,
Stonewall Jackson riding ahead.
Under his slouched hat left and right
He glanced; the old flag met his sight.
'Halt!' – the dust-brown ranks stood fast.
'Fire!' – out blazed the rifle-blast.
It shivered the window, pane and sash;
It rent the banner with seam and gash.
Quick, as it fell, from the broken staff
Dame Barbara snatched the silken scarf.
She leaned far out on the window-sill,
And shook it forth with a royal will.
'Shoot, if you must, this old gray head,
But spare your country's flag,' she said.

A shade of sadness, a blush of shame,
Over the face of the leader came;
The nobler nature within him stirred
To life at that woman's deed and word;
'Who touches a hair of yon gray head
Dies like a dog! March on!' he said.
All day long through Frederick street
Sounded the tread of marching feet:
All day long that free flag tost
Over the heads of the rebel host.
Ever its torn folds rose and fell
On the loyal winds that loved it well;
And through the hill-gaps sunset light
Shone over it with a warm good-night.

Barbara Frietchie's work is o'er,
And the Rebel rides on his raids no more.
Honour to her! and let a tear

Fall, for her sake, on Stonewall's bier.
Over Barbara Frietchie's grave,
Flag of Freedom and Union, wave!
Peace and order and beauty draw
Round thy symbol of light and law;
And ever the stars above look down
On thy stars below in Frederick town!

EDGAR ALLAN POE

The Raven

Once upon a midnight dreary, while I pondered, weak and weary,
Over many a quaint and curious volume of forgotten lore,
While I nodded, nearly napping, suddenly there came a tapping
As of someone gently rapping, rapping at my chamber door.
''Tis some visitor,' I muttered, 'tapping at my chamber door,
     Only this and nothing more.'

Ah, distinctly I remember it was in the bleak December,
And each separate dying ember wrought its ghost upon the floor.
Eagerly I wished the morrow; vainly I had sought to borrow
From my books surcease of sorrow, sorrow for the lost Lenore –
For the rare and radiant maiden whom the angels name Lenore –
     Nameless *here* for evermore.

And the silken, sad, uncertain rustling of each purple curtain
Thrilled me – filled me with fantastic terrors never felt before;
So that now, to still the beating of my heart, I stood repeating,
''Tis some visitor entreating entrance at my chamber door –
Some late visitor entreating entrance at my chamber door;
     This it is and nothing more.'

Presently my soul grew stronger; hesitating then no longer,
'Sir,' said I, 'or madam, truly your forgiveness I implore;
But the fact is I was napping, and so gently you came rapping,
And so faintly you came tapping, tapping at my chamber door,
That I scarce was sure I heard you' – here I opened wide the door;
     Darkness there and nothing more.

Deep into that darkness peering, long I stood there wondering,
    fearing,
Doubting, dreaming dreams no mortals ever dared to dream before;
But the silence was unbroken, and the stillness gave no token,

And the only word there spoken was the whispered word 'Lenore!'
This I whispered, and an echo murmured back the word 'Lenore' –
     Merely this and nothing more.

Back into the chamber turning, all my soul within me burning,
Soon again I heard a tapping somewhat louder than before.
'Surely,' said I, 'surely that is something at my window lattice;
Let me see then what thereat is, and this mystery explore –
Let my heart be still a moment and this mystery explore;
     'Tis the wind and nothing more!'

Open here I flung a shutter, when with many a flirt and flutter
In there stepped a stately raven of the saintly days of yore;
Not the least obeisance made he: not a minute stopped or stayed he;
But with mien of lord or lady, perched above my chamber door –
Perched upon a bust of Pallas, just above my chamber door –
     Perched, and sat, and nothing more.

Then this ebony bird beguiling my sad fancy into smiling
By the grave and stern decorum of the countenance it wore,
'Though thy crest be shorn and shaven, thou,' I said, 'art sure no craven,
Ghastly, grim and ancient raven wandering from the nightly shore,
Tell me what thy lordly name is on the night's Plutonian shore':
     Quoth the raven, 'Nevermore!'

Much I marvelled this ungainly fowl to hear discourse so plainly,
Though its answer little meaning – little relevancy bore;
For we cannot help agreeing that no living human being
Ever yet was blest with seeing bird above his chamber door,
Bird or beast upon the sculptured bust above his chamber door,
     With such a name as 'Nevermore'.

But the raven, sitting lonely on the placid bust, spoke only
That one word, as if his soul in that one word he did outpour;
Nothing further then he uttered – not a feather then he fluttered –
Till I scarcely more than muttered, 'Other friends have flown before –
On the morrow *he* will leave me, as my hopes have flown before.'
     Then the bird said, 'Nevermore.'

Startled at the stillness broken by reply so aptly spoken,
'Doubtless,' said I, 'what it utters is its only stock and store,
Caught from some unhappy master whom unmerciful disaster
Followed fast and followed faster, till his songs one burden bore –
Till the dirges of his hope that melancholy burden bore
     Of "Never – nevermore".'

But the raven still beguiling all my fancy into smiling,
Straight I wheeled a cushioned seat in front of bird, and bust, and door;
Then, upon the velvet sinking, I betook myself to linking
Fancy unto fancy, thinking what this ominous bird of yore –
What this grim, ungainly, ghastly, gaunt and ominous bird of yore
  Meant in croaking 'Nevermore.'

This I sat engaged in guessing, but no syllable expressing
To the fowl whose fiery eyes now burnt into my bosom's core;
This and more I sat divining, with my head at ease reclining
On the cushion's velvet lining that the lamp–light gloated o'er,
But whose velvet-violet lining, with the lamp–light gloating o'er,
  She shall press, ah, nevermore!

Then, methought, the air grew denser, perfumed from an unseen censer
Swung by seraphim whose foot-falls tinkled on the tufted floor.
'Wretch,' I cried, 'thy God hath lent thee – by these angels he hath sent thee
Respite – respite and nepenthe from thy memories of Lenore!
Quaff, oh quaff this kind nepenthe, and forget this lost Lenore!'
  Quoth the raven, 'Nevermore.'

'Prophet!' said I, 'thing of evil! – prophet still, if bird or devil!
Whether tempter sent, or whether tempest tossed thee here ashore,
Desolate yet all undaunted, on this desert land enchanted –
On this home by horror haunted – tell me truly, I implore –
Is there – *is* there balm in Gilead? tell me – tell me, I implore!'
  Quoth the raven, 'Nevermore.'

'Prophet!' said I, 'thing of evil – prophet still, if bird or devil!
By that heaven that bends above us, by that God we both adore –
Tell this soul, with sorrow laden, if within the distant Aidenn
It shall clasp a sainted maiden whom the angels name Lenore –
Clasp a rare and radiant maiden whom the angels name Lenore.'
  Quoth the raven, 'Nevermore.'

'Be that word our sign of parting, bird or fiend!' I shrieked upstarting –
'Get thee back into the tempest and the night's Plutonian shore!
Leave no black plume as a token of that lie thy soul hath spoken!
Leave my loneliness unbroken, quit the bust above my door!
Take thy beak from out my heart and take thy form from off my door!'
  Quoth the raven, 'Nevermore.'

And the raven, never flitting, still is sitting, *still* is sitting,
On the pallid bust of Pallas just above my chamber door;
And his eyes have all the seeming of a demon's that is dreaming,
And the lamp–light o'er him streaming throws his shadow on the floor;
And my soul from out that shadow that lies floating on the floor
  Shall be lifted – nevermore!

ALFRED, LORD TENNYSON

Morte d'Arthur

So all day long the noise of battle rolled
Among the mountains by the winter sea;
Until King Arthur's table, man by man,
Had fall'n in Lyonnesse about their Lord,
King Arthur: then, because his wound was deep,
The bold Sir Bedivere uplifted him,
Sir Bedivere, the last of all his knights,
And bore him to a chapel nigh the field,
A broken chancel with a broken cross,
That stood on a dark strait of barren land.
On one side lay the Ocean, and on one
Lay a great water, and the moon was full.
    Then spake King Arthur to Sir Bedivere:
'The sequel of today unsolders all
The goodliest fellowship of famous knights
Whereof this world holds record. Such a sleep
They sleep – the men I loved. I think that we
Shall never more, at any future time,
Delight our souls with talk of knightly deeds,
Walking about the gardens and the halls
Of Camelot, as in the days that were.
I perish by this people which I made, –
Tho' Merlin sware that I should come again
To rule once more – but let what will be, be.
I am so deeply smitten thro' the helm
That without help I cannot last till morn.
Thou therefore take my brand Excalibur,
Which was my pride: for thou rememberest how
In those old days, one summer noon, an arm
Rose up from out the bosom of the lake,
Clothed in white samite, mystic, wonderful,
Holding the sword – and how I rowed across
And took it, and have worn it, like a king:
And, wheresoever I am sung or told
In aftertime, this also shall be known:
But now delay not: take Excalibur,
And fling him far into the middle mere:
Watch what thou seest, and lightly bring me word.'
    To him replied the bold Sir Bedivere:
'It is not meet, Sir King, to leave thee thus,
Aidless, alone, and smitten thro' the helm.
A little thing may harm a wounded man.
Yet I thy hest will all perform at full,

Watch what I see, and lightly bring thee word.'
  So saying, from the ruined shrine he stepped
And in the moon athwart the place of tombs,
Where lay the mighty bones of ancient men,
Old knights, and over them the sea-wind sang
Shrill, chill, with flakes of foam. He, stepping down
By zig-zag paths, and juts of pointed rock,
Came on the shining levels of the lake.
  There drew he forth the brand Excalibur,
And o'er him, drawing it, the winter moon,
Brightening the skirts of a long cloud, ran forth
And sparkled keen with frost against the hilt:
For all the haft twinkled with diamond sparks,
Myriads of topaz-lights, and jacinth-work
Of subtlest jewellery. He gazed so long
That both his eyes were dazzled, as he stood,
This way and that dividing the swift mind,
In act to throw: but at the last it seemed
Better to leave Excalibur concealed
There in the many-knotted waterflags,
That whistled stiff and dry about the marge.
So strode he back slow to the wounded King.
  Then spake King Arthur to Sir Bedivere:
'Hast thou performed my mission which I gave?
What is it thou hast seen? or what hast heard?'
  And answer made the bold Sir Bedivere:
'I heard the ripple washing in the reeds,
And the wild water lapping on the crag.'
  To whom replied King Arthur, faint and pale:
'Thou hast betrayed thy nature and thy name,
Not rendering true answer, as beseemed
Thy fealty, nor like a noble knight:
For surer sign had followed, either hand,
Or voice, or else a motion of the mere.
This is a shameful thing for men to lie.
Yet now, I charge thee, quickly go again
As thou art lief and dear, and do the thing
I bad thee, watch, and lightly bring me word.'
  Then went Sir Bedivere the second time
Across the ridge, and paced beside the mere,
Counting the dewy pebbles, fixed in thought;
But when he saw the wonder of the hilt,
How curiously and strangely chased, he smote
His palms together, and he cried aloud,
  'And if indeed I cast the brand away,
Surely a precious thing, one worthy note,
Should thus be lost for ever from the earth,

Which might have pleased the eyes of many men.
What good should follow this, if this were done?
What harm, undone? deep harm to disobey,
Seeing obedience is the bond of rule.
Were it well to obey then, if a king demand
An act unprofitable, against himself?
The King is sick, and knows not what he does.
What record, or what relic of my lord
Should be to aftertime, but empty breath
And rumours of a doubt? But were this kept,
Stored in some treasure-house of mighty kings,
Some one might show it at a joust of arms,
Saying, "King Arthur's sword, Excalibur,
Wrought by the lonely maiden of the Lake,
Nine years she wrought it, sitting in the deeps
Upon the hidden bases of the hills."
So might some old man speak in the aftertime
To all the people, winning reverence.
But now much honour and much fame were lost.'
   So spake he, clouded with his own conceit,
And hid Excalibur the second time,
And so strode back slow to the wounded King.
   Then spoke King Arthur, breathing heavily:
'What is it thou hast seen? or what hast heard?'
   And answer made the bold Sir Bedivere:
'I heard the water lapping on the crag,
And the long ripple washing in the reeds.'
   To whom replied King Arthur, much in wrath:
'Ah, miserable and unkind, untrue,
Unknightly, traitor-hearted! Woe is me!
Authority forgets a dying king,
Laid widowed of the power in his eye
That bowed the will. I see thee what thou art,
For thou, the latest-left of all my knights,
In whom should meet the offices of all,
Thou wouldst betray me for the precious hilt;
Either from lust of gold, or like a girl
Valuing the giddy pleasure of the eyes.
Yet, for a man may fail in duty twice,
And the third time may prosper, get thee hence:
But, if thou spare to fling Excalibur,
I will arise and slay thee with my hands.'
   Then quickly rose Sir Bedivere, and ran,
And, leaping down the ridges lightly, plunged
Among the bulrush-beds, and clutched the sword,
And strongly wheeled and threw it. The great brand
Made lightnings in the splendour of the moon,

And flashing round and round, and whirled in an arch,
Shot like a streamer of the northern morn,
Seen where the moving isles of winter shock
By night, with noises of the northern sea.
So flashed and fell the brand Excalibur:
But ere he dipped the surface, rose an arm
Clothed in white samite, mystic, wonderful,
And caught him by the hilt, and brandished him
Three times, and drew him under in the mere.
And lightly went the other to the King.

Then spoke King Arthur, drawing thicker breath:
'Now see I by thine eyes that this is done.
Speak out: what is it thou hast heard, or seen?'

And answer made the bold Sir Bedivere:
'Sir King, I closed mine eyelids, lest the gems
Should blind my purpose, for I never saw,
Nor shall see, here or elsewhere, till I die,
Not tho' I live three lives of mortal men,
So great a miracle as yonder hilt.
Then with both hands I flung him, wheeling him:
But when I looked again, behold an arm,
Clothed in white samite, mystic, wonderful,
That caught him by the hilt, and brandished him
Three times, and drew him under in the mere.'

And answer made King Arthur, breathing hard;
'My end draws nigh: 'tis time that I were gone.
Make broad thy shoulders to receive my weight,
And bear me to the margin; yet I fear
My wound hath taken cold, and I shall die.'

So saying, from the pavement he half rose,
Slowly, with pain, reclining on his arm,
And looking wistfully with wide blue eyes
As in a picture. Him Sir Bedivere
Remorsefully regarded thro' his tears,
And would have spoken, but he found not words,
Then took with care, and kneeling on one knee,
O'er both his shoulders drew the languid hands,
And rising bore him thro' the place of tombs.

But, as he walked, King Arthur panted hard,
Like one that feels a nightmare on his bed
When all the house is mute. So sighed the King,
Muttering and murmuring at his ear, 'Quick, quick!
I fear it is too late, and I shall die.'
But the other swiftly strode from ridge to ridge,
Clothed with his breath, and looking, as he walked,
Larger than human on the frozen hills.
He heard the deep behind him, and a cry

Before. His own thought drove him like a goad.
Dry clashed his harness in the icy caves
And barren chasms, and all to left and right
The bare black cliff clanged round him, as he based
His feet on juts of slippery crag that rang
Sharp-smitten with the dint of armed heels –
And on a sudden, lo! the level lake,
And the long glories of the winter moon.

Then saw they how there hove a dusky barge,
Dark as a funeral scarf from stem to stern,
Beneath them; and descending they were ware
That all the decks were dense with stately forms
Black-stoled, black-hooded, like a dream – by these
Three Queens with crowns of gold – and from them rose
A cry that shivered to the tingling stars,
And, as it were one voice, an agony
Of lamentation, like a wind, that shrills
All night in a waste land, where no one comes,
Or hath come, since the making of the world.

Then murmured Arthur, 'Place me in the barge,'
And to the barge they came. There those three Queens
Put forth their hands, and took the King, and wept.
But she, that rose the tallest of them all
And fairest, laid his head upon her lap,
And loosed the shattered casque, and chafed his hands,
And called him by his name, complaining loud,
And dropping bitter tears against his brow
Striped with dark blood: for all his face was white
And colourless, and like the withered moon
Smote by the fresh beam of the springing east;
And all his greaves and cuisses dashed with drops
Of onset; and the light and lustrous curls –
That made his forehead like a rising sun
High from the dais-throne – were parched with dust;
Or, clotted into points and hanging loose,
Mixed with the knightly growth that fringed his lips.
So like a shattered column lay the King;
Not like that Arthur who, with lance in rest,
From spur to plume a star or tournament,
Shot through the lists at Camelot, and charged
Before the eyes of ladies and of kings.

Then loudly cried the bold Sir Bedivere,
'Ah! my Lord Arthur, whither shall I go?
Where shall I hide my forehead and my eyes?
For now I see the true old times are dead,
When every morning brought a noble chance,
And every chance brought out a noble knight.

Such times have been not since the light that led
The holy Elders with the gift of myrrh.
But now the whole Round Table is dissolved
Which was an image of the mighty world;
And I, the last, go forth companionless,
And the days darken round me, and the years,
Among new men, strange faces, other minds.'
    And slowly answered Arthur from the barge:
'The old order changeth, yielding place to new,
And God fulfils Himself in many ways,
Lest one good custom should corrupt the world.
Comfort thyself: what comfort is in me?
I have lived my life, and that which I have done
May He within Himself make pure! but thou,
If thou shouldst never see my face again,
Pray for my soul. More things are wrought by prayer
Than this world dreams of. Wherefore, let thy voice
Rise like a fountain for me night and day.
For what are men better than sheep or goats
That nourish a blind life within the brain,
If, knowing God, they lift not hands of prayer
Both for themselves and those who call them friend?
For so the whole round earth is every way
Bound by gold chains about the feet of God.
But now farewell. I am going a long way
With these thou seest – if indeed I go –
(For all my mind is clouded with a doubt)
To the island-valley of Avilion;
Where falls not hail, or rain, or any snow,
Nor ever wind blows loudly; but it lies
Deep-meadowed, happy, fair with orchard-lawns
And bowery hollows crowned with summer sea,
Where I will heal me of my grievous wound.'
    So said he, and the barge with oar and sail
Moved from the brink, like some full-breasted swan
That, fluting a wild carol ere her death,
Ruffles her pure cold plume, and takes the flood
With swarthy webs. Long stood Sir Bedivere
Revolving many memories, till the hull
Looked one black dot against the verge of dawn,
And on the mere the wailing died away.

The Revenge

At Flores in the Azores Sir Richard Grenville lay,
And a pinnace, like a fluttered bird, came flying from far away:

'Spanish ships of war at sea! we have sighted fifty-three!'
Then sware Lord Thomas Howard: ''Fore God I am no coward;
But I cannot meet them here, for my ships are out of gear,
And the half my men are sick. I must fly, but follow quick.
We are six ships of the line; can we fight with fifty-three?'

Then spake Sir Richard Grenville: 'I know you are no coward;
You fly them for a moment to fight with them again.
But I've ninety men and more that are lying sick ashore.
I should count myself the coward if I left them, my Lord Howard,
To these Inquisition dogs and the devildoms of Spain.'

So Lord Howard past away with five ships of war that day,
Till he melted like a cloud in the silent summer heaven;
But Sir Richard bore in hand all his sick men from the land
Very carefully and slow,
Men of Bideford in Devon,
And we laid them on the ballast down below;
For we brought them all aboard,
And they blest him in their pain, that they were not left to Spain,
To the thumbscrew and the stake, for the glory of the Lord.

He had only a hundred seamen to work the ship and to fight,
And he sailed away from Flores till the Spaniard came in sight,
With his huge sea-castles heaving upon the weather bow.
'Shall we fight or shall we fly?
Good Sir Richard, tell us now,
For to fight is but to die!
There'll be little of us left by the time this sun be set.'
And Sir Richard said again: 'We be all good English men.
Let us bang these dogs of Seville, the children of the devil,
For I never turned my back upon Don or devil yet.'

Sir Richard spoke and he laughed, and we roared a hurrah, and so
The little Revenge ran on sheer into the heart of the foe,
With her hundred fighters on deck, and her ninety sick below;
For half of their fleet to the right and half to the left were seen,
And the little Revenge ran on through the long sea-lane between.

Thousands of their soldiers looked down from their decks and laughed,
Thousands of their seamen made mock at the mad little craft
Running on and on, till delayed
By their mountain-like San Philip that, of fifteen hundred tons,
And up-shadowing high above us with her yawning tiers of guns,
Took the breath from our sails, and we stayed.

And while now the great San Philip hung above us like a cloud

Whence the thunderbolt will fall
Long and loud,
Four galleons drew away
From the Spanish fleet that day,
And two upon the larboard and two upon the starboard lay,
And the battle-thunder broke from them all.

But anon the great San Philip, she bethought herself and went
Having that within her womb that had left her ill content;
And the rest they came aboard us, and they fought us hand to hand,
For a dozen times they came with their pikes and musqueteers,
And a dozen times we shook 'em off as a dog that shakes his ears
When he leaps from the water to the land.

And the sun went down, and the stars came out far over the summer sea,
But never a moment ceased the fight of the one and the fifty-three.
Ship after ship, the whole night long, their high-built galleons came,
Ship after ship, the whole night long, with her battle-thunder and flame;
Ship after ship, the whole night long, drew back with her dead and her
    shame.
For some were sunk and many were shattered, and so could fight us no
    more –
God of battles, was ever a battle like this in the world before?

For he said 'Fight on! fight on!'
Though his vessel was all but a wreck;
And it chanced that, when half of the short summer night was gone,
With a grisly wound to be drest he had left the deck,
But a bullet struck him that was dressing it suddenly dead,
And himself he was wounded again in the side and the head,
And he said 'Fight on! fight on!'

And the night went down, and the sun smiled out far over the summer
    sea,
And the Spanish fleet with broken sides lay round us all in a ring;
But they dared not touch us again, for they feared that we still could
    sting,
So they watched what the end would be.
And we had not fought them in vain,
But in perilous plight were we,
Seeing forty of our poor hundred were slain,
And half of the rest of us maimed for life
In the crash of the cannonades and the desperate strife;
And the sick men down in the hold were most of them stark and cold,
And the pikes were all broken or bent, and the powder was all of it spent;
And the masts and the rigging were lying over the side;
But Sir Richard cried in his English pride,

'We have fought such a fight for a day and a night
As may never be fought again!
We have won great glory, my men!
And a day less or more
At sea or ashore,
We die – does it matter when?
Sink me the ship, Master Gunner – sink her, split her in twain!
Fall into the hands of God, not into the hands of Spain!'

And the gunner said 'Ay, ay,' but the seamen made reply:
'We have children, we have wives,
And the Lord hath spared our lives.
We will make the Spaniard promise, if we yield, to let us go;
We shall live to fight again and to strike another blow.'
And the lion there lay dying, and they yielded to the foe.

And the stately Spanish men to their flagship bore him then,
Where they laid him by the mast, old Sir Richard caught at last,
And they praised him to his face with their courtly foreign grace;
But he rose upon their decks, and he cried:
'I have fought for Queen and Faith like a valiant man and true;
I have only done my duty as a man is bound to do:
With a joyful spirit I Sir Richard Grenville die!'
And he fell upon their decks, and he died.

And they stared at the dead that had been so valiant and true,
And had holden the power and glory of Spain so cheap
That he dared her with one little ship and his English few;
Was he devil or man? He was devil for aught they knew,
But they sank his body with honour down into the deep,
And they manned the Revenge with a swarthier alien crew,
And away she sailed with her loss and longed for her own;
When a wind from the lands they had ruined awoke from sleep,
And the water began to heave and the weather to moan,
And or ever that evening ended a great gale blew,
And a wave like the wave that is raised by an earthquake grew,
Till it smote on their hulls and their sails and their masts and their flags,
And the whole sea plunged and fell on the shot-shattered navy of Spain,
And the little Revenge herself went down by the island crags
To be lost evermore in the main.

EDWARD LEAR

The Dong with a Luminous Nose

When awful darkness and silence reign
Over the great Gromboolian plain,
   Through the long, long wintry nights;
When the angry breakers roar
As they beat on the rocky shore;
   When storm-clouds brood on the towering heights
Of the hills of the Chankly Bore:
Then, through the vast and gloomy dark,
There moves what seems a fiery spark,
   A lonely spark with silvery rays
   Piercing the coal-black night,
   A meteor strange and bright:
Hither and thither the vision strays,
   A single lurid light.

Slowly it wanders, – pauses, – creeps,
Anon it sparkles, – flashes and leaps;
And ever as onward it gleaming goes
A light on the Bong-tree stems it throws.
And those who watch at that midnight hour
From hall or terrace, or lofty tower,
Cry, as the wild light passes along,
     'The Dong! – the Dong!
   The wandering Dong through the forest goes!
    The Dong! the Dong!
   The Dong with a luminous Nose!'

    Long years ago
   The Dong was happy and gay,
Till he fell in love with a Jumbly Girl
   Who came to those shores one day,
For the Jumblies came in a sieve, they did,
Landing at eve near the Zemmery Fidd
    Where the Oblong Oysters grow,
   And the rocks are smooth and gray.
And all the woods and the valleys rang
With the Chorus they daily and nightly sang,
      'Far and few, far and few,
      Are the lands where the Jumblies live;
      Their heads are green, and their hands are blue
      And they went to sea in a sieve.'

Happily, happily passed those days!

While the cheerful Jumblies stayed;
They danced in circlets all night long,
To the plaintive pipe of the lively Dong,
In moonlight, shine, or shade.
For day and night he was always there
By the side of the Jumbly Girl so fair,
With her sky-blue hands, and her sea-green hair.
Till the morning came of that hateful day
When the Jumblies sailed in their sieve away,
And the Dong was left on the cruel shore
Gazing – gazing for evermore,
Ever keeping his weary eyes on
That pea-green sail on the far horizon,
Singing the Jumbly Chorus still
As he sate all day on the grassy hill,
'Far and few, far and few,
Are the lands where the Jumblies live;
Their heads are green, and their hands are blue,
And they went to sea in a sieve.'

But when the sun was low in the West,
The Dong arose and said:
'What little sense I once possessed
Has quite gone out of my head!'
And since that day he wanders still
By lake and forest, marsh and hill,
Singing – 'O somewhere, in valley or plain
Might I find my Jumbly Girl again!
For ever I'll seek by lake and shore
Till I find my Jumbly Girl once more!'

Playing a pipe with silvery squeaks,
Since then his Jumbly Girl he seeks,
And because by night he could not see,
He gathered the bark of the Twangum Tree
On the flowery plain that grows.
And he wove him a wondrous Nose,
A Nose as strange as a Nose could be!
Of vast proportions and painted red,
And tied with cords to the back of his head.
In a hollow rounded space it ended
With a luminous Lamp within suspended,
All fenced about
With a bandage stout
To prevent the wind from blowing it out;
And with holes all round to send the light
In gleaming rays on the dismal night.

And now each night, and all night long,
Over those plains still roams the Dong;
And above the wail of the Chimp and Snipe
You may hear the squeak of his plaintive pipe
While ever he seeks, but seeks in vain
To meet with his Jumbly Girl again;
Lonely and wild – all night he goes,
The Dong with a luminous Nose!
And all who watch at the midnight hour,
From hall or terrace, or lofty tower,
Cry, as they trace the meteor bright,
Moving along through the dreary night,
   'This is the hour when forth he goes,
   The Dong with a luminous Nose!
   Yonder – over the plain he goes;
     He goes!
     He goes;
The Dong with a luminous Nose!'

ROBERT BROWNING

My Last Duchess

[FERRARA]

That's my last Duchess painted on the wall,
Looking as if she were alive. I call
That piece a wonder, now: Frà Pandolf's hands
Worked busily a day, and there she stands.
Will't please you sit and look at her? I said
'Frà Pandolf' by design, for never read
Strangers like you that pictured countenance,
The depth and passion of its earnest glance,
But to myself they turned (since none puts by
The curtain I have drawn for you, but I)
And seemed as they would ask me, if they durst,
How such a glance came there; so, not the first
Are you to turn and ask thus. Sir, 'twas not
Her husband's presence only, called that spot
Of joy into the Duchess' cheek: perhaps
Frà Pandolf chanced to say 'Her mantle laps
Over my lady's wrist too much,' or 'Paint
Must never hope to reproduce the faint
Half-flush that dies along her throat': such stuff

Was courtesy, she thought, and cause enough
For calling up that spot of joy. She had
A heart – how shall I say? – too soon made glad,
Too easily impressed; she liked whate'er
She looked on, and her looks went everywhere.
Sir, 'twas all one! My favour at her breast,
The dropping of the daylight in the West,
The bough of cherries some officious fool
Broke in the orchard for her, the white mule
She rode with round the terrace – all and each
Would draw from her alike the approving speech,
Or blush, at least. She thanked men, – good! but thanked
Somehow – I know not how – as if she ranked
My gift of a nine-hundred-years-old name
With anybody's gift. Who'd stoop to blame
This sort of trifling? Even had you skill
In speech – (which I have not) – to make your will
Quite clear to such an one, and say, 'Just this
Or that in you disgusts me; here you miss,
Or there exceed the mark' – and if she let
Herself be lessoned so, nor plainly set
Her wits to yours, forsooth, and made excuse
– E'en then would be some stooping; and I choose
Never to stoop. Oh sir, she smiled, no doubt,
Whene'er I passed her; but who passed without
Much the same smile? This grew; I gave commands;
Then all smiles stopped together. There she stands
As if alive. Will't please you rise? We'll meet
The company below, then. I repeat,
The Count your master's known munificence
Is ample warrant that no just pretence
Of mine for dowry will be disallowed;
Though his fair daughter's self, as I avowed
At starting, is my object. Nay, we'll go
Together down, sir. Notice Neptune, though,
Taming a sea-horse, thought a rarity,
Which Claus of Innsbruck cast in bronze for me.

The Pied Piper of Hamelin

Hamelin Town's in Brunswick,
    By famous Hanover city;
The river Weser, deep and wide,
Washes its wall on the southern side;
A pleasanter spot you never spied;
    But, when begins my ditty,
Almost five hundred years ago,

To see the townsfolk suffer so
   From vermin, was a pity.

  Rats!
They fought the dogs and killed the cats,
   And bit the babies in the cradles,
And ate the cheeses out of the vats,
   And licked the soup from the cooks' own ladles,
Split open the kegs of salted sprats,
Made nests inside men's Sunday hats,
And even spoiled the women's chats
      By drowning their speaking
      With shrieking and squeaking
In fifty different sharps and flats.

At last the people in a body
   To the Town Hall came flocking:
''Tis clear,' cried they, 'our Mayor's a noddy;
   And as for our Corporation – shocking
To think we buy gowns lined with ermine
For dolts that can't or won't determine
What's best to rid us of our vermin!
You hope, because you're old and obese,
To find in the furry civic robe ease?
Rouse up, sirs! Give your brains a racking
To find the remedy we're lacking,
Or, sure as fate, we'll send you packing!'
At this the Mayor and Corporation
Quaked with a mighty consternation.

An hour they sat in council,
   At length the Mayor broke silence:
'For a guilder I'd my ermine gown sell,
   I wish I were a mile hence!
It's easy to bid one rack one's brain – ·
I'm sure my poor head aches again,
I've scratched it so, and all in vain.
Oh for a trap, a trap, a trap!'
Just as he said this, what should hap
At the chamber door but a gentle tap?
'Bless us,' cried the Mayor, 'what's that?'
(With the Corporation as he sat,
Looking little though wondrous fat;
Nor brighter was his eye, nor moister
Than a too-long-opened oyster,
Save when at noon his paunch grew mutinous
For a plate of turtle, green and glutinous)

'Only a scraping of shoes on the mat?
Anything like the sound of a rat
Makes my heart go pit-a-pat!'

'Come in!' the Mayor cried, looking bigger:
And in did come the strangest figure!
His queer long coat from heel to head
Was half of yellow and half of red,
And he himself was tall and thin,
With sharp blue eyes, each like a pin,
And light loose hair, yet swarthy skin,
No tuft on cheek nor beard on chin,
But lips where smiles went out and in;
There was no guessing his kith and kin:
And nobody could enough admire
The tall man and his quaint attire.
Quoth one: 'It's as my great-grandsire,
Starting up at the Trump of Doom's tone,
Had walked this way from his painted tombstone!'

He advanced to the council-table:
And, 'Please your honours,' said he, 'I'm able,
By means of a secret charm, to draw
    All creatures living beneath the sun,
    That creep or swim or fly or run,
After me so as you never saw!
And I chiefly use my charm
On creatures that do people harm,
The mole and toad and newt and viper;
And people call me the Pied Piper.'
(And here they noticed round his neck
    A scarf of red and yellow stripe,
To match with his coat of the self-same check;
    And at the scarf's end hung a pipe;
And his fingers, they noticed, were ever straying
As if impatient to be playing
Upon this pipe, as low it dangled
Over his vesture so old-fangled.)
'Yet,' said he, 'poor piper as I am,
In Tartary I freed the Cham,
    Last June, from his huge swarms of gnats;
I eased in Asia the Nizam
    Of a monstrous brood of vampire-bats:
And as for what your brain bewilders,
    If I can rid your town of rats
Will you give me a thousand guilders?'
'One? fifty thousand!' – was the exclamation
Of the astonished Mayor and Corporation.

Into the street the Piper stept,
    Smiling first a little smile,
As if he knew what magic slept
    In his quiet pipe the while;
Then, like a musical adept,
To blow the pipe his lips he wrinkled,
And green and blue his sharp eyes twinkled,
Like a candle-flame where salt is sprinkled;
And ere three shrill notes the pipe uttered,
You heard as if an army muttered;
And the muttering grew to a grumbling;
And the grumbling grew to a mighty rumbling;
And out of the houses the rats came tumbling.
Great rats, small rats, lean rats, brawny rats,
Brown rats, black rats, grey rats, tawny rats,
Grave old plodders, gay young friskers,
    Fathers, mothers, uncles, cousins,
Cocking tails and pricking whiskers,
    Families by tens and dozens,
Brothers, sisters, husbands, wives –
Followed the Piper for their lives.
From street to street he piped advancing,
And step for step they followed dancing,
Until they came to the river Weser,
    Wherein all plunged and perished!
– Save one who, stout as Julius Caesar,
Swam across and lived to carry
    (As he, the manuscript he cherished)
To Rat-land home his commentary:
Which was, 'At the first shrill notes of the pipe,
I heard a sound as of scraping tripe,
And putting apples, wondrous ripe,
Into a cider-press's gripe:
And a moving away of pickle-tub-boards,
And a leaving ajar of conserve-cupboards,
And a drawing the corks of train-oil-flasks,
And a breaking the hoops of butter-casks;
And it seemed as if a voice
    (Sweeter far than by harp or by psaltery
Is breathed) called out, "Oh rats, rejoice!
    The world is grown to one vast drysaltery!
So munch on, crunch on, take your nuncheon,
Breakfast, supper, dinner, luncheon!"
And just as a bulky sugar-puncheon,
All ready staved, like a great sun shone
Glorious scarce an inch before me,

Just as methought it said, "Come, bore me!"
– I found the Weser rolling o'er me.'

You should have heard the Hamelin people
Ringing the bells till they rocked the steeple.
'Go,' cried the Mayor, 'and get long poles,
Poke out the nests and block up the holes!
Consult with carpenters and builders,
And leave in our town not even a trace
Of the rats!' – when suddenly, up the face
Of the Piper perked in the market-place,
With a 'First, if you please, my thousand guilders!'

A thousand guilders! The Mayor looked blue;
So did the Corporation too.
For council dinners made rare havoc
With Claret, Moselle, Vin-de-Grave, Hock;
And half the money would replenish
Their cellar's biggest butt with Rhenish.
To pay this sum to a wandering fellow
With a gipsy coat of red and yellow!
'Beside,' quoth the Mayor with a knowing wink,
'Our business was done at the river's brink;
We saw with our eyes the vermin sink,
And what's dead can't come to life, I think.
So, friend, we're not the folks to shrink
From the duty of giving you something for drink,
And a matter of money to put in your poke;
But as for the guilders, what we spoke
Of them, as you very well know, was in joke.
Besides, our losses have made us thrifty.
A thousand guilders! Come, take fifty!'

The Piper's face fell, and he cried
'No trifling! I can't wait, beside!
I've promised to visit by dinnertime
Baghdad, and accept the prime
Of the Head-Cook's pottage, all he's rich in,
For having left, in the Caliph's kitchen,
Of a nest of scorpions no survivor:
With him I proved no bargain-driver,
With you, don't think I'll bate a stiver!
And folks who put me in a passion
May find me pipe after another fashion.'

'How?' cried the Mayor, 'd'ye think I brook
Being worse treated than a cook?

Insulted by a lazy ribald
With idle pipe and vesture piebald?
You threaten us, fellow? Do your worst,
Blow your pipe there till you burst!'

Once more he stepped into the street
    And to his lips again
    Laid his long pipe of smooth straight cane;
And ere he blew three notes (such sweet
Soft notes as yet musician's cunning
    Never gave the enraptured air)
There was a rustling that seemed like a bustling
Of merry crowds justling at pitching and hustling,
Small feet were pattering, wooden shoes clattering,
Little hands clapping and little tongues chattering,
And, like fowls in a farmyard when barley is scattering,
Out came the children running.
All the little boys and girls,
With rosy cheeks and flaxen curls,
And sparkling eyes and teeth like pearls,
Tripping and skipping, ran merrily after
The wonderful music with shouting and laughter.

The Mayor was dumb, and the Council stood
As if they were changed into blocks of wood,
Unable to move a step, or cry
To the children merrily skipping by
– Could only follow with the eye
That joyous crowd at the Piper's back.
But how the Mayor was on the rack,
And the wretched Council's bosoms beat,
As the Piper turned from the High Street
To where the Weser rolled its waters
Right in the way of their sons and daughters!
However he turned from south to west,
And to Koppelberg Hill his steps addressed,
And after him the children pressed;
Great was the joy in every breast.
'He never can cross that mighty top!
He's forced to let the piping drop,
And we shall see our children stop!'
When, lo, as they reached the mountain-side,
A wondrous portal opened wide,
As if a cavern was suddenly hollowed;
And the Piper advanced and the children followed,
And when all were in to the very last,
The door in the mountain-side shut fast.

Did I say, all? No! One was lame,
  And could not dance the whole of the way;
And in after years, if you would blame
  His sadness, he was used to say –
'It's dull in our town since my playmates left!
I can't forget that I'm bereft
Of all the pleasant sights they see,
Which the Piper also promised me.
For he led us, he said, to a joyous land,
Joining the town and just at hand,
Where waters gushed and fruit trees grew
And flowers put forth a fairer hue,
And everything was strange and new;
The sparrows were brighter than peacocks here,
And their dogs outran our fallow deer,
And honey-bees had lost their stings,
And horses were born with eagles' wings:
And just as I became assured
My lame foot would be speedily cured,
The music stopped and I stood still,
And found myself outside the hill,
Left alone against my will,
To go now limping as before,
And never hear of that country more!'

Alas, alas for Hamelin!
  There came into many a burgher's pate
  A text which says that heaven's gate
  Opes to the rich at as easy rate
As the needle's eye takes a camel in!
The Mayor sent east, west, north, and south,
To offer the Piper, by word of mouth,
  Wherever it was men's lot to find him,
Silver and gold to his heart's content,
If he'd only return the way he went,
  And bring the children behind him.
But when they saw 'twas a lost endeavour,
And Piper and dancers were gone for ever,
They made a decree that lawyers never
  Should think their records dated duly
If, after the day of the month and year,
These words did not as well appear,
'And so long after what happened here
  On the Twenty-second of July,
Thirteen hundred and seventy-six':
And the better in memory to fix
The place of the children's last retreat,

They called it the Pied Piper's Street –
Where anyone playing on pipe or tabor
Was sure for the future to lose his labour.
Nor suffered they hostelry or tavern
   To shock with mirth a street so solemn;
But opposite the place of the cavern
   They wrote the story on a column;
And on the great church-window painted
The same, to make the world acquainted
How their children were stolen away,
And there it stands to this very day.
And I must not omit to say
That in Transylvania there's a tribe
Of alien people who ascribe
The outlandish ways and dress
On which their neighbours lay such stress,
To their fathers and mothers having risen
Out of some subterraneous prison
Into which they were trepanned
Long time ago in a mighty band
Out of Hamelin town in Brunswick land,
But how or why, they don't understand.

How They Brought the Good News from Ghent to Aix

I sprang to the stirrup, and Joris, and he;
I galloped, Dirck galloped, we galloped all three;
'Good speed!' cried the watch, as the gate-bolts undrew;
'Speed!' echoed the wall to us galloping through;
Behind shut the postern, the lights sank to rest,
And into the midnight we galloped abreast.

Not a word to each other; we kept the great pace,
Neck by neck, stride by stride, never changing our place.
I turned in my saddle and made its girths tight,
Then shortened each stirrup, and set the pique right,
Rebuckled the cheek-strap, chained slacker the bit,
Nor galloped less steadily Roland a whit.

'Twas moonset at starting; but while we drew near
Lokeren, the cocks crew and twilight dawned clear;
At Boom, a great yellow star came out to see;
At Düffeld, 'twas morning as plain as could be;
And from Mecheln church-steeple we heard the half-chime,
So, Joris broke silence with, 'Yet there is time!'

At Aershot, up leaped of a sudden the sun,
And against him the cattle stood black every one,
To stare through the mist at us galloping past,
And I saw my stout galloper Roland at last,
With resolute shoulders, each butting away
The haze, as some bluff river headland its spray:

And his low head and crest, just one sharp ear bent back
For my voice, and the other pricked out on his track;
And one eye's black intelligence – ever that glance
O'er its white edge at me, his own master, askance!
And the thick heavy spume-flakes which aye and anon
His fierce lips shook upwards in galloping on.

By Hasselt, Dirck groaned; and cried Joris, 'Stay spur!
Your Roos galloped bravely, the fault's not in her,
We'll remember at Aix' – for one heard the quick wheeze
Of her chest, saw the stretched neck and staggering knees,
And sunk tail, and horrible heave of the flank,
As down on her haunches she shuddered and sank.

So, we were left galloping, Joris and I,
Past Looz and past Tongres, no cloud in the sky;
The broad sun above laughed a pitiless laugh,
'Neath our feet broke the brittle bright stubble like chaff;
Till over by Dalhem a dome-spire sprang white,
And 'Gallop,' gasped Joris, 'for Aix is in sight!'

'How they'll greet us!' – and all in a moment his roan
Rolled neck and croup over, lay dead as a stone;
And there was my Roland to bear the whole weight
Of the news which alone could save Aix from her fate,
With his nostrils like pits full of blood to the brim,
And with circles of red for his eye-sockets' rim.

Then I cast loose my buffcoat, each holster let fall,
Shook off both my jack-boots, let go belt and all,
Stood up in the stirrup, leaned, patted his ear,
Called my Roland his pet-name, my horse without peer;
Clapped my hands, laughed and sang, any noise, bad or good,
Till at length into Aix Roland galloped and stood.

And all I remember is – friends flocking round
As I sat with his head 'twixt my knees on the ground;
And no voice but was praising this Roland of mine,
As I poured down his throat our last measure of wine,
Which (the burgesses voted by common consent)
Was no more than his due who brought good news from Ghent.

MATTHEW ARNOLD

Sohrab and Rustum

And the first grey of morning filled the east,
And the fog rose out of the Oxus stream.
But all the Tartar camp along the stream
Was hushed, and still the men were plunged in sleep:
Sohrab alone, he slept not: all night long
He had lain wakeful, tossing on his bed;
But when the grey dawn stole into his tent,
He rose, and clad himself, and girt his sword,
And took his horseman's cloak, and left his tent,
And went abroad into the cold wet fog,
Through the dim camp to Peran-Wisa's tent.
   Through the black Tartar tents he passed, which stood
Clustering like bee-hives on the low flat strand
Of Oxus, where the summer floods o'erflow
When the sun melts the snows in high Pamere:
Through the black tents he passed, o'er that low strand,
And to a hillock came, a little back
From the stream's brink, the spot where first a boat,
Crossing the stream in summer, scrapes the land.
The men of former times had crowned the top
With a clay fort: but that was fall'n; and now
The Tartars built there Peran-Wisa's tent,
A dome of laths, and o'er it felts were spread.
And Sohrab came there, and went in, and stood
Upon the thick-piled carpets in the tent,
And found the old man sleeping on his bed
Of rugs and felts, and near him lay his arms.
And Peran-Wisa heard him, though the step
Was dulled; for he slept light, an old man's sleep;
And he rose quickly on one arm, and said:
   'Who art thou? for it is not yet clear dawn.
Speak! is there news, or any night alarm?'
   But Sohrab came to the bedside, and said:
'Thou know'st me Peran-Wisa: it is I.
The sun is not yet risen, and the foe
Sleep; but I sleep not; all night long I lie
Tossing and wakeful, and I come to thee.
For so did King Afrasiab bid me seek
Thy counsel, and to heed thee as thy son,
In Samarcand, before the army marched;
And I will tell thee what my heart desires.
Thou know'st if, since from Ader-baijan first
I came among the Tartars, and bore arms,

I have still served Afrasiab well, and shown,
At my boy's years, the courage of a man.
This too thou know'st, that, while I still bear on
The conquering Tartar ensigns through the world,
And beat the Persians back on every field,
I seek one man, one man, and one alone –
Rustum, my father; who, I hoped, should greet,
Should one day greet, upon some well-fought field,
His not unworthy, not inglorious son.
So I long hoped, but him I never find.
Come then, hear now, and grant me what I ask.
Let the two armies rest today: but I
Will challenge forth the bravest Persian lords
To meet me, man to man: if I prevail,
Rustum will surely hear it; if I fall –
Old man, the dead need no one, claim no kin.
Dim is the rumour of a common fight,
Where host meets host, and many names are sunk:
But of a single combat fame speaks clear.'
    He spoke: and Peran-Wisa took the hand
Of the young man in his, and sighed, and said:
    'O Sohrab, an unquiet heart is thine!
Canst thou not rest among the Tartar chiefs,
And share the battle's common chance with us
Who love thee, but must press for ever first,
In single fight incurring single risk,
To find a father thou hast never seen?
That were far best, my son, to stay with us
Unmurmuring; in our tents, while it is war,
And when 'tis truce, then in Afrasiab's towns.
But, if this one desire indeed rules all,
To seek out Rustum – seek him not through fight:
Seek him in peace, and carry to his arms,
O Sohrab, carry an unwounded son!
But far hence seek him, for he is not here.
For now it is not as when I was young,
When Rustum was in front of every fray:
But now he keeps apart, and sits at home,
In Seistan, with Zal, his father old.
Whether that his own mighty strength at last
Feels the abhorred approaches of old age;
Or in some quarrel with the Persian King.
There go: – Thou wilt not? Yet my heart forebodes
Danger or death awaits thee on this field.
Fain would I know thee safe and well, though lost
To us: fain therefore send thee hence, in peace
To seek thy father, not seek single fights

In vain: – but who can keep the lion's cub
From ravening? and who govern Rustum's son?
Go: I will grant thee what thy heart desires.'
    So said he, and dropped Sohrab's hand, and left
His bed, and the warm rugs whereon he lay,
And o'er his chilly limbs his woollen coat
He passed, and tied his sandals on his feet,
And threw a white cloak round him, and he took
In his right hand a ruler's staff, no sword;
And on his head he set his sheep-skin cap,
Black, glossy, curled, the fleece of Kara-Kul;
And raised the curtain of his tent, and called
His herald to his side, and went abroad.
    The sun, by this, had risen, and cleared the fog
From the broad Oxus and the glittering sands:
And from their tents the Tartar horsemen filed
Into the open plain; so Haman bade;
Haman, who next to Peran-Wisa ruled
The host, and still was in his lusty prime.
From their black tents, long files of horse, they streamed:
As when, some grey November morn, the files,
In marching order spread, of long-necked cranes
Stream over Casbin and the southern slopes
Of Elburz, from the Aralian estuaries,
Or some frore Caspian reed-bed, southward bound   *frozen*
For the warm Persian sea-board: so they streamed.
The Tartars of the Oxus, the King's guard,
First, with black sheep-skin caps and with long spears;
Large men, large steeds; who from Bokhara come
And Khiva, and ferment the milk of mares.
Next the more temperate Toorkmuns of the south,
The Tukas, and the lances of Salore,
And those from Attruck and the Caspian sands;
Light men, and on light steeds, who only drink
The acrid milk of camels, and their wells.
And then a swarm of wandering horse, who came
From far, and a more doubtful service owned;
The Tartars of Ferghana, from the banks
Of the Jaxartes, men with scanty beards
And close-set skull-caps; and those wilder hordes
Who roam o'er Kipchak and the northern waste,
Kalmuks and unkemped Kuzzaks, tribes who stray
Nearest the Pole, and wandering Kirghizzes,
Who come on shaggy ponies from Pamere.
These all filed out from camp into the plain.
And on the other side the Persians formed:
First a light cloud of horse, Tartars they seemed,

The Ilyats of Khorassan: and behind,
The royal troops of Persia, horse and foot,
Marshalled battalions bright in burnished steel.
But Peran-Wisa with his herald came
Threading the Tartar squadrons to the front,
And with his staff kept back the foremost ranks.
And when Ferood, who led the Persians, saw
That Peran-Wisa kept the Tartars back,
He took his spear, and to the front he came,
And checked his ranks, and fixed them where they stood.
And the old Tartar came upon the sand
Betwixt the silent hosts, and spake, and said:
   'Ferood, and ye, Persians and Tartars, hear!
Let there be truce between the hosts today.
But choose a champion from the Persian lords
To fight our champion Sohrab, man to man.'
   As, in the country, on a morn in June,
When the dew glistens on the pearled ears,
A shiver runs through the deep corn for joy –
So, when they heard what Peran-Wisa said,
A thrill through all the Tartar squadrons ran
Of pride and hope for Sohrab, whom they loved.
   But as a troop of pedlars, from Cabool,
Cross underneath the Indian Caucasus,
That vast sky-neighbouring mountain of milk snow;
Crossing so high, that, as they mount, they pass
Long flocks of travelling birds dead on the snow,
Choked by the air, and scarce can they themselves
Slake their parched throats with sugared mulberries –
In single file they move, and stop their breath,
For fear they should dislodge the o'erhanging snows –
So the pale Persians held their breath with fear.
   And to Ferood his brother chiefs came up
To counsel: Gudurz and Zoarrah came,
And Feraburz, who ruled the Persian host
Second, and was the uncle of the King:
These came and counselled; and then Gudurz said:
   'Ferood, shame bids us take their challenge up,
Yet champion have we none to match this youth.
He has the wild stag's foot, the lion's heart.
But Rustum came last night; aloof he sits
And sullen, and has pitched his tents apart:
Him will I seek, and carry to his ear
The Tartar challenge, and this young man's name.
Haply he will forget his wrath, and fight.
Stand forth the while, and take the challenge up.'
   So spake he; and Ferood stood forth and cried:

'Old man, be it agreed as thou hast said.
Let Sohrab arm, and we will find a man.'
   He spake; and Peran-Wisa turned, and strode
Back through the opening squadrons to his tent.
But through the anxious Persians Gudurz ran,
And crossed the camp which lay behind, and reached,
Out on the sands beyond it, Rustum's tents.
Of scarlet cloth they were, and glittering gay,
Just pitched: the high pavilion in the midst
Was Rustum's, and his men lay camped around.
And Gudurz entered Rustum's tent, and found
Rustum: his morning meal was done, but still
The table stood before him, charged with food;
A side of roasted sheep, and cakes of bread,
And dark green melons; and there Rustum sate
Listless, and held a falcon on his wrist,
And played with it; but Gudurz came and stood
Before him; and he looked, and saw him stand;
And with a cry sprang up, and dropped the bird,
And greeted Gudurz with both hands, and said:
   'Welcome! these eyes could see no better sight.
What news? but sit down first, and eat and drink.'
   But Gudurz stood in the tent door, and said:
'Not now: a time will come to eat and drink,
But not today: today has other needs.
The armies are drawn out, and stand at gaze:
For from the Tartars is a challenge brought
To pick a champion from the Persian lords
To fight their champion – and thou know'st his name –
Sohrab men call him, but his birth is hid.
O Rustum, like thy might is this young man's!
He has the wild stag's foot, the lion's heart.
And he is young, and Iran's chiefs are old,
Or else too weak; and all eyes turn to thee.
Come down and help us, Rustum, or we lose.'
   He spoke: but Rustum answered with a smile:
'Go to! if Iran's chiefs are old, then I
Am older: if the young are weak, the King
Errs strangely: for the King, for Kai-Khosroo,
Himself is young, and honours younger men,
And lets the aged moulder to their graves.
Rustum he loves no more, but loves the young –
The young may rise at Sohrab's vaunts, not I.
For what care I, though all speak Sohrab's fame?
For would that I myself had such a son,
And not that one slight helpless girl I have,
A son so famed, so brave, to send to war,

And I to tarry with the snow-haired Zal,
My father, whom the robber Afghans vex,
And clip his borders short, and drive his herds,
And he has none to guard his weak old age.
There would I go, and hang my armour up,
And with my great name fence that weak old man,
And spend the goodly treasures I have got,
And rest my age, and hear of Sohrab's fame,
And leave to death the hosts of thankless kings,
And with these slaughterous hands draw sword no more.'
   He spoke, and smiled; and Gudurz made reply:
'What then, O Rustum, will men say to this,
When Sohrab dares our bravest forth, and seeks
Thee most of all, and thou, whom most he seeks,
Hidest thy face? Take heed, lest men should say,
Like some old miser, Rustum hoards his fame,
And shuns to peril it with younger men.'
   And, greatly moved, then Rustum made reply:
'O Gudurz, wherefore dost thou say such words?
Thou knowest better words than this to say.
What is one more, one less, obscure or famed,
Valiant or craven, young or old, to me?
Are not they mortal, am not I myself?
But who for men of naught would do great deeds?
Come, thou shalt see how Rustum hoards his fame.
But I will fight unknown, and in plain arms;
Let not men say of Rustum, he was matched
In single fight with any mortal man.'
   He spoke, and frowned; and Gudurz turned, and ran
Back quickly through the camp in fear and joy,
Fear at his wrath, but joy that Rustum came.
But Rustum strode to his tent door, and called
His followers in, and bade them bring his arms,
And clad himself in steel: the arms he chose
Were plain, and on his shield was no device,
Only his helm was rich, inlaid with gold,
And from the fluted spine atop a plume
Of horsehair waved, a scarlet horsehair plume.
So armed he issued forth; and Ruksh, his horse,
Followed him, like a faithful hound, at heel,
Ruksh, whose renown was noised through all the earth,
The horse, whom Rustum on a foray once
Did in Bokhara by the river find
A colt beneath its dam, and drove him home,
And reared him; a bright bay, with lofty crest;
Dight with a saddle-cloth of broidered green
Crusted with gold, and on the ground were worked

All beasts of chase, all beasts which hunters know:
So followed, Rustum left his tents, and crossed
The camp, and to the Persian host appeared.
And all the Persians knew him, and with shouts
Hailed; but the Tartars knew not who he was.
And dear as the wet diver to the eyes
Of his pale wife who waits and weeps on shore,
By sandy Bahrein, in the Persian Gulf,
Plunging all day in the blue waves, at night,
Having made up his tale of precious pearls,
Rejoins her in their hut upon the sands –
So dear to the pale Persians Rustum came.

And Rustum to the Persian front advanced,
And Sohrab armed in Haman's tent, and came.
And as afield the reapers cut a swathe
Down through the middle of a rich man's corn,
And on each side are squares of standing corn,
And in the midst a stubble, short and bare;
So on each side were squares of men, with spears
Bristling, and in the midst, the open sand.
And Rustum came upon the sand, and cast
His eyes towards the Tartar tents, and saw
Sohrab come forth, and eyed him as he came.

As some rich woman, on a winter's morn,
Eyes through her silken curtains the poor drudge
Who with numb blackened fingers makes her fire –
At cock-crow, on a starlit winter's morn,
When the frost flowers the whitened window panes –
And wonders how she lives, and what the thoughts
Of that poor drudge may be; so Rustum eyed
The unknown adventurous youth, who from afar
Came seeking Rustum, and defying forth
All the most valiant chiefs: long he perused
His spirited air, and wondered who he was.
For very young he seemed, tenderly reared;
Like some young cypress, tall, and dark, and straight,
Which in a queen's secluded garden throws
Its slight dark shadow on the moonlit turf,
By midnight, to a bubbling fountain's sound –
So slender Sohrab seemed, so softly reared.
And a deep pity entered Rustum's soul
As he beheld him coming; and he stood,
And beckoned to him with his hand, and said:

'O thou young man, the air of Heaven is soft,
And warm and pleasant; but the grave is cold.
Heaven's air is better than the cold dead grave.
Behold me: I am vast, and clad in iron,

And tried; and I have stood on many a field
Of blood, and I have fought with many a foe:
Never was that field lost, or that foe saved.
O Sohrab, wherefore wilt thou rush on death?
Be governed: quit the Tartar host, and come
To Iran, and be as my son to me,
And fight beneath my banner till I die.
There are no youths in Iran brave as thou.'
　　So he spake, mildly: Sohrab heard his voice,
The mighty voice of Rustum; and he saw
His giant figure planted on the sand,
Sole, like some single tower, which a chief
Has builded on the waste in former years
Against the robbers; and he saw that head,
Streaked with its first grey hairs: hope filled his soul;
And he ran forward and embraced his knees,
And clasped his hand within his own and said:
　'Oh, by thy father's head! by thine own soul!
Art thou not Rustum? Speak! art thou not he?'
　　But Rustum eyed askance the kneeling youth,
And turned away, and spake to his own soul:
　'Ah me, I muse what this young fox may mean.
False, wily, boastful, are these Tartar boys.
For if I now confess this thing he asks,
And hide it not, but say *Rustum is here*,
He will not yield indeed, nor quit our foes,
But he will find some pretext not to fight,
And praise my fame, and proffer courteous gifts,
A belt or sword perhaps, and go his way.
And on a feast-tide, in Afrasiab's hall,
In Samarcand, he will arise and cry –
"I challenged once, when the two armies camped
Beside the Oxus, all the Persian lords
To cope with me in single fight; but they
Shrank; only Rustum dared: then he and I
Changed gifts, and went on equal terms away."
So will he speak, perhaps, while men applaud.
Then were the chiefs of Iran shamed through me.'
　　And then he turned, and sternly spake aloud:
'Rise! wherefore dost thou vainly question thus
Of Rustum? I am here, whom thou hast called
By challenge forth: make good thy vaunt, or yield.
Is it with Rustum only thou wouldst fight?
Rash boy, men look on Rustum's face and flee,
For well I know, that did great Rustum stand
Before thy face this day, and were revealed,
There would be then no talk of fighting more.

But being what I am, I tell thee this;
Do thou record it in thine inmost soul:
Either thou shalt renounce thy vaunt, and yield;
Or else thy bones shall strew this sand, till winds
Bleach them, or Oxus with his summer floods,
Oxus in summer wash them all away.'
  He spoke: and Sohrab answered, on his feet:
'Art thou so fierce? Thou wilt not fright me so.
I am no girl, to be made pale by words.
Yet this thou hast said well, did Rustum stand
Here on this field, there were no fighting then.
But Rustum is far hence, and we stand here.
Begin: thou art more vast, more dread than I,
And thou art proved, I know, and I am young –
But yet success sways with the breath of Heaven.
And though thou thinkest that thou knowest sure
Thy victory, yet thou canst not surely know.
For we are all, like swimmers in the sea,
Poised on the top of a huge wave of fate,
Which hangs uncertain to which side to fall.
And whether it will heave us up to land,
Or whether it will roll us out to sea,
Back out to sea, to the deep waves of death,
We know not, and no search will make us know:
Only the event will teach us in its hour.'
  He spoke; and Rustum answered not, but hurled
His spear: down from the shoulder, down it came,
As on some partridge in the corn a hawk
That long has towered in the airy clouds
Drops like a plummet: Sohrab saw it come,
And sprang aside, quick as a flash: the spear
Hissed, and went quivering down into the sand,
Which sent it flying wide: then Sohrab threw
In turn, and full struck Rustum's shield: sharp rang,
The iron plates rang sharp, but turned the spear.
And Rustum seized his club, which none but he
Could wield: an unlopped trunk it was, and huge,
Still rough; like those which men in treeless plains
To build them boats fish from the flooded rivers,
Hyphasis or Hydaspes, when, high up
By their dark springs, the wind in winter-time
Has made in Himalayan forests wrack,
And strewn the channels with torn boughs; so huge
The club which Rustum lifted now, and struck
One stroke; but again Sohrab sprang aside
Lithe as the glancing snake, and the club came
Thundering to earth, and leapt from Rustum's hand.

And Rustum followed his own blow, and fell
To his knees, and with his fingers clutched the sand:
And now might Sohrab have unsheathed his sword,
And pierced the mighty Rustum while he lay
Dizzy, and on his knees, and choked with sand:
But he looked on, and smiled, nor bared his sword,
But courteously drew back, and spoke, and said:
  'Thou strik'st too hard: that club of thine will float
Upon the summer floods, and not my bones.
But rise, and be not wroth; not wroth am I:
No, when I see thee, wrath forsakes my soul.
Thou sayest thou art not Rustum: be it so.
Who art thou then, that canst so touch my soul?
Boy as I am, I have seen battles too;
Have waded foremost in their bloody waves,
And heard their hollow roar of dying men;
But never was my heart thus touched before.
Are they from Heaven, these softenings of the heart?
O thou old warrior, let us yield to Heaven!
Come, plant we here in earth our angry spears,
And make a truce, and sit upon this sand,
And pledge each other in red wine, like friends,
And thou shalt talk to me of Rustum's deeds.
There are enough foes in the Persian host
Whom I may meet, and strike, and feel no pang;
Champions enough Afrasiab has, whom thou
Mayst fight; fight them, when they confront thy spear.
But oh, let there be peace 'twixt thee and me!'
  He ceased: but while he spake, Rustum had risen,
And stood erect, trembling with rage: his club
He left to lie, but had regained his spear,
Whose fiery point now in his mailed right-hand
Blazed bright and baleful, like that autumn star,
The baleful sign of fevers: dust had soiled
His stately crest, and dimmed his glittering arms.
His breast heaved; his lips foamed; and twice his voice
Was choked with rage: at last these words broke way:
  'Girl! nimble with thy feet, not with thy hands!
Curled minion, dancer, coiner of sweet words!
Fight; let me hear thy hateful voice no more!
Thou art not in Afrasiab's gardens now
With Tartar girls, with whom thou art wont to dance;
But on the Oxus sands, and in the dance
Of battle, and with me, who make no play
Of war: I fight it out, and hand to hand.
Speak not to me of truce, and pledge, and wine!
Remember all thy valour: try thy feints

And cunning: all the pity I had is gone:
Because thou hast shamed me before both the hosts
With thy light skipping tricks, and thy girl's wiles.'
   He spoke; and Sohrab kindled at his taunts,
And he too drew his sword: at once they rushed
Together, as two eagles on one prey
Come rushing down together from the clouds,
One from the east, one from the west: their shields
Dashed with a clang together, and a din
Rose, such as that the sinewy woodcutters
Make often in the forest's heart at morn,
Of hewing axes, crashing trees: such blows
Rustum and Sohrab on each other hailed.
And you would say that sun and stars took part
In that unnatural conflict; for a cloud
Grew suddenly in Heaven, and darked the sun
Over the fighters' heads; and a wind rose
Under their feet, and moaning swept the plain,
And in a sandy whirlwind wrapped the pair.
In gloom they twain were wrapped, and they alone;
For both the on-looking hosts on either hand
Stood in broad daylight, and the sky was pure,
And the sun sparkled on the Oxus stream.
But in the gloom they fought, with bloodshot eyes
And labouring breath; first Rustum struck the shield
Which Sohrab held stiff out; the steel-spiked spear
Rent the tough plates, but failed to reach the skin,
And Rustum plucked it back with angry groan.
Then Sohrab with his sword smote Rustum's helm,
Nor clove its steel quite through; but all the crest
He shore away, and that proud horsehair plume,
Never till now defiled, sank to the dust;
And Rustum bowed his head; but then the gloom
Grew blacker: thunder rumbled in the air,
And lightnings rent the cloud; and Ruksh, the horse,
Who stood at hand, uttered a dreadful cry:
No horse's cry was that, most like the roar
Of some pained desert lion, who all day
Has trailed the hunter's javelin in his side,
And comes at night to die upon the sand:
The two hosts heard that cry, and quaked for fear,
And Oxus curdled as it crossed his stream.
But Sohrab heard, and quailed not, but rushed on,
And struck again; and again Rustum bowed
His head; but this time all the blade, like glass,
Sprang in a thousand shivers on the helm,
And in his hand the hilt remained alone.

Then Rustum raised his head: his dreadful eyes
Glared, and he shook on high his menacing spear,
And shouted, *Rustum!* Sohrab heard that shout,
And shrank amazed: back he recoiled one step,
And scanned with blinking eyes the advancing form:
And then he stood bewildered; and he dropped
His covering shield, and the spear pierced his side.
He reeled, and staggering back, sank to the ground.
And then the gloom dispersed, and the wind fell,
And the bright sun broke forth, and melted all
The cloud; and the two armies saw the pair;
Saw Rustum standing, safe upon his feet,
And Sohrab, wounded, on the bloody sand.
   Then, with a bitter smile, Rustum began:
'Sohrab, thou thoughtest in thy mind to kill
A Persian lord this day, and strip his corpse,
And bear thy trophies to Afrasiab's tent.
Or else that the great Rustum would come down
Himself to fight, and that thy wiles would move
His heart to take a gift, and let thee go.
And then that all the Tartar host would praise
Thy courage or thy craft, and spread thy fame,
To glad thy father in his weak old age.
Fool! thou art slain, and by an unknown man!
Dearer to the red jackals shalt thou be,
Than to thy friends, and to thy father old.'
   And, with a fearless mien, Sohrab replied:
'Unknown thou art; yet thy fierce vaunt is vain.
Thou dost not slay me, proud and boastful man!
No! Rustum slays me, and this filial heart.
For were I matched with ten such men as thee,
And I were that which till today I was,
They should be lying here, I standing there.
But that beloved name unnerved my arm –
That name, and something, I confess, in thee,
Which troubles all my heart, and made my shield
Fall; and thy spear transfixed an unarmed foe.
And now thou boastest, and insult'st my fate.
But hear thou this, fierce man, tremble to hear!
The mighty Rustum shall avenge my death!
My father, whom I seek through all the world,
He shall avenge my death, and punish thee!'
   As when some hunter in the spring hath found
A breeding eagle sitting on her nest,
Upon the craggy isle of a hill lake,
And pierced her with an arrow as she rose,
And followed her to find her where she fell

Far off; – anon her mate comes winging back
From hunting, and a great way off descries
His huddling young left sole; at that, he checks
His pinion, and with short uneasy sweeps
Circles above his eyry, with loud screams
Chiding his mate back to her nest; but she
Lies dying, with the arrow in her side,
In some far stony gorge out of his ken,
A heap of fluttering feathers: never more
Shall the lake glass her, flying over it;
Never the black and dripping precipices
Echo her stormy scream as she sails by: –
As that poor bird flies home, nor knows his loss –
So Rustum knew not his own loss, but stood
Over his dying son, and knew him not.
  But with a cold, incredulous voice, he said:
'What prate is this of fathers and revenge?
The mighty Rustum never had a son.'
  And, with a failing voice, Sohrab replied:
'Ah yes, he had! and that lost son am I.
Surely the news will one day reach his ear,
Reach Rustum, where he sits, and tarries long,
Somewhere, I know not where, but far from here;
And pierce him like a stab, and make him leap
To arms, and cry for vengeance upon thee.
Fierce man, bethink thee, for an only son!
What will that grief, what will that vengeance be!
Oh, could I live, till I that grief had seen!
Yet him I pity not so much, but her,
My mother, who in Ader-baijan dwells
With that old King, her father, who grows grey
With age, and rules over the valiant Koords.
Her most I pity, who no more will see
Sohrab returning from the Tartar camp,
With spoils and honour, when the war is done.
But a dark rumour will be bruited up,
From tribe to tribe, until it reach her ear;
And then will that defenceless woman learn
That Sohrab will rejoice her sight no more;
But that in battle with a nameless foe,
By the far-distant Oxus, he is slain.'
  He spoke; and as he ceased he wept aloud,
Thinking of her he left, and his own death.
He spoke; but Rustum listened, plunged in thought.
Nor did he yet believe it was his son
Who spoke, although he called back names he knew;
For he had had sure tidings that the babe,

Which was in Ader-baijan born to him,
Had been a puny girl, no boy at all:
So that sad mother sent him word, for fear
Rustum should take the boy, to train in arms;
And so he deemed that either Sohrab took,
By a false boast, the style of Rustum's son;
Or that men gave it him, to swell his fame.
So deemed he; yet he listened, plunged in thought;
And his soul set to grief, as the vast tide
Of the bright rocking Ocean sets to shore
At the full moon: tears gathered in his eyes;
For he remembered his own early youth,
And all its bounding rapture; as, at dawn,
The shepherd from his mountain lodge descries
A far bright city, smitten by the sun,
Through many rolling clouds; – so Rustum saw
His youth; saw Sohrab's mother, in her bloom;
And that old King, her father, who loved well
His wandering guest, and gave him his fair child
With joy; and all the pleasant life they led,
They three, in that long-distant summer-time –
The castle, and the dewy woods, and hunt
And hound, and morn on those delightful hills
In Ader-baijan. And he saw that youth,
Of age and looks to be his own dear son,
Piteous and lovely, lying on the sand,
Like some rich hyacinth, which by the scythe
Of an unskilful gardener has been cut,
Mowing the garden grass-plots near its bed,
And lies, a fragrant tower of purple bloom,
On the mown, dying grass; – so Sohrab lay,
Lovely in death, upon the common sand.
And Rustum gazed on him with grief, and said:
  'O Sohrab, thou indeed art such a son
Whom Rustum, wert thou his, might well have loved!
Yet here thou errest, Sohrab, or else men
Have told thee false; thou art not Rustum's son.
For Rustum had no son: one child he had –
But one – a girl: who with her mother now
Plies some light female task, nor dreams of us –
Of us she dreams not, nor of wounds, nor war.'
  But Sohrab answered him in wrath; for now
The anguish of the deep-fixed spear grew fierce,
And he desired to draw forth the steel,
And let the blood flow free, and so to die;
But first he would convince his stubborn foe –
And rising sternly on one arm, he said:

'Man, who art thou who dost deny my words?
Truth sits upon the lips of dying men,
And falsehood, while I lived, was far from mine.
I tell thee, pricked upon this arm I bear
That seal which Rustum to my mother gave,
That she might prick it on the babe she bore.'
   He spoke: and all the blood left Rustum's cheeks;
And his knees tottered, and he smote his hand
Against his breast, his heavy mailed hand,
That the hard iron corslet clanked aloud:
And to his heart he pressed the other hand,
And in a hollow voice he spake, and said:
   'Sohrab, that were a proof which could not lie.
If thou show this, then art thou Rustum's son.'
   Then, with weak hasty fingers, Sohrab loosed
His belt, and near the shoulder bared his arm,
And showed a sign in faint vermilion points
Pricked: as a cunning workman, in Pekin,
Pricks with vermilion some clear porcelain vase,
An emperor's gift – at early morn he paints,
And all day long, and, when night comes, the lamp
Lights up his studious forehead and thin hands:
So delicately pricked the sign appeared
On Sohrab's arm, the sign of Rustum's seal.
It was that griffin, which of old reared Zal,
Rustum's great father, whom they left to die
A helpless babe, among the mountain rocks.
Him that kind creature found, and reared, and loved –
Then Rustum took it for his glorious sign.
And Sohrab bared that figure on his arm,
And himself scanned it long with mournful eyes,
And then he touched it with his hand and said:
   'How say'st thou? Is that sign the proper sign
Of Rustum's son, or of some other man's?'
   He spoke: but Rustum gazed and gazed, and stood
Speechless; and then he uttered one sharp cry –
O Boy – thy Father! – and his voice choked there.
And then a dark cloud passed before his eyes,
And his head swam, and he sank down to earth.
But Sohrab crawled to where he lay, and cast
His arms about his neck, and kissed his lips,
And with fond faltering fingers stroked his cheeks,
Trying to call him back to life: and life
Came back to Rustum, and he oped his eyes,
And they stood wide with horror, and he seized
In both his hands the dust which lay around,
And threw it on his head, and smirched his hair,

His hair, and face, and beard, and glittering arms:
And strong convulsive groanings shook his breast,
And his sobs choked him; and he clutched his sword,
To draw it, and for ever let life out.
But Sohrab saw his thought, and held his hands,
And with a soothing voice he spoke, and said:
  'Father, forbear: for I but meet today
The doom that at my birth was written down
In Heaven, and thou art Heaven's unconscious hand.
Surely my heart cried out that it was thou,
When first I saw thee; and thy heart spoke too,
I know it: but fate trod those promptings down
Under its iron heel; fate, fate engaged
The strife, and hurled me on my father's spear.
But let us speak no more of this: I find
My father; let me feel that I have found.
Come, sit beside me on this sand, and take
My head betwixt thy hands, and kiss my cheeks,
And wash them with thy tears, and say, *My Son!*
Quick! quick! for numbered are my sands of life,
And swift; for like the lightning to this field
I came, and like the wind I go away –
Sudden, and swift, and like a passing wind.
But it was writ in Heaven that this should be.'
  So said he: and his voice released the heart
Of Rustum, and his tears broke forth; he cast
His arms round his son's neck, and wept aloud,
And kissed him. And awe fell on both the hosts
When they saw Rustum's grief: and Ruksh, the horse,
With his head bowing to the ground, and mane
Sweeping the dust, came near, and in mute woe
First to the one then to the other moved
His head, as if inquiring what their grief
Might mean; and from his dark compassionate eyes,
The big warm tears rolled down, and caked the sand.
But Rustum chid him with stern voice, and said:
  'Ruksh, now thou grievest; but, O Ruksh, thy feet
Should first have rotted on their nimble joints,
Or ere they bore thy master to this field.'
  But Sohrab looked upon the horse and said:
'Is this then Ruksh? How often, in past days,
My mother told me of thee, thou brave steed!
My terrible father's terrible horse; and said,
That I should one day find thy lord and thee.
Come, let me lay my hand upon thy mane.
O Ruksh, thou art more fortunate than I;
For thou hast gone where I shall never go,

And snuffed the breezes of my father's home.
And thou hast trod the sands of Seistan,
And seen the river of Helmund, and the lake
Of Zirrah; and the aged Zal himself
Has often stroked thy neck, and given thee food,
Corn in a golden platter soaked with wine,
And said – *O Ruksh! bear Rustum well!* – but I
Have never known my grandsire's furrowed face,
Nor seen his lofty house in Seistan,
Nor slaked my thirst at the clear Helmund stream:
But lodged among my father's foes, and seen
Afrasiab's cities only, Samarcand,
Bokhara, and lone Khiva in the waste,
And the black Toorkmun tents; and only drunk
The desert rivers, Moorghab and Tejend,
Kohik, and where the Kalmuks feed their sheep,
The northern Sir; and this great Oxus stream –
The yellow Oxus, by whose brink I die.'
   Then, with a heavy groan, Rustum bewailed:
'Oh that its waves were flowing over me!
Oh that I saw its grains of yellow silt
Roll tumbling in the current o'er my head!'
   And with a grave mild voice, Sohrab replied:
'Desire not that, my father; thou must live.
For some are born to do great deeds, and live,
As some are born to be obscured, and die.
Do thou the deeds I die too young to do,
And reap a second glory in thine age.
Thou art my father, and thy gain is mine.
But come: thou seest this great host of men
Which follow me; I pray thee, slay not these:
Let me entreat for them: what have they done?
They followed me, my hope, my fame, my star.
Let them all cross the Oxus back in peace.
But me thou must bear hence, not send with them,
But carry me with thee to Seistan,
And place me on a bed, and mourn for me,
Thou, and the snow-haired Zal, and all thy friends.
And thou must lay me in that lovely earth,
And heap a stately mound above my bones,
And plant a far-seen pillar over all:
That so the passing horseman on the waste
May see my tomb a great way off, and cry –
Sohrab, the mighty Rustum's son, lies there,
Whom his great father did in ignorance kill –
And I be not forgotten in my grave.'
   And, with a mournful voice, Rustum replied:

'Fear not; as thou hast said, Sohrab, my son,
So shall it be: for I will burn my tents,
And quit the host, and bear thee hence with me,
And carry thee away to Seistan,
And place thee on a bed, and mourn for thee,
With the snow-headed Zal, and all my friends.
And I will lay thee in that lovely earth,
And heap a stately mound above thy bones,
And plant a far-seen pillar over all:
And men shall not forget thee in thy grave.
And I will spare thy host: yea, let them go:
Let them all cross the Oxus back in peace.
What should I do with slaying any more?
For would that all whom I have ever slain
Might be once more alive; my bitterest foes,
And they who were called champions in their time,
And through whose death I won that fame I have;
And I were nothing but a common man,
A poor, mean soldier, and without renown,
So thou mightest live too, my son, my son!
Or rather would that I, even I myself,
Might now be lying on this bloody sand,
Near death, and by an ignorant stroke of thine,
Not thou of mine; and I might die, not thou;
And I, not thou, be borne to Seistan;
And Zal might weep above my grave, not thine;
And say – O son, I weep thee not too sore,
For willingly, I know, thou met'st thine end. –
But now in blood and battles was my youth,
And full of blood and battles is my age;
And I shall never end this life of blood.'
     Then, at the point of death, Sohrab replied:
'A life of blood indeed, thou dreadful man!
But thou shalt yet have peace; only not now:
Not yet: but thou shalt have it on that day,
When thou shalt sail in a high-masted ship,
Thou and the other peers of Kai-Khosroo,
Returning home over the salt blue sea,
From laying thy dear master in his grave.'
     And Rustum gazed on Sohrab's face, and said:
'Soon be that day, my son, and deep that sea!
Till then, if fate so wills, let me endure.'
     He spoke; and Sohrab smiled on him, and took
The spear, and drew it from his side, and eased
His wound's imperious anguish; but the blood
Came welling from the open gash, and life
Flowed with the stream: all down his cold white side

The crimson torrent ran, dim now, and soiled,
Like the soiled tissue of white violets
Left, freshly gathered, on their native bank,
By romping children, whom their nurses call
From the hot fields at noon: his head drooped low,
His limbs grew slack; motionless, white, he lay –
White, with eyes closed; only when heavy gasps,
Deep, heavy gasps, quivering through all his frame,
Convulsed him back to life, he opened them,
And fixed them feebly on his father's face:
Till now all strength was ebbed, and from his limbs
Unwillingly the spirit fled away,
Regretting the warm mansion which it left,
And youth and bloom, and this delightful world.
     So, on the bloody sand, Sohrab lay dead.
And the great Rustum drew his horseman's cloak
Down o'er his face, and sate by his dead son.
As those black granite pillars, once high-reared
By Jemshid in Persepolis, to bear
His house, now, mid their broken flights of steps,
Lie prone, enormous, down the mountain side –
So in the sand lay Rustum by his son.
     And night came down over the solemn waste,
And the two gazing hosts, and that sole pair,
And darkened all; and a cold fog, with night,
Crept from the Oxus. Soon a hum arose,
As of a great assembly loosed, and fires
Began to twinkle through the fog: for now
Both armies moved to camp, and took their meal:
The Persians took it on the open sands
Southward; the Tartars by the river marge:
And Rustum and his son were left alone.
     But the majestic river floated on,
Out of the mist and hum of that low land,
Into the frosty starlight, and there moved,
Rejoicing, through the hushed Chorasmian waste,
Under the solitary moon: he flowed
Right for the Polar Star, past Orgunjè,
Brimming, and bright, and large: then sands begin
To hem his watery march, and dam his streams,
And split his currents; that for many a league
The shorn and parcelled Oxus strains along
Through beds of sand and matted rushy isles –
Oxus, forgetting the bright speed he had
In his high mountain-cradle in Pamere,
A foiled circuitous wanderer: till at last
The longed-for dash of waves is heard, and wide

His luminous home of waters opens, bright
And tranquil, from whose floor the new-bathed stars
Emerge, and shine upon the Aral Sea.

GEORGE MEREDITH
King Harald's Trance

Sword in length a reaping-hook amain
Harald sheared his field, blood up to shank:
 'Mid the swathes of slain,
 First at moonrise drank.

Thereof hunger, as for meats the knife,
Pricked his ribs, in one sharp spur to reach
 Home and his young wife,
 Nigh the sea-ford beach.

After battle keen to feed was he:
Smoking flesh the thresher washed down fast,
 Like an angry sea
 Ships from keel to mast.

Name us glory, singer, name us pride
Matching Harald's in his deeds of strength;
 Chiefs, wife, sword by side,
 Foemen stretched their length!

Half a winter night the toasts hurrahed,
Crowned him, clothed him, trumpeted him high,
 Till awink he bade
 Wife to chamber fly.

Twice the sun had mounted, twice had sunk,
Ere his ears took sound; he lay for dead;
 Mountain on his trunk,
 Ocean on his head.

Clamped to couch, his fiery hearing sucked
Whispers that at heart made iron-clang:
 Here fool-women clucked,
 There men held harangue.

Burial to fit their lord of war
They decreed him: hailed the kingling: ha!
 Hateful! but this Thor
 Failed a weak lamb's baa.

King they hailed a branchlet, shaped to fare,
Weighted so, like quaking shingle spume,
    When his blood's own heir
    Ripened in the womb!

Still he heard, and doglike, hoglike, ran
Nose of hearing till his blind sight saw:
    Woman stood with man
    Mouthing low, at paw.

Woman, man, they mouthed; they spake a thing
Armed to split a mountain, sunder seas;
    Still the frozen king
    Lay and felt him freeze.

Doglike, hoglike, horselike now he raced,
Riderless, in ghost across a ground
    Flint of breast, blank-faced,
    Past the fleshly bound.

Smell of brine his nostrils filled with might:
Nostrils quickened eyelids, eyelids hand:
    Hand for sword at right
    Groped, the great haft spanned.

Wonder struck to ice his people's eyes:
Him they saw, the prone upon the bier,
    Sheer from backbone rise,
    Sword uplifting peer.

Sitting did he breathe against the blade,
Standing kiss it for that proof of life:
    Strode, as netters wade,
    Straightway to his wife.

Her he eyed: his judgement was one word,
Foulbed! and she fell: the blow clove two.
    Fearful for the third,
    All their breath indrew.

Morning danced along the waves to beach;
Dumb his chiefs fetched breath for what might hap:
    Glassily on each
    Stared the iron cap.

Sudden, as it were a monster oak
Split to yield a limb by stress of heat,
    Strained he, staggered, broke
    Doubled at their feet.

LEWIS CARROLL

From *The Hunting of the Snark*

THE BARRISTER'S DREAM

They sought it with thimbles, they sought it with care;
    They pursued it with forks and hope;
They threatened its life with a railway-share;
    They charmed it with smiles and soap.

But the Barrister, weary of proving in vain
    That the Beaver's lace-making was wrong,
Fell asleep, and in dreams saw the creature quite plain
    That his fancy had dwelt on so long.

He dreamed that he stood in a shadowy Court,
    Where the Snark, with a glass in its eye,
Dressed in gown, bands, and wig, was defending a pig
    On the charge of deserting its sty.

The Witnesses proved, without error or flaw,
    That the sty was deserted when found:
And the Judge kept explaining the state of the law
    In a soft under-current of sound.

The indictment had never been clearly expressed,
    And it seemed that the Snark had begun,
And had spoken three hours, before any one guessed
    What the pig was supposed to have done.

The Jury had each formed a different view
    (Long before the indictment was read),
And they all spoke at once, so that none of them knew
    One word that the others had said.

'You must know – ' said the Judge: but the Snark exclaimed 'Fudge!
    That statute is obsolete quite!
Let me tell you, my friends, the whole question depends
    On an ancient manorial right.

'In the matter of Treason the pig would appear
    To have aided, but scarcely abetted:
While the charge of Insolvency fails, it is clear,
    If you grant the plea "never indebted".

'The fact of Desertion I will not dispute:

But its guilt, as I trust, is removed
(So far as relates to the costs of this suit)
  By the Alibi which has been proved.

'My poor client's fate now depends on your votes.'
  Here the speaker sat down in his place,
And directed the Judge to refer to his notes
  And briefly to sum up the case.

But the Judge said he never had summed up before;
  So the Snark undertook it instead,
And summed it so well that it came to far more
  Than the Witnesses ever had said!

When the verdict was called for, the Jury declined,
  As the word was so puzzling to spell;
But they ventured to hope that the Snark wouldn't mind
  Undertaking that duty as well.

So the Snark found the verdict, although, as it owned,
  It was spent with the toils of the day:
When it said the word 'guilty!' the Jury all groaned,
  And some of them fainted away.

Then the Snark pronounced sentence, the Judge being quite
  Too nervous to utter a word:
When it rose to its feet, there was silence like night,
  And the fall of a pin might be heard.

'Transportation for life' was the sentence it gave,
  'And *then* to be fined forty pound.'
The Jury all cheered, though the Judge said he feared
  That the phrase was not legally sound.

But their wild exultation was suddenly checked
  When the jailer informed them, with tears,
Such a sentence would have not the slightest effect,
  As the pig had been dead for some years.

The Judge left the Court, looking deeply disgusted:
  But the Snark, though a little aghast,
As the lawyer to whom the defence was entrusted,
  Went bellowing on to the last.

Thus the Barrister dreamed, while the bellowing seemed
  To grow every moment more clear:
Till he woke to the knell of a furious bell,
  Which the Bellman rang close to his ear.

WILLIAM MORRIS

The Haystack in the Floods

Had she come all the way for this,
To part at last without a kiss?
Yea, had she borne the dirt and rain
That her own eyes might see him slain
Beside the haystack in the floods?

Along the dripping leafless woods,
The stirrup touching either shoe,
She rode astride as troopers do;
With kirtle kilted to her knee,
To which the mud splashed wretchedly;
And the wet dripped from every tree
Upon her head and heavy hair,
And on her eyelids broad and fair;
The tears and rain ran down her face.
By fits and starts they rode apace,
And very often was his place
Far off from her; he had to ride
Ahead, to see what might betide
When the roads crossed; and sometimes, when
There rose a murmuring from his men,
Had to turn back with promises;
Ah me! she had but little ease;
And often for pure doubt and dread
She sobbed, made giddy in the head
By the swift riding; while, for cold,
Her slender fingers scarce could hold
The wet reins; yea, and scarcely, too,
She felt the foot within her shoe,
Against the stirrup: all for this,
To part at last without a kiss
Beside the haystack in the floods.

For when they neared that old soaked hay,
They saw across the only way
That Judas, Godmar, and the three
Red running lions dismally
Grinned from his pennon, under which
In one straight line along the ditch,
They counted thirty heads.
                              So then,
While Robert turned round to his men,
She saw at once the wretched end,

And, stooping down, tried hard to rend
Her coif the wrong way from her head,
And hid her eyes; while Robert said:
'Nay, love, 'tis scarcely two to one,
At Poictiers where we made them run
So fast – why, sweet my love, good cheer.
The Gascon frontier is so near,
Nought after this.'
          But, 'O,' she said,
'My God! my God! I have to tread
The long way back without you; then
The court at Paris; those six men;
The gratings of the Chatelet;
The swift Seine on some rainy day
Like this, and people standing by,
And laughing, while my weak hands try
To recollect how strong men swim,
All this, or else a life with him,
For which I should be damned at last,
Would God that this next hour were past!'

He answered not, but cried his cry,
'St George for Marny!' cheerily;
And laid his hand upon her rein.
Alas! no man of all his train
Gave back that cheery cry again;
And, while for rage his thumb beat fast
Upon his sword-hilts, some one cast
About his neck a kerchief long,
And bound him.
          Then they went along
To Godmar; who said: 'Now Jehane,
Your lover's life is on the wane
So fast, that, if this very hour
You yield not as my paramour,
He will not see the rain leave off –
Nay, keep your tongue from gibe and scoff,
Sir Robert, or I slay you now.'

She laid her hand upon her brow,
Then gazed upon the palm, as though
She thought her forehead bled, and – 'No,'
She said, and turned her head away,
As there were nothing else to say,
And everything were settled. Red
Grew Godmar's face from chin to head:
'Jehane, on yonder hill there stands

My castle, guarding well my lands:
What hinders me from taking you,
And doing that I list to do
To your fair wilful body, while
Your knight lies dead?'
               A wicked smile
Wrinkled her face, her lips grew thin,
A long way out she thrust her chin:
'You know that I should strangle you
While you were sleeping; or bite through
Your throat, by God's help – ah!' she said,
'Lord Jesus, pity your poor maid!
For in such wise they hem me in,
I cannot choose but sin and sin,
Whatever happens: yet I think
They could not make me eat or drink,
And so should I just reach my rest.'
'Nay, if you do not my behest,
O Jehane! though I love you well,'
Said Godmar, 'would I fail to tell
All that I know.' 'Foul lies,' she said,
'Eh? lies my Jehane? by God's head,
At Paris folks would deem them true!
Do you know, Jehane, they cry for you,
"Jehane the brown! Jehane the brown!
Give us Jehane to burn or drown!" –
Eh – gag me Robert! – sweet my friend,
This were indeed a piteous end
For those long fingers, and long feet,
And long neck, and smooth shoulders sweet;
An end that few men would forget
That saw it – So, an hour yet:
Consider Jehane, which to take
Of life or death!'
             So scarce awake,
Dismounting, did she leave that place,
And totter some yards. With her face
Turned upward to the sky she lay,
Her head on a wet heap of hay,
And fell asleep: and while she slept,
And did not dream, the minutes crept
Round to twelve again: but she,
Being waked at last, sighed quietly,
And strangely childlike came, and said:
'I will not.' Straightway Godmar's head,
As though it hung on strong wires, turned
Most sharply round, and his face burned.

For Robert – both his eyes were dry,
He could not weep, but gloomily
He seemed to watch the rain; yea, too,
His lips were firm; he tried once more
To touch her lips; she reached out, sore
And vain desire so tortured them,
The poor grey lips, and now the hem
Of his sleeve brushed them.
               With a start
Up Godmar rose, thrust them apart;
From Robert's throat he loosed the bands
Of silk and mail; with empty hands
Held out, she stood and gazed, and saw,
The long bright blade without a flaw
Glide out from Godmar's sheath, his hand
In Robert's hair; she saw him bend
Back Robert's head; she saw him send
The thin steel down; the blow told well,
Right backward the knight Robert fell,
And moaned as dogs do, being half dead,
Unwitting, as I deem: so then
Godmar turned grinning to his men,
Who ran, some five or six, and beat
His head to pieces at their feet.

Then Godmar turned again, and said:
'So Jehane, the first fitte is read!
Take note, my lady, that your way
Lies backward to the Chatelet!'
She shook her head and gazed awhile
At her cold hands with a rueful smile,
As though this thing had made her mad.

This was the parting that they had
Beside the haystack in the floods.

BRET HARTE

The Stage-Driver's Story

It was the stage-driver's story, as he stood with his back to the wheelers,
Quietly flecking his whip, and turning his quid of tobacco;
While on the dusty road, and blent with the rays of the moonlight,
We saw the long curl of his lash and the juice of tobacco descending.

'Danger! Sir, I believe you; indeed, I may say, on that subject,
You your existence might put to the hazard and turn of a wager.
I have seen danger? Oh, no! not me, sir, indeed, I assure you:
'Twas only the man with the dog that is sitting alone in yon waggon.

'It was the Geiger Grade, a mile and a half from the summit:
Black as your hat was the night, and never a star in the heavens.
Thundering down the grade, the gravel and stones we sent flying
Over the precipice side – a thousand feet plumb to the bottom.

'Half-way down the grade I felt, sir, a thrilling and creaking,
Then a lurch to one side, as we hung on the bank of the cañon;
Then, looking up the road, I saw, in the distance behind me,
The off hind wheel of the coach, just loosed from its axle, and following.

'One glance alone I gave, then gathered together my ribbons,
Shouted, and flung them, outspread, on the straining necks of my
    cattle;
Screamed at the top of my voice, and lashed the air in my frenzy,
While down the Geiger Grade, on *three* wheels, the vehicle thundered.

'Speed was our only chance, when again came the ominous rattle:
Crack, and another wheel slipped away, and was lost in the darkness.
Two only now were left; yet such was our fearful momentum,
Upright, erect, and sustained on *two* wheels, the vehicle thundered.

'As some huge bowlder, unloosed from its rocky shelf on the mountain,
Drives before it the hare and the timorous squirrel, far leaping,
So down the Geiger Grade rushed the Pioneer coach, and before it
Leaped the wild horses, and shrieked in advance of the danger impending.

'But to be brief in my tale. Again, ere we came to the level,
Slipped from its axle a wheel; so that, to be plain in my statement,
A matter of twelve hundred yards or more, as the distance may be,
We travelled upon *one* wheel, until we drove up to the station.

'Then, sir, we sank in a heap; but, picking myself from the ruins,
I heard a noise up the grade; and looking, I saw in the distance
The three wheels following still, like moons on the horizon whirling,
Till, circling, they gracefully sank on the road at the side of the station.

'This is my story, sir; a trifle, indeed, I assure you.
Much more, perchance, might be said – but I hold him of all men
    most lightly
Who swerves from the truth in his tale. No, thank you – Well, since
    you *are* pressing,
Perhaps I don't care if I do: you may give me the same, Jim – no
    sugar.'

Plain Language from Truthful James

Which I wish to remark,
   And my language is plain,
That for ways that are dark
   And for tricks that are vain,
The heathen Chinee is peculiar,
   Which the same I would rise to explain.

Ah Sin was his name;
   And I shall not deny,
In regard to the same,
   What that name might imply;
But his smile it was pensive and childlike,
   As I frequent remarked to Bill Nye.

It was August the third,
   And quite soft was the skies;
Which it might be inferred
   That Ah Sin was likewise;
Yet he played it that day upon William
   And me in a way I despise.

Which we had a small game,
   And Ah Sin took a hand:
It was Euchre. The same
   He did not understand;
But he smiled as he sat by the table,
   With the smile that was childlike and bland.

Yet the cards they were stocked
   In a way that I grieve,
And my feelings were shocked
   At the state of Nye's sleeve,
Which was stuffed full of aces and bowers,
   And the same with intent to deceive.

But the hands that were played

By that heathen Chinee,
And the points that he made,
    Were quite frightful to see, –
Till at last he put down a right bower,
    Which the same Nye had dealt unto me.

Then I looked up at Nye,
    And he gazed upon me;
And he rose with a sigh,
    And said, 'Can this be?
We are ruined by Chinese cheap labour' –
    And he went for that heathen Chinee.

In the scene that ensued
    I did not take a hand,
But the floor it was strewed
    Like the leaves on the strand
With the cards that Ah Sin had been hiding,
    In the game 'he did not understand'.

In his sleeves, which were long,
    He had twenty-four jacks –
Which was coming it strong,
    Yet I state but the facts;
And we found on his nails, which were taper,
    What is frequent in tapers – that's wax.

Which is why I remark,
    And my language is plain,
That for ways that are dark
    And for tricks that are vain,
The heathen Chinee is peculiar, –
    Which the same I am free to maintain.

ANONYMOUS

Frankie and Johnny

Frankie and Johnny were lovers, O lordy how they could love.
Swore to be true to each other, true as the stars above;
He was her man, but he done her wrong.

Frankie she was his woman, everybody knows.
She spent one hundred dollars for a suit of Johnny's clothes.

He was her man, but he done her wrong.

Frankie and Johnny went walking, Johnny in his bran' new suit,
'O good Lawd,' says Frankie, 'but don't my Johnny look cute?'
He was her man, but he done her wrong.

Frankie went down to Memphis; she went on the evening train.
She paid one hundred dollars for Johnny a watch and chain.
He was her man, but he done her wrong.

Frankie went down to the corner, to buy a glass of beer;
She says to the fat bartender, 'Has my loving man been here?
He was my man, but he done me wrong.'

'Ain't going to tell you no story, ain't going to tell you no lie,
I seen your man 'bout an hour ago with a girl named Alice Bly –
If he's your man, he's doing you wrong.'

Frankie went back to the hotel, she didn't go there for fun,
Under her long red kimono she toted a forty-four gun.
He was her man, but he done her wrong.

Frankie went down to the hotel, looked in the window so high,
There was her lovin' Johnny a-lovin' up Alice Bly;
He was her man, but he done her wrong.

Frankie went down to the hotel, she rang that hotel bell,
'Stand back all of you floozies or I'll blow you all to hell,
I want my man, he's doin' me wrong.'

Frankie threw back her kimono; took out the old forty-four;
Roota-toot-toot, three times she shot, right through that hotel door.
She shot her man, 'cause he done her wrong.

Johnny grabbed off his Stetson, 'O good Lawd, Frankie, don't
     shoot.'
But Frankie put her finger on the trigger, and the gun went roota-
     toot-toot.
He was her man, but she shot him down.

'Roll me over easy, roll me over slow,
Roll me over easy, boys, 'cause my wounds are hurting me so,
I was her man, but I done her wrong.'

With the first shot Johnny staggered; with the second shot he fell;
When the third bullet hit him, there was a new man's face in hell.
He was her man, but he done her wrong.

Frankie heard a rumbling away down under the ground.
Maybe it was Johnny where she had shot him down.
He was her man, and she done him wrong.

'Oh, bring on your rubber-tyred hearses, bring on your rubber-tyred
    hacks,
They're takin' my Johnny to the buryin' groun' but they'll never
    bring him back.
He was my man, but he done me wrong.'

The judge he said to the jury, 'It's plain as plain can be.
This woman shot her man, so it's murder in the second degree.
He was her man, though he done her wrong.'

Now it wasn't murder in the second degree, it wasn't murder in the
    third.
Frankie simply dropped her man, like a hunter drops a bird.
He was her man, but he done her wrong.

'Oh, put me in that dungeon. Oh, put me in that cell.
Put me where the northeast wind blows from the southeast corner of
    hell.
I shot my man 'cause he done me wrong.'

Frankie walked up to the scaffold, as calm as a girl could be,
She turned her eyes to heaven and said, 'Good Lord, I'm coming to
    thee.
He was my man, and I done him wrong.'

W. S. GILBERT

The Yarn of the 'Nancy Bell'

'Twas on the shores that round our coast
    From Deal to Ramsgate span,
That I found alone on a piece of stone
    An elderly naval man.

His hair was weedy, his beard was long,
    And weedy and long was he,
And I heard this wight on the shore recite,
    In a singular minor key:

'Oh, I am a cook and a captain bold,

And the mate of the *Nancy* brig,
And a bo'sun tight, and a midshipmite,
   And the crew of the captain's gig.'

And he shook his fists and he tore his hair,
   Till I really felt afraid,
For I couldn't help thinking the man had been drinking,
   And so I simply said:

'Oh elderly man, it's little I know
   Of the duties of men of the sea,
And I'll eat my hand if I understand
   How you can possibly be

'At once a cook, and a captain bold,
   And the mate of the *Nancy* brig,
And a bo'sun tight, and a midshipmite,
   And the crew of the captain's gig.'

Then he gave a hitch to his trousers, which
   Is a trick all seamen larn,
And having got rid of a thumping quid,
   He spun this painful yarn:

''Twas in the good ship *Nancy Bell*
   That we sailed to the Indian Sea,
And there on a reef we come to grief,
   Which has often occurred to me.

'And pretty nigh all the crew was drowned
   (There was seventy-seven o' soul),
And only ten of the *Nancy*'s men
   Said "Here" to the muster-roll.

'There was me and the cook and the captain bold,
   And the mate of the *Nancy* brig,
And the bo'sun tight, and a midshipmite,
   And the crew of the captain's gig.

'For a month we'd neither wittles nor drink,
   Till a-hungry we did feel,
So we drawed a lot, and accordin' shot
   The captain for our meal.

'The next lot fell to the *Nancy*'s mate,
   And a delicate dish he made;
Then our appetite with the midshipmite
   We seven survivors stayed.

'And then we murdered the bo'sun tight,
   And he much resembled pig;
Then we wittled free, did the cook and me,
   On the crew of the captain's gig.

'Then only the cook and me was left,
   And the delicate question, "Which
Of us two goes to the kettle?" arose,
   And we argued it out as sich.

'For I loved that cook as a brother, I did,
   And the cook he worshipped me;
But we'd both be blowed if we'd either be stowed
   In the other chap's hold, you see.

' "I'll be eat if you dines off me," says Tom.
   "Yes, that," says I, "you'll be, –
I'm boiled if I die, my friend," quoth I,
   And "Exactly so," quoth he.

'Says he, "Dear James, to murder me
   Were a foolish thing to do,
For don't you see that you can't cook *me*,
   While I can – and will – cook *you*!"

'So he boils the water, and takes the salt
   And the pepper in portions true
(Which he never forgot), and some chopped shallot,
   And some sage and parsley too.

' "Come here," says he, with a proper pride,
   Which his smiling features tell,
"'Twill soothing be if I let you see
   How extremely nice you'll smell."

'And he stirred it round and round and round,
   And he sniffed at the foaming froth;
When I ups with his heels, and smothers his squeals
   In the scum of the boiling broth.

'And I eat that cook in a week or less,
   And – as I eating be
The last of his chops, why, I almost drops,
   For a wessel in sight I see.

★

'And I never grin, and I never smile,
    And I never larf nor play,
But I sit and croak, and a single joke
    I have – which is to say:

'Oh, I am a cook and a captain bold,
    And the mate of the *Nancy* brig,
And a bo'sun tight, and a midshipmite,
    And the crew of the captain's gig.'

ALGERNON CHARLES SWINBURNE

From *Tristram of Lyonesse*

[KING MARK, TRISTRAM, AND PALAMEDE][1]

On the mid stairs, between the light and dark,
Before the main tower's portal stood King Mark,
Crowned: and his face was as the face of one
Long time athirst and hungering for the sun
In barren thrall of bitter bonds, who now
Thinks here to feel its blessing on his brow.
A swart lean man, but kinglike, still of guise,
With black streaked beard and cold unquiet eyes,
Close-mouthed, gaunt-cheeked, wan as a morning moon,
Though hardly time on his worn hair had strewn
The thin first ashes from a sparing hand:
Yet little fire there burnt upon the brand,
And way-worn seemed he with life's wayfaring.
So between shade and sunlight stood the king,
And his face changed nor yearned not towards his bride;
But fixed between mild hope and patient pride
Abode what gift of rare or lesser worth
This day might bring to all his days on earth.
But at the glory of her when she came
His heart endured not: very fear and shame
Smote him, to take her by the hand and kiss,
Till both were molten in the burning bliss,
And with a thin flame flushing his cold face
He led her silent to the bridal place.
There were they wed and hallowed of the priest,

[1] Iseult is brought by Tristram to Cornwall, to marry King Mark; but
meanwhile, under the influence of a magic potion, she and Tristram have
fallen in love with each other.

And all the loud time of the marriage feast
One thought within three hearts was as a fire,
Where craft and faith took counsel with desire.
For when the feast had made a glorious end
They gave the new queen for her maids to tend
At dawn of bride-night, and thereafter bring
With marriage music to the bridegroom king.
Then by device of craft between them laid
To him went Brangwain delicately, and prayed
That this thing even for love's sake might not be,
But without sound or light or eye to see
She might come in to bride-bed: and he laughed,
As one that wist not well of wise love's craft,
And bade all bridal things be as she would.
Yet of his gentleness he gat not good;
For clothed and covered with the nuptial dark
Soft like a bride came Brangwain to King Mark,
And to the queen came Tristram; and the night
Fled, and ere danger of detective light
From the king sleeping Brangwain slid away,
And where had lain her handmaid Iseult lay.
And the king waking saw beside his head
That face yet passion-coloured, amorous red
From lips not his, and all that strange hair shed
Across the tissued pillows, fold on fold,
Innumerable, incomparable, all gold,
To fire men's eyes with wonder, and with love
Men's hearts; so shone its flowering crown above
The brows enwound with that imperial wreath,
And framed with fragrant radiance round the face beneath.
    And the king marvelled, seeing with sudden start
Her very glory, and said out of his heart:
'What have I done of good for God to bless
That all this he should give me, tress on tress,
All this great wealth and wondrous? Was it this
That in mine arms I had all night to kiss,
And mix with me this beauty? this that seems
More fair than heaven doth in some tired saint's dreams,
Being part of that same heaven? yea, more, for he,
Though loved of God so, yet but seems to see,
But to me sinful such great grace is given
That in mine hands I hold this part of heaven,
Not to mine eyes lent merely. Doth God make
Such things so godlike for man's mortal sake?
Have I not sinned, that in this fleshly life
Have made of her a mere man's very wife?'

So the king mused and murmured; and she heard
The faint sound trembling of each breathless word,
And laughed into the covering of her hair.
    And many a day for many a month as fair
Slid over them like music; and as bright
Burned with love's offerings many a secret night.
And many a dawn to many a fiery noon
Blew prelude, when the horn's heart-kindling tune
Lit the live woods with sovereign sound of mirth
Before the mightiest huntsman hailed on earth
Lord of its lordliest pleasure, where he rode
Hard by her rein whose peerless presence glowed
Not as that white queen's of the virgin hunt
Once, whose crown-crescent braves the night-wind's brunt,
But with the sun for frontlet of a queenlier front.
For where the flashing of her face was turned
As lightning was the fiery light that burned
From eyes and brows enkindled more with speed
And rapture of the rushing of her steed
Than once with only beauty; and her mouth
Was as a rose athirst that pants for drouth
Even while it laughs for pleasure of desire,
And all her heart was as a leaping fire.
Yet once more joy they took of woodland ways
Than came of all those flushed and fiery days
When the loud air was mad with life and sound,
Through many a dense green mile, of horn and hound
Before the king's hunt going along the wind,
And ere the timely leaves were changed or thinned,
Even in mid maze of summer. For the knight
Forth was once ridden toward some frontier fight
Against the lewd folk of the Christless lands
That warred with wild and intermittent hands
Against the king's north border; and there came
A knight unchristened yet of unknown name,
Swart Palamede, upon a secret quest,
To high Tintagel, and abode as guest
In likeness of a minstrel with the king.
Nor was there man could sound so sweet a string,
Save Tristram only, of all held best on earth.
And one loud eve, being full of wine and mirth,
Ere sunset left the walls and waters dark,
To that strange minstrel strongly swore King Mark,
By all that makes a knight's faith firm and strong,
That he for guerdon of his harp and song
Might crave and have his liking. Straight there came
Up the swart cheek a flash of swarthier flame,

And the deep eyes fulfilled of glittering night
Laughed out in lightnings of triumphant light
As the grim harper spake: 'O king, I crave
No gift of man that king may give to slave,
But this thy crowned queen only, this thy wife,
Whom yet unseen I loved, and set my life
On this poor chance to compass, even as here,
Being fairer famed than all save Guenevere.'
Then as the noise of seaward storm that mocks
With roaring laughter from reverberate rocks
The cry from ships near shipwreck, harsh and high
Rose all the wrath and wonder in one cry
Through all the long roof's hollow depth and length
That hearts of strong men kindled in their strength
May speak in laughter lion-like, and cease,
Being wearied: only two men held their peace
And each glared hard on other: but King Mark
Spake first of these: 'Man, though thy craft be dark
And thy mind evil that begat this thing,
Yet stands the word once plighted of a king
Fast: and albeit less evil it were for me
To give my life up than my wife, or be
A landless man crowned only with a curse,
Yet this in God's and all men's sight were worse,
To live soul-shamed, a man of broken troth,
Abhorred of men as I abhor mine oath
Which yet I may forswear not.' And he bowed
His head, and wept: and all men wept aloud,
Save one, that heard him weeping: but the queen
Wept not: and statelier yet than eyes had seen
That ever looked upon her queenly state
She rose, and in her eyes her heart was great
And full of wrath seen manifest and scorn
More strong than anguish to go thence forlorn
Of all men's comfort and her natural right.
And they went forth into the dawn of night.
Long by wild ways and clouded light they rode,
Silent; and fear less keen at heart abode
With Iseult than with Palamede: for awe
Constrained him, and the might of love's high law,
That can make lewd men loyal; and his heart
Yearned on her, if perchance with amorous art
And soothfast skill of very love he might
For courtesy find favour in her sight
And comfort of her mercies: for he wist
More grace might come of that sweet mouth unkissed
Than joy for violence done it, that should make

223

His name abhorred for shame's disloyal sake.
And in the stormy starlight clouds were thinned
And thickened by short gusts of changing wind
That panted like a sick man's fitful breath:
And like a moan of lions hurt to death
Came the sea's hollow noise along the night.
But ere its gloom from aught but foam had light
They halted, being aweary: and the knight
As reverently forbore her where she lay
As one that watched his sister's sleep till day.
Nor durst he kiss or touch her hand or hair
For love and shamefast pity, seeing how fair
She slept, and fenceless from the fitful air.
And shame at heart stung nigh to death desire,
But grief at heart burned in him like a fire
For hers and his own sorrowing sake, that had
Such grace for guerdon as makes glad men sad,
To have their will and want it. And the day
Sprang: and afar along the wild waste way
They heard the pulse and press of hurrying horse hoofs play:
And like the rushing of a ravenous flame
Whose wings make tempest of the darkness, came
Upon them headlong as in thunder borne
Forth of the darkness of the labouring morn
Tristram: and up forthright upon his steed
Leapt, as one blithe for battle, Palamede,
And mightily with shock of horse and man
They lashed together: and fair that fight began
As fair came up that sunrise; to and fro,
With knees nigh staggered and stout heads bent low
From each quick shock of spears on either side,
Reeled the strong steeds heavily, haggard-eyed
And heartened high with passion of their pride
As sheer the stout spears shocked again, and flew
Sharp-splintering: then, his sword as each knight drew,
They flashed and foined full royally, so long
That but to see so fair a strife and strong
A man might well have given out of his life
One year's void space forlorn of love or strife.
As when a bright north-easter, great of heart,
Scattering the strengths of squadrons, hurls apart
Ship from ship labouring violently, in such toil
As earns but ruin – with even so strong recoil
Back were the steeds hurled from the spear-shock, fain
And foiled of triumph: then with tightened rein
And stroke of spur, inveterate, either knight
Bore in again upon his foe with might,

Heart-hungry for the hot-mouthed feast of fight
And all athirst of mastery: but full soon
The jarring notes of that tempestuous tune
Fell, and its mighty music made of hands
Contending, clamorous through the loud waste lands,
Broke off at once; and shattered from his steed
Fell, as a mainmast ruining, Palamede,
Stunned: and those lovers left him where he lay,
And lightly through green lawns they rode away.

THOMAS HARDY

The Burghers

[17—]

The sun had wheeled from Grey's to Dammer's Crest,
And still I mused on that thing imminent:
At length I sought the High-street to the West.

The level flare raked pane and pediment
And my wrecked face, and shaped my nearing friend
Like one of those the Furnace held unshent.

'I've news concerning her,' he said. 'Attend.
They fly tonight at the late moon's first gleam:
Watch with thy steel: two righteous thrusts will end

'Her shameless visions and his passioned dream.
I'll watch with thee, to testify thy wrong –
To aid, maybe. Law consecrates the scheme.'

I started, and we paced the flags along
Till I replied: 'Since it has come to this
I'll do it! But alone. I can be strong.'

Three hours past Curfew, when the Froom's mild hiss
Reigned sole, undulled by whirr of merchandise,
From Pummery-Tout to where the Gibbet is,

I crossed my pleasaunce hard by Glyd'path Rise,
And stood beneath the wall. Eleven strokes went,
And to the door they came, contrariwise,

And met in clasp so close I had but bent
My lifted blade on either to have let
Their two souls loose upon the firmament.

But something held my arm. 'A moment yet
As pray-time ere you wantons die!' I said;
And then they saw me. Swift her gaze was set

With eye and cry of love illimited
Upon her heart-king. Never upon me
Had she thrown look of love so thoroughsped!

At once she flung her faint form shieldingly
On his, against the vengeance of my vows;
The which o'erruling, her shape shielded he.

Blanked by such love, I stood as in a drowse,
And the slow moon edged from the upland nigh,
My sad thoughts moving thuswise: 'I may house

'And I may husband her, yet what am I
But licensed tyrant to this bonded pair?
Says charity, "Do as ye would be done by." '

Hurling my iron to the bushes there,
I bade them stay. And, as if brain and breast
Were passive, they walked with me to the stair.

Inside the house none watched; and on we prest
Before a mirror, in whose gleam I read
Her beauty, his; and mine own mien unblest;

Till at her room I turned. 'Madam,' I said,
'Have you the wherewithal for this? Pray speak.
Love fills no cupboard. You'll need daily bread.'

'We've nothing, sire,' she lipped; 'and nothing seek.
'Twere base in me to rob my lord unware;
Our hands will earn a pittance week by week.'

And next I saw she had piled her raiment rare
Within the garde-robes, and her household purse,
Her jewels, her least lace of personal wear;

And stood in homespun. Now grown wholly hers,
I handed her the gold, her jewels all,
And him the choicest of her robes diverse.

'I'll take you to the doorway in the wall,
And then adieu,' I told them. 'Friends, withdraw.'
They did so; and she went – beyond recall.

And as I paused beneath the arch I saw
Their moonlit figures – slow as in surprise –
Descend the slope, and vanish on the haw.

' "Fool," some will say,' I thought. 'But who is wise,
Save God alone, to weigh my reasons why?'
'Hast thou struck home?' came with the bough's night-sighs.

It was my friend. 'I have struck well. They fly,
But carry wounds that none can cicatrise.'
'Not mortal?' said he. 'Lingering – worse,' said I.

SIDNEY LANIER

The Revenge of Hamish

It was three slim does and a ten-tined buck in the bracken lay;
    And all of a sudden the sinister smell of a man,
    Awaft on a wind-shift, wavered and ran
Down the hill-side and sifted along through the bracken and passed
    that way.

Then Nan got a-tremble at nostril; she was the daintiest doe;
    In the print of her velvet flank on the velvet fern
    She reared, and rounded her ears in turn.
Then the buck leapt up, and his head as a king's to a crown did go

Full high in the breeze, and he stood as if Death had the form of a
    deer;
    And the two slim does long lazily stretching arose,
    For their day-dream slowlier came to a close,
Till they woke and were still, breath-bound with waiting and wonder
    and fear.

Then Alan the huntsman sprang over the hillock, the hounds shot by,
    The does and the ten-tined buck made a marvellous bound,
    The hounds swept after with never a sound,
But Alan loud winded his horn in sign that the quarry was nigh.

For at dawn of that day proud Maclean of Lochbuy to the hunt had
    waxed wild,
      And he cursed at old Alan till Alan fared off with the hounds
      For to drive him the deer to the lower glen-grounds:
'I will kill a red deer,' quoth Maclean, 'in the sight of the wife and the
    child.'

So gaily he paced with the wife and the child to his chosen stand;
      But he hurried tall Hamish the henchman ahead: 'Go turn,' –
      Cried Maclean – 'if the deer seek to cross to the burn,
Do thou turn them to me: nor fail, lest thy back be red as thy hand.'

Now hard-fortuned Hamish, half blown of his breath with the height
    of the hill,
      Was white in the face when the ten-tined buck and the does
      Drew leaping to burn-ward; huskily rose
His shouts, and his nether lip twitched, and his legs were o'er-weak
    for his will.

So the deer darted lightly by Hamish and bounded away to the burn.
      But Maclean never bating his watch tarried waiting below.
      Still Hamish hung heavy with fear for to go
All the space of an hour; then he went, and his face was greenish and
    stern,

And his eye sat back in the socket, and shrunken the eyeballs shone,
      As withdrawn from a vision of deeds it were shame to see.
      'Now, now, grim henchman, what is't with thee?'
Brake Maclean, and his wrath rose red as a beacon the wind hath
    upblown.

'Three does and a ten-tined buck made out,' spoke Hamish, full mild,
      'And I ran for to turn, but my breath it was blown, and they
          passed;
      I was weak, for ye called ere I broke me my fast.'
Cried Maclean: 'Now a ten-tined buck in the sight of the wife and the
    child

I had killed if the gluttonous kern had not wrought me a snail's own
    wrong!'
      Then he sounded, and down came kinsmen and clansmen all:
      'Ten blows, for ten tine, on his back let fall,
And reckon no stroke if the blood follow not at the bite of thong!'

So Hamish made bare, and took him his strokes; at the last he smiled.
      'Now I'll to the burn,' quoth Maclean, 'for it still may be,
      If a slimmer-paunched henchman will hurry with me,

I shall kill me the ten-tined buck for a gift to the wife and the child!'

Then the clansmen departed, by this path and that; and over the hill
    Sped Maclean with an outward wrath for an inward shame;
    And that place of the lashing full quiet became;
And the wife and the child stood sad; and bloody-backed Hamish sat
  still.

But look! red Hamish has risen; quick about and about turns he.
    'There is none betwixt me and the crag-top!' he screams under
      breath.
    Then, livid as Lazarus lately from death,
He snatches the child from the mother, and clambers the crag toward
  the sea.

Now the mother drops breath; she is dumb, and her heart goes dead
  for a space,
    Till the motherhood, mistress of death, shrieks, shrieks through
      the glen,
    And that place of the lashing is live with men,
And Maclean, and the gillie that told him, dash up in a desperate race.

Not a breath's time for asking; an eye-glance reveals all the tale
  untold.
    They follow mad Hamish afar up the crag toward the sea,
    And the lady cries: 'Clansmen, run for a fee! –
Yon castle and lands to the two first hands that shall hook him and
  hold

Fast Hamish back from the brink!' – and ever she flies up the steep,
    And the clansmen pant, and they sweat, and they jostle and
      strain.
    But, mother, 'tis vain; but, father, 'tis vain;
Stern Hamish stands bold on the brink, and dangles the child o'er the
  deep.

Now a faintness falls on the men that run, and they all stand still.
    And the wife prays Hamish as if he were God, on her knees,
    Crying: 'Hamish! O Hamish! but please, but please
For to spare him!' and Hamish still dangles the child, with a wavering
  will.

On a sudden he turns; with a sea-hawk scream, and a gibe, and a
  song,
    Cries: 'So; I will spare ye the child if, in sight of ye all,
    Ten blows on Maclean's bare back shall fall,

And ye reckon no stroke if the blood follow not at the bite of the
   thong!'

Then Maclean he set hardly his tooth to his lip that his tooth was red,
     Breathed short for a space, said: 'Nay, but it never shall be!
     Let me hurl off the damnable hound in the sea!'
But the wife: 'Can Hamish go fish us the child from the sea, if dead?

'Say yea! – Let them lash *me*, Hamish?' – 'Nay' – 'Husband, the
   lashing will heal;
     But, oh, who will heal me the bonny sweet bairn in his grave?
     Could ye cure me my heart with the death of a knave?
Quick! Love! I will bare thee – so – kneel!' Then Maclean 'gan slowly
   to kneel

With never a word, till presently downward he jerked to the earth.
     Then the henchman – he that smote Hamish – would tremble
       and lag;
     'Strike, hard!' quoth Hamish, full stern, from the crag;
Then he struck him, and 'One!' sang Hamish, and danced with the
   child in his mirth.

And no man spake beside Hamish; he counted each stroke with a
   song.
     When the last stroke fell, then he moved him a pace down the
       height,
     And he held forth the child in the heartaching sight
Of the mother, and looked all pitiful grave, as repenting a wrong.

And there as the motherly arms stretched out with the thanksgiving
   prayer –
     And there as the mother crept up with a fearful swift pace,
     Till her finger nigh felt of the bairnie's face –
In a flash fierce Hamish turned round and lifted the child in the air,

And sprang with the child in his arms from the horrible height in the
   sea,
     Shrill screeching, 'Revenge!' in the wind-rush; and pallid
       Maclean,
     Age-feeble with anger, and impotent pain,
Crawled up on the crag, and lay flat, and locked hold of dead roots of
   a tree –

And gazed hungrily o'er, and the blood from his back drip-dripped in
   the brine,
     And a sea-hawk flung down a skeleton fish as he flew,
     And the mother stared white on the waste of blue,
And the wind drove a cloud to seaward, and the sun began to shine.

GEORGE ROBERT SIMS

Christmas Day in the Workhouse

It is Christmas Day in the workhouse, and the cold, bare walls are
   bright
With garlands of green and holly, and the place is a pleasant sight;
For with clean-washed hands and faces, in a long and hungry line
The paupers sit at the table, for this is the hour they dine.

And the guardians and their ladies, although the wind is east,
Have come in their furs and wrappers, to watch their charges feast;
To smile and be condescending, pudding on pauper plates,
To be hosts at the workhouse banquet they've paid for – with the
   rates.

O, the paupers are meek and lowly with their 'Thank'ee kindly,
   mums;'
So long as they fill their stomachs, what matter it whence it comes?
But one of the old men mutters, and pushes his plate aside:
'Great God!' he cries, 'but it chokes me; for this is the day *she* died!'

The guardians gazed in horror, the master's face went white;
'Did a pauper refuse the pudding? Could their ears believe
   aright?'
Then the ladies clutched their husbands, thinking the man would die,
Struck by a bolt, or something, by the outraged One on high.

But the pauper sat for a moment, then rose 'mid silence grim,
For the others had ceased to chatter, and trembled in every limb.
He looked at the guardians' ladies, then, eyeing their lords, he said:
'I eat not the food of villains whose hands are foul and red;

'Whose victims cry for vengeance from their dank, unhallowed
   graves.'
'He's drunk,' said the workhouse master, 'or else he's mad and raves.'
'Not drunk or mad,' cried the pauper, 'but only a hunted beast,
Who, torn by the hounds and mangled, declines the vulture's feast.

'I care not a curse for the guardians, and I won't be dragged away.
Just let me have the fit out, it's only on Christmas Day
That the black past comes to goad me and prey on my burning brain;
I'll tell you the rest in a whisper – I swear I won't shout again.

'Keep your hands off me, curse you! Hear me right out to the end.
You come here to see how paupers the season of Christmas spend.
You come here to watch us feeding, as they watch the captured beast.

Hear why a penniless pauper spits on your paltry feast.

'Do you think I will take your bounty and let you smile and think
You're doing a noble action with the parish's meat and drink?
Where is my wife, you traitors – the poor old wife you slew?
Yes, by the God above us, my Nance was killed by you.

'Last Winter my wife lay dying, starved in a filthy den.
I had never been to the parish – I came to the parish then.
I swallowed my pride in coming, for ere the ruin came
I held up my head as a trader, and I bore a spotless name.

'I came to the parish, craving bread for a starving wife –
Bread for the woman who'd loved me through fifty years of life;
And what do you think they told me, mocking my awful grief?
That "the House" was open to us, but they wouldn't "give out relief".

'I slunk to the filthy alley – 'twas a cold, raw Christmas eve –
And the bakers' shops were open, tempting a man to thieve;
But I clenched my fists together, holding my head awry,
So I came to her empty-handed and mournfully told her why.

'Then I told her "the House" was open; she had heard of the ways of
  that,
For her bloodless cheeks went crimson, and up in her rags she sat,
Crying, "Bide the Christmas here, John, we've never had one apart;
I think I can bear the hunger – the other would break my heart."

'All through that eve I watched her, holding her hand in mine,
Praying the Lord and weeping till my lips were salt as brine;
I asked her once if she hungered, and as she answered "No",
The moon shone in at the window, set in a wreath of snow.

'Then the room was bathed in glory, and I saw in my darling's eyes
The far-way look of wonder that comes when the spirit flies;
And her lips were parched and parted, and her reason came and went.
For she raved of our home in Devon, where our happiest years were
  spent.

'And the accents, long forgotten, came back to the tongue once
  more.
For she talked like the country lassie I wooed by the Devon shore;
Then she rose to her feet and trembled, and fell on the rags and
  moaned,
And, "Give me a crust – I'm famished – for the love of God," she
  groaned.

'I rushed from the room like a madman, and flew to the workhouse
   gate,
Crying, "Food for a dying woman!" and the answer came, "Too
   late";
They drove me away with curses; then I fought with a dog in the
   street,
And tore from the mongrel's clutches a crust he was trying to eat.

'Back through the filthy by-lanes! Back through the trampled slush!
Up to the crazy garret, wrapped in an awful hush.
My heart sank down at the threshold, and I paused with a sudden
   thrill,
For there, in the silvery moonlight, my Nance lay, cold and still.

'Up to the blackened ceiling the sunken eyes were cast –
I knew on those lips, all bloodless, my name had been the last;
She'd called for her absent husband – O God! Had I but known –
Had called in vain, and, in anguish, had died in that den – *alone*.

'Yes, there in a land of plenty, lay a loving woman dead,
Cruelly starved and murdered for a loaf of the parish bread.
At yonder gate, last Christmas, I craved for a human life,
You, who would feed us paupers, *what of my murdered wife?*

'There, get ye gone to your dinners; don't mind me in the least.
Think of the happy paupers eating your Christmas feast;
And when you recount their blessings in your smug parochial way,
Say what you did for *me*, too, only last Christmas Day.'

ROBERT LOUIS STEVENSON

Ticonderoga: a Legend of the West Highlands

This is the tale of the man
   Who heard a word in the night
In the land of the heathery hills,
   In the days of the feud and the fight.
By the sides of the rainy sea,
   Where never a stranger came,
On the awful lips of the dead,
   He heard the outlandish name.
It sang in his sleeping ears,
   It hummed in his waking head:
The name – Ticonderoga,
   The utterance of the dead.

THE SAYING OF THE NAME

'On the loch-sides of Appin,
　　When the mist blew from the sea,
A Stewart stood with a Cameron:
　　An angry man was he.
The blood beat in his ears,
　　The blood ran hot to his head,
The mist blew from the sea,
　　And there was the Cameron dead.

'O, what have I done to my friend,
　　O, what have I done to mysel',
That he should be cold and dead,
　　And I in the danger of all?

'Nothing but danger about me,
　　Danger behind and before,
Death at wait in the heather
　　In Appin and Mamore,
Hate at all of the ferries
　　And death at each of the fords,
Camerons priming gunlocks
　　And Camerons sharpening swords.'

But this was a man of counsel,
　　This was a man of a score,
There dwelt no pawkier Stewart
　　In Appin or Mamore.
He looked on the blowing mist,
　　He looked on the awful dead,
And there came a smile on his face
　　And there slipped a thought in his head.

Out over cairn and moss,
　　Out over scrog and scaur,
He ran as runs the clansman
　　That bears the cross of war.
His heart beat in his body,
　　His hair clove to his face,
When he came at last in the gloaming
　　To the dead man's brother's place.
The east was white with the moon,
　　The west with the sun was red,
And there, in the house-doorway,
　　Stood the brother of the dead.

'I have slain a man to my danger,
  I have slain a man to my death,
I put my soul in your hands,'
  The panting Stewart saith.
'I lay it bare in your hands,
  For I know your hands are leal;
And be you my targe and bulwark
  From the bullet and the steel.'

Then up and spoke the Cameron,
  And gave him his hand again:
'There shall never a man in Scotland
  Set faith in me in vain;
And whatever man you have slaughtered,
  Of whatever name or line,
By my sword and yonder mountain,
  I make your quarrel mine.
I bid you in to my fireside,
  I share with you house and hall;
It stands upon my honour
  To see you safe from all.'

It fell in the time of midnight,
  When the fox barked in the den,
And the plaids were over the faces
  In all the houses of men,
That as the living Cameron
  Lay sleepless on his bed,
Out of the night and the other world
  Came in to him the dead.

'My blood is on the heather,
  My bones are on the hill;
There is joy in the home of ravens
  That the young shall eat their fill.
My blood is poured in the dust,
  My soul is spilled in the air;
And the man that has undone me
  Sleeps in my brother's care.'

'I'm wae for your death, my brother,
  But if all of my house were dead,
I couldnae withdraw the plighted hand
  Nor break the word once said.'

'O, what shall I say to our father,
  In the place to which I fare?

O, what shall I say to our mother,
   Who greets to see me there?
And to all the kindly Camerons
   That have lived and died long-syne –
Is this the word you send them,
   Fause-hearted brother mine?'

'It's neither fear nor duty,
   It's neither quick nor dead
Shall gar me withdraw the plighted hand,
   Or break the word once said.'

Thrice in the time of midnight,
   When the fox barked in the den,
And the plaids were over the faces
   In all the houses of men,
Thrice as the living Cameron
   Lay sleepless on his bed,
Out of the night and the other world
   Came in to him the dead,
And cried to him for vengeance
   On the man that laid him low;
And thrice the living Cameron
   Told the dead Cameron, no.

'Thrice have you seen me, brother,
   But now shall see me no more,
Till you meet your angry fathers
   Upon the farther shore.
Thrice have I spoken, and now,
   Before the cock be heard,
I take my leave for ever
   With the naming of a word.
It shall sing in your sleeping ears,
   It shall hum in your waking head,
The name – Ticonderoga,
   And the warning of the dead.'

Now when the night was over
   And the time of people's fears,
The Cameron walked abroad,
   And the word was in his ears.
'Many a name I know,
   But never a name like this;
O, where shall I find a skilly man
   Shall tell me what it is?'
With many a man he counselled

Of high and low degree,
With the herdsmen on the mountains
  And the fishers of the sea.
And he came and went unweary,
  And read the books of yore,
And the runes that were written of old
  On stones upon the moor.
And many a name he was told,
  But never the name of his fears –
Never, in east or west,
  The name that rang in his ears:
Names of men and of clans;
  Names for the grass and the tree,
For the smallest tarn in the mountains,
  The smallest reef in the sea:
Names for the high and low
  The names of the craig and the flat;
But in all the land of Scotland,
  Never a name like that.

THE SEEKING OF THE NAME

And now there was speech in the south,
    And a man of the south that was wise,
A periwigged lord of London,
  Called on the clans to rise.
And the riders rode, and the summons
  Came to the western shore,
To the land of the sea and the heather,
  To Appin and Mamore.
It called on all to gather
  From every scrog and scaur,
That loved their father's tartan
  And the ancient game of war.
And down the watery valley
  And up the windy hill,
Once more, as in the olden,
  The pipes were sounding shrill.
Again in highland sunshine
  The naked steel was bright;
And the lads, once more in tartan,
  Went forth again to fight.

'O, why should I dwell here
  With a weird upon my life,
When the clansmen shout for battle
  And the war-swords clash in strife?
I cannae joy at feast,

I cannae sleep in bed,
For the wonder of the word
   And the warning of the dead.
It sings in my sleeping ears,
   It hums in my waking head,
The name – Ticonderoga,
   The utterance of the dead.
Then up, and with the fighting men
   To march away from here,
Till the cry of the great war-pipe
   Shall drown it in my ear!'

Where flew King George's ensign
   The plaided soldiers went:
They drew the sword in Germany,
   In Flanders pitched the tent.
The bells of foreign cities
   Rang far across the plain:
They passed the happy Rhine,
   They drank the rapid Main.
Through Asiatic jungles
   The Tartans filed their way,
And the neighing of the war-pipes
   Struck terror in Cathay.

'Many a name have I heard,' he thought,
   'In all the tongues of men,
Full many a name both here and there,
   Full many both now and then.
When I was at home in my father's house
   In the land of the naked knee,
Between the eagles that fly in the lift
   And the herrings that swim in the sea,
And now that I am a captain-man
   With a braw cockade in my hat –
Many a name have I heard,' he thought,
   'But never a name like that.'

THE PLACE OF THE NAME

There fell a war in a woody place,
   Lay far across the sea,
A war of the march in the mirk midnight
   And the shot from behind the tree,
The shaven head and the painted face,
   The silent foot in the wood,
In a land of a strange, outlandish tongue
   That was hard to be understood.

It fell about the gloaming,
   The general stood with his staff,
He stood and he looked east and west
   With little mind to laugh.
'Far have I been and much have I seen,
   And kent both gain and loss,
But here we have woods on every hand
   And a kittle water to cross.
Far have I been and much have I seen,
   But never the beat of this;
And there's one must go down to that waterside
   To see how deep it is.'

It fell in the dusk of the night
   When unco things betide,
The skilly captain, the Cameron,
   Went down to that waterside.
Canny and soft the captain went;
   And a man of the woody land,
With the shaven head and the painted face,
   Went down at his right hand.
It fell in the quiet night,
   There was never a sound to ken;
But all the woods to the right and the left
   Lay filled with the painted men.

'Far have I been and much have I seen,
   Both as a man and boy,
But never have I set forth a foot
   On so perilous an employ.'
It fell in the dusk of the night
   When unco things betide,
That he was aware of a captain-man
   Drew near to the waterside.
He was aware of his coming
   Down in the gloaming alone;
And he looked in the face of the man,
   And lo! the face was his own.
'This is my weird,' he said,
   'And now I ken the worst;
For many shall fall with the morn,
   But I shall fall with the first.
O, you of the outland tongue,
   You of the painted face,
This is the place of my death;
   Can you tell me the name of the place?'

'Since the Frenchmen have been here
   They have called it Sault-Marie;
But that is a name for priests,
   And not for you and me.
It went by another word,'
   Quoth he of the shaven head:
'It was called Ticonderoga
   In the days of the great dead.'

And it fell on the morrow's morning,
   In the fiercest of the fight,
That the Cameron bit the dust
   As he foretold at night;
And far from the hills of heather
   Far from the isles of the sea,
He sleeps in the place of the name
   As it was doomed to be.

OSCAR WILDE

From *The Ballad of Reading Gaol*

[THE CONDEMNED MAN]

He did not wear his scarlet coat,
   For blood and wine are red,
And blood and wine were on his hands
   When they found him with the dead,
The poor dead woman whom he loved,
   And murdered in her bed.

He walked amongst the Trial Men
   In a suit of shabby gray;
A cricket cap was on his head,
   And his step seemed light and gay;
But I never saw a man who looked
   So wistfully at the day.

I never saw a man who looked
   With such a wistful eye
Upon that little tent of blue
   Which prisoners call the sky,
And at every drifting cloud that went
   With sails of silver by.

I walked, with other souls in pain,
  Within another ring,
And was wondering if the man had done
  A great or little thing,
When a voice behind me whispered low,
  '*That fellow's got to swing.*'
          . . .

Six weeks our guardsman walked the yard,
  In the suit of shabby gray:
His cricket cap was on his head,
  And his step seemed light and gay,
But I never saw a man who looked
  So wistfully at the day.

I never saw a man who looked
  With such a wistful eye
Upon that little tent of blue
  Which prisoners call the sky,
And at every wandering cloud that trailed
  Its ravelled fleeces by.

He did not wring his hands, as do
  Those witless men who dare
To try to rear the changeling Hope
  In the cave of black Despair:
He only looked upon the sun,
  And drank the morning air.

He did not wring his hands nor weep,
  Nor did he peek or pine,
But he drank the air as though it held
  Some healthful anodyne;
With open mouth he drank the sun
  As though it had been wine!

And I and all the souls in pain,
  Who tramped the other ring,
Forgot if we ourselves had done
  A great or little thing,
And watched with gaze of dull amaze
  The man who had to swing.

And strange it was to see him pass
  With a step so light and gay,
And strange it was to see him look
  So wistfully at the day,
And strange it was to think that he
  Had such a debt to pay.

For oak and elm have pleasant leaves
   That in the spring-time shoot:
But grim to see is the gallows-tree,
   With its adder-bitten root,
And, green or dry, a man must die
   Before it bears its fruit!

The loftiest place is that seat of grace
   For which all worldlings try:
But who would stand in hempen band
   Upon a scaffold high,
And through a murderer's collar take
   His last look at the sky?

It is sweet to dance to violins
   When Love and Life are fair:
To dance to flutes, to dance to lutes
   Is delicate and rare:
But it is not sweet with nimble feet
   To dance upon the air!

So with curious eyes and sick surmise
   We watched him day by day,
And wondered if each one of us
   Would end the self-same way,
For none can tell to what red Hell
   His sightless soul may stray.

At last the dead man walked no more
   Amongst the Trial Men,
And I knew that he was standing up
   In the black dock's dreadful pen,
And that never would I see his face
   In God's sweet world again.

Like two doomed ships that pass in storm
   We had crossed each other's way:
But we made no sign, we said no word,
   We had no word to say;
For we did not meet in the holy night,
   But in the shameful day.

A prison wall was round us both,
   Two outcast men we were:
The world had thrust us from its heart
   And God from out His care:

And the iron gin that waits for Sin
   Had caught us in its snare.

★

In Debtors' Yard the stones are hard,
   And the dripping wall is high,
So it was there he took the air
   Beneath the leaden sky,
And by each side a warder walked,
   For fear the man might die.

Or else he sat with those who watched
   His anguish night and day;
Who watched him when he rose to weep,
   And when he crouched to pray;
Who watched him lest himself should rob
   Their scaffold of its prey.

. . .

And twice a day he smoked his pipe,
   And drank his quart of beer:
His soul was resolute, and held
   No hiding-place for fear;
He often said that he was glad
   The hangman's day was near.

But why he said so strange a thing
   No warder dared to ask:
For he to whom a watcher's doom
   Is given as his task,
Must set a lock upon his lips
   And make his face a mask.

Or else he might be moved, and try
   To comfort or console:
And what should Human Pity do
   Pent up in Murderer's Hole?
What word of grace in such a place
   Could help a brother's soul?

With slouch and swing around the ring
   We trod the Fool's Parade!
We did not care: we knew we were
   The Devil's Own Brigade:
And shaven head and feet of lead
   Make a merry masquerade.

243

We tore the tarry ropes to shreds
  With blunt and bleeding nails;
We rubbed the doors, and scrubbed the floors,
  And cleaned the shining rails:
And, rank by rank, we soaped the plank,
  And clattered with the pails.

We sewed the sacks, we broke the stones,
  We turned the dusty drill:
We banged the tins, and bawled the hymns,
  And sweated on the mill:
But in the heart of every man
  Terror was lying still.

So still it lay that every day
  Crawled like a weed-clogged wave:
And we forgot the bitter lot
  That waits for fool and knave,
Till once, as we tramped in from work,
  We passed an open grave.

With yawning mouth the yellow hole
  Gaped for a living thing;
The very mud cried out for blood
  To the thirsty asphalte ring;
And we knew that ere one dawn grew fair
  Some prisoner had to swing.

Right in we went, with soul intent
  On Death and Dread and Doom:
The hangman, with his little bag,
  Went shuffling through the gloom:
And each man trembled as he crept
  Into his numbered tomb.

That night the empty corridors
  Were full of forms of Fear,
And up and down the iron town
  Stole feet we could not hear,
And through the bars that hide the stars
  White faces seemed to peer.

He lay as one who lies and dreams
  In a pleasant meadow-land,
The watchers watched him as he slept,
  And could not understand

How one could sleep so sweet a sleep
  With a hangman close at hand.

But there is no sleep when men must weep
  Who never yet have wept:
So we – the fool, the fraud, the knave –
  That endless vigil kept,
And through each brain on hands of pain
  Another's terror crept.

            . . .

At last I saw the shadowed bars,
  Like a lattice wrought in lead,
Move right across the whitewashed wall
  That faced my three-plank bed,
And I knew that somewhere in the world
  God's dreadful dawn was red.

At six o'clock we cleaned our cells,
  At seven all was still,
But the sough and swing of a mighty wing
  The prison seemed to fill,
For the Lord of Death with icy breath
  Had entered in to kill.

            . . .

We waited for the stroke of eight:
  Each tongue was thick with thirst:
For the stroke of eight is the stroke of Fate
  That makes a man accursed,
And Fate will use a running noose
  For the best man and the worst.

We had no other thing to do,
  Save to wait for the sign to come:
So, like things of stone in a valley lone,
  Quiet we sat and dumb:
But each man's heart beat thick, and quick,
  Like a madman on a drum!

With sudden shock the prison-clock
  Smote on the shivering air,
And from all the gaol rose up a wail
  Of impotent despair,
Like the sound that frightened marshes hear
  From some leper in his lair.

And as one sees most fearful things
  In the crystal of a dream,

We saw the greasy hempen rope
   Hooked to the blackened beam,
And heard the prayer the hangman's snare
   Strangled into a scream.
     . . .

There is no chapel on the day
   On which they hang a man:
The Chaplain's heart is far too sick,
   Or his face is far too wan,
Or there is that written in his eyes
   Which none should look upon.

So they kept us close till nigh on noon,
   And then they rang the bell,
And the warders with their jingling keys
   Opened each listening cell,
And down the iron stair we tramped,
   Each from his separate Hell.

Out into God's sweet air we went,
   But not in wonted way,
For this man's face was white with fear,
   And that man's face was gray,
And I never saw sad men who looked
   So wistfully at the day.

I never saw sad men who looked
   With such a wistful eye
Upon that little tent of blue
   We prisoners called the sky,
And at every careless cloud that passed
   In happy freedom by.
     . . .

The warders strutted up and down,
   And kept their herd of brutes,
Their uniforms were spick and span,
   And they wore their Sunday suits,
But we knew the work they had been at,
   By the quicklime on their boots.

For where a grave had opened wide,
   There was no grave at all:
Only a stretch of mud and sand
   By the hideous prison-wall,
And a little heap of burning lime,
   That the man should have his pall.
     . . .

For three long years they will not sow
   Or root or seedling there:
For three long years the unblessed spot
   Will sterile be and bare,
And look upon the wondering sky
   With unreproachful stare.

They think a murderer's heart would taint
   Each simple seed they sow.
It is not true! God's kindly earth
   Is kindlier than men know,
And the red rose would blow more red,
   The white rose whiter blow.

JOHN DAVIDSON

A Runnable Stag

When the pods went pop on the broom, green broom,
   And apples began to be golden-skinned,
We harboured a stag in the Priory coomb,
   And we feathered his trail up-wind, up-wind,
   We feathered his trail up-wind –
      A stag of warrant, a stag, a stag,
      A runnable stag, a kingly crop,
      Brow, bay and tray and three on top,
      A stag, a runnable stag.

Then the huntsman's horn rang yap, yap, yap,
   And 'Forwards' we heard the harbourer shout;
But 'twas only a brocket that broke a gap
   In the beechen underwood, driven out,
   From the underwood antlered out
      By warrant and might of the stag, the stag,
      The runnable stag, whose lordly mind
      Was bent on sleep, though beamed and tined
      He stood, a runnable stag.

So we tufted the covert till afternoon
   With Tinkerman's Pup and Bell-of-the-North;
And hunters were sulky and hounds out of tune
   Before we tufted the right stag forth,
   Before we tufted him forth,
      The stag of warrant, the wily stag,

The runnable stag with his kingly crop,
Brow, bay and tray and three on top,
The royal and runnable stag.

It was Bell-of-the-North and Tinkerman's Pup
  That stuck to the scent till the copse was drawn.
'Tally ho! tally ho!' and the hunt was up,
  The tufters whipped and the pack laid on,
  The resolute pack laid on,
    And the stag of warrant away at last,
    The runnable stag, the same, the same,
    His hoofs on fire, his horns like flame,
    A stag, a runnable stag.

'Let your gelding be: if you check or chide
  He stumbles at once and you're out of the hunt;
For three hundred gentlemen, able to ride,
  On hunters accustomed to bear the brunt,
  Accustomed to bear the brunt,
    Are after the runnable stag, the stag,
    The runnable stag with his kingly crop,
    Brow, bay and tray and three on top,
    The right, the runnable stag.'

By perilous paths in coomb and dell,
  The heather, the rocks, and the river-bed,
The pace grew hot, for the scent lay well,
  And a runnable stag goes right ahead,
  The quarry went right ahead –
    Ahead, ahead, and fast and far;
    His antlered crest, his cloven hoof,
    Brow, bay and tray and three aloof,
    The stag, the runnable stag.

For a matter of twenty miles and more,
  By the densest hedge and the highest wall,
Through herds of bullocks he baffled the lore
  Of harbourer, huntsman, hounds and all,
  Of harbourer, hounds and all –
    The stag of warrant, the wily stag,
    For twenty miles, and five and five,
    He ran, and he never was caught alive,
    This stag, this runnable stag.

When he turned at bay in the leafy gloom,
  In the emerald gloom where the brook ran deep,
He heard in the distance the rollers boom,

And he saw in a vision of peaceful sleep,
In a wonderful vision of sleep,
  A stag of warrant, a stag, a stag,
  A runnable stag in a jewelled bed,
  Under the sheltering ocean dead,
  A stag, a runnable stag.

So a fateful hope lit up his eye,
  And he opened his nostrils wide again,
And he tossed his branching antlers high
  As he headed the hunt down the Charlock glen,
  As he raced down the echoing glen
    For five miles more, the stag, the stag,
    For twenty miles, and five and five,
    Not to be caught now, dead or alive,
    The stag, the runnable stag.

Three hundred gentlemen, able to ride,
  Three hundred horses as gallant and free,
Beheld him escape on the evening tide,
  Far out till he sank in the Severn Sea,
  Till he sank in the depths of the sea –
    The stag, the buoyant stag, the stag
    That slept at last in a jewelled bed
    Under the sheltering ocean spread,
    The stag, the runnable stag.

A. E. HOUSMAN

The True Lover

The lad came to the door at night,
  When lovers crown their vows,
And whistled soft and out of sight
  In shadow of the boughs.

'I shall not vex you with my face
  Henceforth, my love, for aye;
So take me in your arms a space
  Before the east is grey.

'When I from hence away am past
  I shall not find a bride,

And you shall be the first and last
　　I ever lay beside.'

She heard and went and knew not why;
　　Her heart to his she laid;
Light was the air beneath the sky
　　But dark under the shade.

'Oh do you breathe, lad, that your breast
　　Seems not to rise and fall,
And here upon my bosom prest
　　There beats no heart at all?'

'O loud, my girl, it once would knock,
　　You should have felt it then;
But since for you I stopped the clock
　　It never goes again.'

'Oh lad, what is it, lad, that drips
　　Wet from your neck on mine?
What is it falling on my lips,
　　My lad, that tastes of brine?'

'Oh like enough 'tis blood, my dear,
　　For when the knife has slit
The throat across from ear to ear
　　'Twill bleed because of it.'

Under the stars the air was light
　　But dark below the boughs,
The still air of the speechless night,
　　When lovers crown their vows.

RUDYARD KIPLING

The Ballad of East and West

Oh, East is East, and West is West, and never the twain shall meet,
Till Earth and Sky stand presently at God's great Judgment Seat;
But there is neither East nor West, Border nor Breed, nor Birth,
When two strong men stand face to face, though they come from the ends of
　　the earth!

Kamal is out with twenty men to raise the Border-side,

And he has lifted the Colonel's mare that is the Colonel's pride.
He has lifted her out of the stable-door between the dawn and the day,
And turned the calkins upon her feet, and ridden her far away.
Then up and spoke the Colonel's son that led a troop of the Guides:
'Is there never a man of all my men can say where Kamal hides?'
Then up and spoke Mohammed Khan, the son of the Ressaldar:
'If ye know the track of the morning mist, ye know where his pickets are.
At dusk he harries the Abazai – at dawn he is into Bonair,
But he must go by Fort Bukloh to his own place to fare.
So if ye gallop to Fort Bukloh as fast as a bird can fly,
By the favour of God ye may cut him off ere he win to the Tongue of Jagai.
But if he be past the Tongue of Jagai, right swiftly turn ye then,
For the length and the breadth of that grisly plain is sown with Kamal's men.
There is rock to the left, and rock to the right, and low lean thorn between,
And ye may hear a breech-bolt snick where never a man is seen.'
The Colonel's son has taken horse, and a raw rough dun was he,
With the mouth of a bell and the heart of Hell and the head of a gallows-tree.
The Colonel's son to the Fort has won, they bid him stay to eat –
Who rides at the tail of a Border thief, he sits not long at his meat.
He's up and away from Fort Bukloh as fast as he can fly,
Till he was aware of his father's mare in the gut of the Tongue of Jagai,
Till he was aware of his father's mare with Kamal upon her back,
And when he could spy the white of her eye, he made the pistol crack.
He has fired once, he has fired twice, but the whistling ball went wide.
'Yet shoot like a soldier,' Kamal said. 'Show now if ye can ride!'
It's up and over the Tongue of Jagai, as blown dust-devils go,
The dun he fled like a stag of ten, but the mare like a barren doe.
The dun he leaned against the bit and slugged his head above,
But the red mare played with the snaffle-bars, as a maiden plays with a glove.
There was rock to the left and rock to the right, and low lean thorn between,
And thrice he heard a breech-bolt snick tho' never a man was seen.
They have ridden the low moon out of the sky, their hoofs drum up the dawn,
The dun he went like a wounded bull, but the mare like a new-roused fawn.
The dun he fell at a water-course – in a woeful heap fell he,

And Kamal has turned the red mare back, and pulled the rider free.
He has knocked the pistol out of his hand – small room was there to
strive,
"Twas only by favour of mine,' quoth he, 'ye rode so long alive:
There was not a rock for twenty mile, there was not a clump of tree,
But covered a man of my own men with his rifle cocked on his knee.
If I had raised my bridle-hand, as I have held it low,
The little jackals that flee so fast were feasting all in a row.
If I had bowed my head on my breast, as I have held it high,
The kite that whistles above us now were gorged till she could not fly.'
Lightly answered the Colonel's son: 'Do good to bird and beast,
But count who come for the broken meats before thou makest a
feast.
If there should follow a thousand swords to carry my bones away,
Belike the price of a jackal's meal were more than a thief could pay.
They will feed their horse on the standing crop, their men on the
garnered grain.
The thatch of the byres will serve their fires when all the cattle are
slain.
But if thou thinkest the price be fair – thay brethren wait to sup,
The hound is kin to the jackal-spawn – howl, dog, and call them up!
And if thou thinkest the price be high, in steer and gear and stack,
Give me my father's mare again, and I'll fight my own way back!'
Kamal has gripped him by the hand and set him upon his feet.
'No talk shall be of dogs,' said he, 'when wolf and grey wolf meet.
May I eat dirt if thou hast hurt of me in deed or breath;
What dam of lances brought thee forth to jest at the dawn with
Death?'
Lightly answered the Colonel's son: 'I hold by the blood of my clan:
Take up the mare for my father's gift – by God, she has carried a
man!'
The red mare ran to the Colonel's son, and nuzzled against his breast;
'We be two strong men,' said Kamal then, 'but she loveth the
younger best.
So she shall go with a lifter's dower, my turquoise-studded rein,
My 'broidered saddle and saddle-cloth, and silver stirrups twain.'
The Colonel's son a pistol drew, and held it muzzle-end,
'Ye have taken the one from a foe,' said he. 'Will ye take the mate
from a friend?'
'A gift for a gift,' said Kamal straight; 'a limb for the risk of a limb.
Thy father has sent his son to me, I'll send my son to him!'
With that he whistled his only son, that dropped from a mountain-
crest –
He trod the ling like a buck in spring, and he looked like a lance in
rest.
'Now here is thy master,' Kamal said, 'who leads a troop of the
Guides,

And thou must ride at his left side as shield on shoulder rides.
Till Death or I cut loose the tie, at camp and board and bed,
Thy life is his – thy fate it is to guard him with thy head.
So, thou must eat the White Queen's meat, and all her foes are thine,
And thou must harry thy father's hold for the peace of the
    Border-line.
And thou must make a trooper tough and hack thy way to power –
Belike they will raise thee to Ressaldar when I am hanged in
    Peshawur!'

They have looked each other between the eyes, and there they found
    no fault.
They have taken the Oath of the Brother-in-Blood on leavened bread
    and salt:
They have taken the Oath of the Brother-in-Blood on fire and fresh-
    cut sod,
On the hilt and the haft of the Khyber knife, and the Wondrous
    Names of God.
The Colonel's son he rides the mare and Kamal's boy the dun,
And two have come back to Fort Bukloh where there went forth but
    one.
And when they drew to the Quarter-Guard, full twenty swords flew
    clear –
There was not a man but carried his feud with the blood of the
    mountaineer.
'Ha' done! ha' done!' said the Colonel's son. 'Put up the steel at your
    sides!
Last night ye had struck at a Border thief – tonight 'tis a man of the
    Guides!'

Oh, East is East, and West is West, and never the twain shall meet,
Till Earth and Sky stand presently at God's great Judgment Seat;
But there is neither East nor West, Border, nor Breed, nor Birth,
When two strong men stand face to face, though they come from the ends of
    the earth!

W. B. YEATS

The Three Bushes

(An incident from the *Historia mei Temporis* of the Abbé Michel de Bourdeille)

Said lady once to lover,
'None can rely upon

253

A love that lacks its proper food;
And if your love were gone
How could you sing those songs of love?
I should be blamed, young man.
  O my dear, O my dear.

'Have no lit candles in your room,'
That lovely lady said,
'That I at midnight by the clock,
May creep into your bed,
For if I saw myself creep in
I think I should drop dead.'
  O my dear, O my dear.

'I love a man in secret,
Dear chambermaid,' said she.
'I know that I must drop down dead
If he stop loving me,
Yet what could I but drop down dead
If I lost my chastity?
  O my dear, O my dear.

'So you must lie beside him
And let him think me there.
And maybe we are all the same
Where no candles are,
And maybe we are all the same
That strip the body bare.'
  O my dear, O my dear.

But no dogs barked, and midnights chimed,
And through the chime she'd say,
'That was a lucky thought of mine,
My lover looked so gay';
But heaved a sigh if the chambermaid
Looked half-asleep all day.
  O my dear, O my dear.

'No, not another song,' said he,
'Because my lady came
A year ago for the first time
At midnight to my room,
And I must lie between the sheets
When the clock begins to chime.'
  O my dear, O my dear.

'A laughing, crying, sacred song,
A leching song,' they said.
Did ever men hear such a song?
No, but that day they did.
Did ever man ride such a race?
No, not until he rode.
O my dear, O my dear.

But when his horse had put its hoof
Into a rabbit-hole
He dropped upon his head and died.
His lady saw it all
And dropped and died thereon, for she
Loved him with her soul.
O my dear, O my dear.

The chambermaid lived long, and took
Their graves into her charge,
And there two bushes planted
That when they had grown large
Seemed sprung from but a single root
So did their roses merge.
O my dear, O my dear.

When she was old and dying,
The priest came where she was;
She made a full confession.
Long looked he in her face,
And O he was a good man
And understood her case.
O my dear, O my dear.

He bade them take and bury her
Beside her lady's man,
And set a rose-tree on her grave,
And now none living can,
When they have plucked a rose there,
Know where its roots began.
O my dear, O my dear.

J. MILTON HAYES

The Green Eye of the Yellow God

There's a one-eyed yellow idol to the north of Khatmandu.
There's a little marble cross below the town;
There's a broken-hearted woman tends the grave of Mad Carew,
And the Yellow God forever gazes down.

He was known as Mad Carew by the subs at Khatmandu,
He was hotter than they felt inclined to tell;
But for all his foolish pranks, he was worshipped in the ranks,
And the Colonel's daughter smiled on him as well.

He had loved her all along, with a passion of the strong,
The fact that she loved him was plain to all.
She was nearly twenty-one and arrangements had begun
To celebrate her birthday with a ball.

He wrote to ask what present she would like from Mad Carew;
They met next day as he dismissed a squad;
And jestingly she told him then that nothing else would do
But the green eye of the little Yellow God.

On the night before the dance, Mad Carew seemed in a trance.
And they chaffed him as they puffed at their cigars;
But for once he failed to smile, and he sat alone awhile,
Then went out into the night beneath the stars.

He returned before the dawn, with his shirt and tunic torn,
And a gash across his temple dripping red;
He was patched up right away, and he slept through all the day,
And the Colonel's daughter watched beside his bed.

He woke at last and asked if they could send his tunic through;
She brought it, and he thanked her with a nod;
He bade her search the pocket saying, 'That's from Mad Carew',
And she found the little green eye of the god.

She upbraided poor Carew in the way that women do,
Though both her eyes were strangely hot and wet;
But she wouldn't take the stone and Mad Carew was left alone
With the jewel that he'd chanced his life to get.

When the ball was at its height, on that still and tropic night,
She thought of him and hastened to his room;

As she crossed the barrack square, she could hear the dreamy air
Of a waltz tune softly stealing through the gloom.

His door was open wide, with silver moonlight shining through;
The place was wet and slippery where she trod;
An ugly knife lay buried in the heart of Mad Carew,
'Twas the 'Vengeance of the Little Yellow God'.·

There's a one-eyed yellow idol to the north of Khatmandu,
There's a little marble cross below the town;
There's a broken-hearted woman tends the grave of Mad Carew,
And the Yellow God forever gazes down.

CHARLOTTE MEW

The Farmer's Bride

Three Summers since I chose a maid,
Too young maybe – but more's to do
At harvest-time than bide and woo.
    When us was wed she turned afraid
Of love and me and all things human;
Like the shut of a winter's day
Her smile went out, and 'twadn't a woman –
    More like a little frightened fay.
    One night, in the Fall, she runned away.

'Out 'mong the sheep, her be,' they said,
'Should properly have been abed;
But sure enough she wadn't there
Lying awake with her wide brown stare.
So over seven-acre field and up-along across the down
    We chased her, flying like a hare
Before our lanterns. To Church-Town
    All in a shiver and a scare
We caught her, fetched her home at last
    And turned the key upon her, fast.

She does the work about the house
As well as most, but like a mouse:
    Happy enough to chat and play
    With birds and rabbits and such as they,
    So long as men-folk keep away.

'Not near, not near!' her eyes beseech
When one of us comes within reach.
  The women say that beasts in stall
  Look round like children at her call.
  I've hardly heard her speak at all.

Shy as a leveret, swift as he,
Straight and slight as a young larch tree,
Sweet as the first wild violets she,
To her wild self. But what to me?

The short days shorten and the oaks are brown,
  The blue smoke rises to the low grey sky,
One leaf in the still air falls slowly down,
  A magpie's spotted feathers lie
On the black earth spread white with rime,
The berries redden up to Christmas-time.
  What's Christmas-time without there be
  Some other in the house than we!

  She sleeps up in the attic there
  Alone, poor maid. 'Tis but a stair
Betwixt us. Oh! my God! the down,
The soft young down of her, the brown,
The brown of her – her eyes, her hair, her hair!

EDWIN ARLINGTON ROBINSON

Mr Flood's Party

Old Eben Flood, climbing alone one night
Over the hill between the town below
And the forsaken upland hermitage
That held as much as he should ever know
On earth again of home, paused warily.
The road was his with not a native near;
And Eben, having leisure, said aloud,
For no man else in Tilbury Town to hear:

'Well, Mr Flood, we have the harvest moon
Again, and we may not have many more;
The bird is on the wing, the poet says
And you and I have said it here before.
Drink to the bird.' He raised up to the light

The jug that he had gone so far to fill,
And answered huskily: 'Well, Mr Flood,
Since you propose it, I believe I will.'
Alone, as if enduring to the end
A valiant armour of scarred hopes outworn,
He stood there in the middle of the road
Like Roland's ghost winding a silent horn.
Below him, in the town among the trees,
Where friends of other days had honoured him,
A phantom salutation of the dead
Rang thinly till old Eben's eyes were dim.

Then, as a mother lays her sleeping child
Down tenderly, fearing it may awake,
He set the jug down slowly at his feet
With trembling care, knowing that most things break;
And only when assured that on firm earth
It stood, as the uncertain lives of men
Assuredly did not, he paced away,
And with his hand extended paused again:

'Well, Mr Flood, we have not met like this
In a long time; and many a change has come
To both of us, I fear, since last it was
We had a drop together. Welcome home!'
Convivially returning with himself,
Again he raised the jug up to the light;
And with an acquiescent quaver said:
'Well, Mr Flood, if you insist, I might.

'Only a very little, Mr Flood –
For auld lang syne. No more, sir; that will do.'
So, for the time, apparently it did,
And Eben evidently thought so too;
For soon amid the silver loneliness
Of night he lifted up his voice and sang,
Secure, with only two moons listening,
Until the whole harmonious landscape rang –

'For auld lang syne.' The weary throat gave out,
The last word wavered, and the song was done.
He raised again the jug regretfully
And shook his head, and was again alone.
There was not much that was ahead of him,
And there was nothing in the town below –
Where strangers would have shut the many doors
That many friends had opened long ago.

HILAIRE BELLOC

Jim
Who Ran Away From His Nurse, and Was Eaten by a Lion

There was a Boy whose name was Jim;
His Friends were very good to him.
They gave him Tea, and Cakes, and Jam,
And slices of delicious Ham,
And Chocolate with pink inside,
And little Tricycles to ride,
And read him Stories through and through,
And even took him to the Zoo –
But there it was the dreadful Fate
Befell him, which I now relate.

You know – at least you ought to know,
For I have often told you so –
That Children never are allowed
To leave their Nurses in a Crowd;
Now this was Jim's especial Foible,
He ran away when he was able,
And on this inauspicious day
He slipped his hand and ran away!
He hadn't gone a yard when – Bang!
With open Jaws, a Lion sprang,
And hungrily began to eat
The Boy: beginning at his feet.

Now, just imagine how it feels
When first your toes and then your heels,
And then by gradual degrees,
Your shins and ankles, calves and knees,
Are slowly eaten, bit by bit.
No wonder Jim detested it!
No wonder that he shouted 'Hi'!
The Honest Keeper heard his cry,
Though very fat he almost ran
To help the little gentleman.
'Ponto!' he ordered as he came
(For Ponto was the Lion's name),
'Ponto!' he cried, with angry Frown.
'Let go, Sir! Down, Sir! Put it down!'

The Lion made a sudden Stop,
He let the Dainty Morsel drop,
And slunk reluctant to his Cage,

Snarling with Disappointed Rage.
But when he bent him over Jim,
The Honest Keeper's Eyes were dim.
The Lion having reached his Head,
The Miserable Boy was dead!
When Nurse informed his Parents, they
Were more Concerned than I can say: –
His Mother, as she dried her eyes,
Said, 'Well – it gives me no surprise,
He would not do as he was told!'
His Father, who was self-controlled,
Bade all the children round attend
To James' miserable end,
And always keep a-hold of Nurse
For fear of finding something worse.

J. M. SYNGE

Danny

One night a score of Erris men,
A score I'm told and nine,
Said, 'We'll get shut of Danny's noise
Of girls and widows dyin'.

'There's not his like from Binghamstown
To Boyle and Ballycroy,
At playing hell on decent girls,
At beating man and boy.

'He's left two pairs of female twins
Beyond in Killacreest,
And twice in Crossmolina fair
He's struck the parish priest.

'But we'll come round him in the night
A mile beyond the Mullet;
Ten will quench his bloody eyes,
And ten will choke his gullet.'

It wasn't long till Danny came,
From Bangor making way,
And he was damning moon and stars
And whistling grand and gay.

Till in a gap of hazel glen –
And not a hare in sight –
Out lepped the nine-and-twenty lads
Along his left and right.

Then Danny smashed the nose on Byrne,
He split the lips on three,
And bit across the right-hand thumb
On one Red Shawn Magee.

But seven tripped him up behind,
And seven kicked before,
And seven squeezed around his throat
Till Danny kicked no more.

Then some destroyed him with their heels,
Some tramped him in the mud,
Some stole his purse and timber pipe,
And some washed off his blood.

And when you're walking out the way
From Bangor to Belmullet,
You'll see a flat cross on a stone,
Where men choked Danny's gullet.

G. K. CHESTERTON

Lepanto

White founts falling in the Courts of the sun,
And the Soldan of Byzantium is smiling as they run;
There is laughter like the fountains in that face of all men feared,
It stirs the forest darkness, the darkness of his beard,
It curls the blood-red crescent, the crescent of his lips,
For the inmost sea of all the earth is shaken with his ships.
They have dared the white republics up the capes of Italy,
They have dashed the Adriatic round the Lion of the Sea,
And the Pope has cast his arms abroad for agony and loss,
And called the kings of Christendom for swords about the Cross.
The cold queen of England is looking in the glass,
The shadow of the Valois is yawning at the Mass;
From evening isles fantastical rings faint the Spanish gun,
And the Lord upon the Golden Horn is laughing in the sun.

Dim drums throbbing, in the hills half heard,
Where only on a nameless throne a crownless prince has stirred,
Where, risen from a doubtful seat and half attainted stall,
The last knight of Europe takes weapons from the wall,
The last and lingering troubadour to whom the bird has sung,
That once went singing southward when all the world was young.
In that enormous silence, tiny and unafraid,
Comes up along a winding road the noise of the Crusade.
Strong gongs groaning as the guns boom far,
Don John of Austria is going to the war,
Stiff flags straining in the night-blasts cold
In the gloom black-purple, in the glint old-gold,
Torchlight crimson on the copper kettle-drums,
Then the tuckets, then the trumpets, then the cannon, and he comes.
Don John laughing in the brave beard curled,
Spurning of his stirrups like the thrones of all the world,
Holding his head up for a flag of all the free.
Love-light of Spain – hurrah!
Deathlight of Africa!
Don John of Austria
Is riding to the sea.

Mahound is in his paradise above the evening star,
(*Don John of Austria is going to the war.*)
He moves a mighty turban on the timeless houri's knees,
His turban that is woven of the sunsets and the seas.
He shakes the peacock gardens as he rises from his ease,
And he strides among the tree-tops and is taller than the trees,
And his voice through all the garden is a thunder sent to bring
Black Azrael and Ariel and Ammon on the wing.
Giants and the Genii,
Multiplex of wing and eye,
Whose strong obedience broke the sky
When Solomon was king.

They rush in red and purple from the red clouds of the morn,
From temples where the yellow gods shut up their eyes in scorn;
They rise in green robes roaring from the green hells of the sea
Where fallen skies and evil hues and eyeless creatures be;
On them the sea-valves cluster and the grey sea-forests curl,
Splashed with a splendid sickness, the sickness of the pearl;
They swell in sapphire smoke out of the blue cracks of the ground –
They gather and they wonder and give worship to Mahound.
And he saith, 'Break up the mountains where the hermit-folk can
        hide,
And sift the red and silver sands lest bone of saint abide,
And chase the Giaours flying night and day, not giving rest,

For that which was our trouble comes again out of the west.
We have set the seal of Solomon on all things under sun,
Of knowledge and of sorrow and endurance of things done;
But a noise is in the mountains, in the mountains, and I know
The voice that shook our palaces – four hundred years ago:
It is he that saith not 'Kismet'; it is he that knows not Fate;
It is Richard, it is Raymond, it is Godfrey in the gate!
It is he whose loss is laughter when he counts the wager worth:
Put down your feet upon him, that our peace be on the earth.'
For he heard drums groaning and he heard guns jar,
(*Don John of Austria is going to the war.*)
Sudden and still – hurrah!
Bolt from Iberia!
Don John of Austria
Is gone by Alcalar.

St Michael's on his Mountain in the sea-roads of the north
(*Don John of Austria is girt and going forth.*)
Where the grey seas glitter and the sharp tides shift
And the sea-folk labour and the red sails lift.
He shakes his lance of iron and he claps his wings of stone;
The noise is gone through Normandy; the noise is gone alone;
The North is full of tangled things and texts and aching eyes,
And dead is all the innocence of anger and surprise,
And Christian killeth Christian in a narrow dusty room,
And Christian dreadeth Christ that hath a newer face of doom,
And Christian hateth Mary that God kissed in Galilee,
But Don John of Austria is riding to the sea.
Don John calling through the blast and the eclipse,
Crying with the trumpet, with the trumpet of his lips,
Trumpet that sayeth ha!
Domino gloria!
Don John of Austria
Is shouting to the ships.

King Philip's in his closet with the Fleece about his neck,
(*Don John of Austria is armed upon the deck.*)
The walls are hung with velvet that is black and soft as sin,
And little dwarfs creep out of it and little dwarfs creep in.
He holds a crystal phial that has colours like the moon,
He touches, and it tingles, and he trembles very soon,
And his face is as a fungus of a leprous white and grey,
Like plants in the high houses that are shuttered from the day,
And death is in the phial, and the end of noble work,
But Don John of Austria has fired upon the Turk.
Don John's hunting, and his hounds have bayed –
Booms away past Italy the rumour of his raid.

Gun upon gun, ha! ha!
Gun upon gun, hurrah!
Don John of Austria
Has loosed the cannonade.

The Pope was in his chapel before day or battle broke
(*Don John of Austria is hidden in the smoke.*)
The hidden room in man's house where God sits all the year,
The secret window whence the world looks small and very dear.
He sees as in a mirror on the monstrous twilight sea
The crescent of his cruel ships whose name is mystery;
They fling great shadows foe-wards, making Cross and Castle dark;
They veil the plumed lions on the galleys of St Mark;
And above the ships are palaces of brown, black-bearded chiefs,
And below the ships are prisons, where with multitudinous griefs,
Christian captives sick and sunless, all a labouring race repines
Like a race in sunken cities, like a nation in the mines.
They are lost like slaves that swat, and in the skies of morning hung
The stairways of the tallest gods when tyranny was young.
They are countless, voiceless, hopeless as those fallen or fleeing on
Before the high Kings' horses in the granite of Babylon.
And many a one grows witless in his quiet room in hell,
Where a yellow face looks inward through the lattice of his cell,
And he finds his God forgotten, and he seeks no more a sign –
(*But Don John of Austria has burst the battle line!*)
Don John pounding from the slaughter-painted poop,
Purpling all the ocean like a bloody pirate's sloop,
Scarlet running over on the silvers and the golds,
Breaking of the hatches up and bursting of the holds,
Thronging of the thousands up that labour under sea,
White for bliss and blind for sun and stunned for liberty.
Vivat Hispania!
Domino gloria!
Don John of Austria
Has set his people free!

Cervantes on his galley sets the sword back in the sheath,
(*Don John of Austria rides homeward with a wreath.*)
And he sees across a weary land a straggling road in Spain,
Up which a lean and foolish knight forever rides in vain,
And he smiles, but not as Sultans smile, and settles back the
    blade . . .
(*But Don John of Austria rides home from the Crusade.*)

HARRY GRAHAM

Breakfast

The perfect breakfast, all must own,
Is that which man enjoys alone;
Peace, perfect peace, is found, they say,
Only with loved ones far away,
And there is naught but solitude
That suits the matutinal mood.
But there, alas! are tactless folk
Who choose that hour to jest and joke,
Whose conversation, brisk and bright,
Just bearable perhaps at night,
Fills with intolerable gloom
The self-respecting breakfast-room.
Thus, as I verily suspect,
Are many happy households wrecked;
So when you break your morning fast
Let no one share that first repast!

Dean Cope, the eminent divine,
Was breakfasting at half-past nine,
Perusing (as he munched his toast)
'The Anglican or Churchman's Post',
When in there blew, to his distress,
The Bishop of the Diocese
(Most typical in size and girth
Of the Church Militant on Earth)
Who shouted 'Cheerio, old chap!'
And gave the Dean a playful slap.
Alas! What ill-timed *bonhomie*!
The Dean inhaled his kedjeree,
And turning, with his face all black,
He slapped the breezy Bishop back!
Both lost their tempers there and then,
And in a trice these holy men
Began (with the most unholy zeal)
To throw the remnants of the meal
At one another! Buttered eggs
Bespattered aprons, gaitered legs
Were splashed with bacon; bits of sole
Fell thick on cassock, alb, and stole!
The dining-room became a sea
Of struggling Christianity,
And when at last the luckless Dean

Slipped on a pat of margarine,
The Bishop took a careful shot
And brained him with the mustard-pot!
A sight to make the angels weep!
How scandalized the local sheep
Who read descriptions of the scene
In ev'ry Parish Magazine!

The Diocese was deeply shocked;
The Dean, degraded and unfrocked,
Found refuge in a City slum,
Lay-reader to the Deaf and Dumb!
The Bishop lost his see, and sank
To rural Prebendary's rank!
No longer in his breezy way
He reads the Collect for the Day,
Or chants what proper hymns there be
For those of Riper Years at Sea!
At Matins and at Evensong
His cry goes up: 'How long! How long!'
His groans are heard through aisle and apse
Bewailing his untimely lapse,
As he repents him of the crime
Of being bright at breakfast time.

ROBERT SERVICE

The Shooting of Dan McGrew

A bunch of boys were whooping it up in the Malamute saloon;
The kid that handles the music-box was hitting a rag-time tune;
Back of the bar, in a solo game, sat Dangerous Dan McGrew,
And watching his luck was his light-o'-love, the lady that's known as
    Lou.

When out of the night, which was fifty below, and into the din and
    the glare,
There stumbled a miner fresh from the creeks, dog-dirty and loaded
    for bear.
He looked like a man with a foot in the grave, and scarcely the
    strength of a louse,
Yet he tilted a poke of dust on the bar, and he called for drinks for the
    house.

There was none could place the stranger's face, though we searched
 ourselves for a clue;
But we drank his health, and the last to drink was Dangerous Dan
 McGrew.

There's men that somehow just grip your eyes, and hold them hard
 like a spell;
And such was he, and he looked to me like a man who had lived in
 hell;
With a face most hair, and the dreary stare of a dog whose day is
 done,
As he watered the green stuff in his glass, and the drops fell one by
 one.
Then I got to figgering who he was, and wondering what he'd do,
And I turned my head – and there watching him was the lady that's
 known as Lou.

His eyes went rubbering round the room, and he seemed in a kind of
 daze,
Till at last that old piano fell in the way of his wandering gaze.
The rag-time kid was having a drink; there was no one else on the
 stool,
So the stranger stumbles across the room, and flops down there like a
 fool.
In a buckskin shirt that was glazed with dirt he sat, and I saw him
 sway;
Then he clutched the keys with his talon hands – my God! but that
 man could play!

Were you ever out in the Great Alone, when the moon was awful
 clear,
And the icy mountains hemmed you in with a silence you most could
 hear;
With only the howl of a timber wolf, and you camped there in the
 cold,
A half-dead thing in a stark, dead world, clean made for the muck
 called gold;
While high overhead, green, yellow, and red, the North Lights swept
 in bars –
Then you've a hunch what the music meant . . . hunger and night
 and the stars.

And hunger not of the belly kind, that's banished with bacon and
 beans;
But the gnawing hunger of lonely men for a home and all that it
 means;
For a fireside far from the cares that are, four walls and a roof above;

But oh! so cramful of cosy joy, and crowned with a woman's love;
A woman dearer than all the world, and true as Heaven is true –
(God! how ghastly she looks through her rouge – the lady that's
    known as Lou.)

Then on a sudden the music changed, so soft that you scarce could
    hear;
But you felt that your life had been looted clean of all that it once
    held dear;
That some-one had stolen the woman you loved; that her love was a
    devil's lie;
That your guts were gone, and the best for you was to crawl away
    and die.
'Twas the crowning cry of a heart's despair, and it thrilled you
    through and through –
'I guess I'll make it a spread misere,' said Dangerous Dan McGrew.

The music almost died away . . . then it burst like a pent-up flood;
And it seemed to say, 'Repay, repay,' and my eyes were blind with
    blood.
The thought came back of an ancient wrong, and it stung like a
    frozen lash,
And the lust awoke to kill, to kill . . . then the music stopped with a
    crash,

And the stranger turned, and his eyes they burned in a most peculiar
    way;
In a buckskin shirt that was glazed with dirt he sat, and I saw him
    sway;
Then his lips went in in a kind of grin, and he spoke, and his voice
    was calm;
And, 'Boys,' says he, 'you don't know me, and none of you care a
    damn;
But I want to state, and my words are straight and I'll bet my poke
    they're true,
That one of you is a hound of hell . . . and that one is Dan McGrew.'

Then I ducked my head, and the lights went out, and two guns
    blazed in the dark;
And a woman screamed, and the lights went up, and two men lay
    stiff and stark;
Pitched on his head, and pumped full of lead, was Dangerous Dan
    McGrew,
While the man from the creeks lay clutched to the breast of the lady
    that's known as Lou.

These are the simple facts of the case, and I guess I ought to know;

They say that the stranger was crazed with 'hooch', and I'm not
    denying it's so.
I'm not so wise as the lawyer guys, but strictly between us two –
The woman that kissed him and – pinched his poke – was the lady
    that's known as Lou.

ROBERT FROST

Paul's Wife

To drive Paul out of any lumber camp
All that was needed was to say to him,
'How is the wife, Paul?' – and he'd disappear.
Some said it was because he had no wife,
And hated to be twitted on the subject;
Others because he'd come within a day
Or so of having one, and then been jilted;
Others because he'd had one once, a good one,
Who'd run away with someone else and left him;
And others still because he had one now
He only had to be reminded of, –
He was all duty to her in a minute:
He had to run right off to look her up,
As if to say, 'That's so, how is my wife?
I hope she isn't getting into mischief.'
No one was anxious to get rid of Paul.
He'd been the hero of the mountain camps
Ever since, just to show them, he had slipped
The bark of a whole tamarack off whole,
As clean as boys do off a willow twig
To make a willow whistle on a Sunday
In April by subsiding meadow brooks.
They seemed to ask him just to see him go,
'How is the wife, Paul?' and he always went.
He never stopped to murder anyone
Who asked the question. He just disappeared –
Nobody knew in what direction,
Although it wasn't usually long
Before they heard of him in some new camp,
The same Paul at the same old feats of logging.
The question everywhere was why should Paul
Object to being asked a civil question –
A man you could say almost anything to
Short of a fighting word. You have the answers.

And there was one more not so fair to Paul:
That Paul had married a wife not his equal.
Paul was ashamed of her. To match a hero,
She would have had to be a heroine;
Instead of which she was some half-breed squaw.
But if the story Murphy told was true,
She wasn't anything to be ashamed of.

You know Paul could do wonders. Everyone's
Heard how he thrashed the horses on a load
That wouldn't budge until they simply stretched
Their rawhide harness from the load to camp.
Paul told the boss the load would be all right,
'The sun will bring your load in' – and it did –
By shrinking the rawhide to natural length.
That's what is called a stretcher. But I guess
The one about his jumping so's to land
With both his feet at once against the ceiling,
And then land safely right side up again,
Back on the floor, is fact or pretty near fact.
Well, this is such a yarn. Paul sawed his wife
Out of a white-pine log. Murphy was there,
And, as you might say, saw the lady born.
Paul worked at anything in lumbering.
He'd been hard at it taking boards away
For – I forget – the last ambitious sawyer
To want to find out if he couldn't pile
The lumber on Paul till Paul begged for mercy.
They'd sliced the first slab off a big butt log,
And the sawyer had slammed the carriage back
To slam end on again against the saw teeth.
To judge them by the way they caught themselves
When they saw what had happened to the log,
They must have had a guilty expectation
Something was going to go with their slambanging.
Something had left a broad black streak of grease
On the new wood the whole length of the log
Except, perhaps, a foot at either end.
But when Paul put his finger in the grease,
It wasn't grease at all, but a long slot.
The log was hollow. They were sawing pine.
'First time I ever saw a hollow pine.
That comes of having Paul around the place.
Take it to hell for me,' the sawyer said.
Everyone had to have a look at it,
And tell Paul what he ought to do about it.
(They treated it as his.) 'You take a jack-knife,

And spread the opening, and you've got a dug-out
All dug to go a-fishing in.' To Paul
The hollow looked too sound and clean and empty
Ever to have housed birds or beasts or bees.
There was no entrance for them to get in by.
It looked to him like some new kind of hollow
He thought he'd *better* take his jack-knife to.
So after work that evening he came back
And let enough light into it by cutting
To see if it was empty. He made out in there
A slender length of pith, or was it pith?
It might have been the skin a snake had cast
And left stood up on end inside the tree
The hundred years the tree must have been growing.
More cutting and he had this in both hands,
And, looking from it to the pond nearby,
Paul wondered how it would respond to water.
Not a breeze stirred, but just the breath of air
He made in walking slowly to the beach
Blew it once off his hands and almost broke it.
He laid it at the edge where it could drink.
At the first drink it rustled and grew limp.
At the next drink it grew invisible.
Paul dragged the shallows for it with his fingers,
And thought it must have melted. It was gone.
And then beyond the open water, dim with midges,
Where the log drive lay pressed against the boom,
It slowly rose a person, rose a girl,
Her wet hair heavy on her like a helmet,
Who, leaning on a log looked back at Paul.
And that made Paul in turn look back
To see if it was anyone behind him
That she was looking at instead of him.
Murphy had been there watching all the time,
But from a shed where neither of them could see him.
There was a moment of suspense in birth
When the girl seemed too water-logged to live,
Before she caught her first breath with a gasp
And laughed. Then she climbed slowly to her feet,
And walked off talking to herself or Paul
Across the logs like backs of alligators,
Paul taking after her around the pond.

Next evening Murphy and some other fellows
Got drunk, and tracked the pair up Catamount,
From the bare top of which there is a view
To other hills across a kettle valley.

And there, well after dark, let Murphy tell it,
They saw Paul and his creature keeping house.
It was the only glimpse that anyone
Has had of Paul and her since Murphy saw them
Falling in love across the twilight mill-pond.
More than a mile across the wilderness
They sat together halfway up a cliff
In a small niche let into it, the girl
Brightly, as if a star played on the place,
Paul darkly, like her shadow. All the light
Was from the girl herself, though, not from a star,
As was apparent from what happened next.
All those great ruffians put their throats together,
And let out a loud yell, and threw a bottle,
As a brute tribute of respect to beauty.
Of course the bottle fell short by a mile,
But the shout reached the girl and put her light out.
She went out like a firefly, and that was all.

So there were witnesses that Paul was married,
And not to anyone to be ashamed of.
Everyone had been wrong in judging Paul.
Murphy told me Paul put on all those airs
About his wife to keep her to himself.
Paul was what's called a terrible possessor.
Owning a wife with him meant owning her.
She wasn't anybody else's business,
Either to praise her, or so much as name her,
And he'd thank people not to think of her.
Murphy's idea was that a man like Paul
Wouldn't be spoken to about a wife
In any way the world knew how to speak.

OLIVER ST JOHN GOGARTY

Leda and the Swan

Though her mother told her
    Not to go a-bathing,
Leda loved the river
    And she could not keep away:
Wading in its freshets
    When the noon was heavy;
Walking by the water
    At the close of day.

Where between its waterfalls,
  Underneath the beeches,
Gently flows a broader
  Hardly moving stream,
And the balanced trout lie
  In the quiet reaches;
Taking all her clothes off,
  Leda went to swim.

There was not a flag-leaf
  By the river's margin
That might be a shelter
  From a passer-by;
And a sudden whiteness
  In the quiet darkness,
Let alone the splashing,
  Was enough to catch an eye.

But the place was lonely,
  And her clothes were hidden;
Even cattle walking
  In the ford had gone away;
Every single farm-hand
  Sleeping after dinner, –
What's the use of talking?
  There was no one in the way.

In, without a stitch on,
  Peaty water yielded,
Till her head was lifted
  With its ropes of hair;
It was more surprising
  Than a lily gilded,
Just to see how golden
  Was her body there:

Lolling in the water,
  Lazily uplifting
Limbs that on the surface
  Whitened into snow;
Leaning on the water,
  Indolently drifting,
Hardly any faster
  Than the foamy bubbles go.

You would say to see her
  Swimming in the lonely
Pool, or after, dryer,
  Putting on her clothes:
'O but she is lovely,
  Not a soul to see her,
And how lovely only
  Leda's mother knows!'

Under moving branches
  Leisurely she dresses,
And the leafy sunlight
  Made you wonder were
All its woven shadows
  But her golden tresses,
Or a smock of sunlight
  For her body bare.

When on earth great beauty
  Goes exempt from danger,
It will be endangered
  From a source on high;
When unearthly stillness
  Falls on leaves, the ranger,
In his wood-lore anxious,
  Gazes at the sky.

While her hair was drying,
  Came a gentle languor,
Whether from the bathing
  Or the breeze she didn't know.
Anyway she lay there,
  And her mother's anger
(Worse if she had wet hair)
  Could not make her dress and go.

Whitest of all earthly
  Things, the white that's rarest,
Is the snow on mountains
  Standing in the sun;
Next the clouds above them,
  Then the down is fairest
On the breast and pinions
  Of a proudly sailing swan.

And she saw him sailing
  On the pool where lately

She had stretched unnoticed,
  As she thought, and swum;
And she never wondered
  Why, erect and stately,
Where no river weed was
  Such a bird had come.

What was it she called him:
  Goosey-goosey gander?
For she knew no better
  Way to call a swan;
And the bird responding
  Seemed to understand her,
For he left his sailing
  For the bank to waddle on.

Apple blossoms under
  Hills of Lacedaemon,
With the snow beyond them
  In the still blue air,
To the swan who hid them
  With his wings asunder,
Than the breasts of Leda,
  Were not lovelier!

Of the tales that daughters
  Tell their poor old mothers,
Which by all accounts are
  Often very odd:
Leda's was a story
  Stranger than all others.
What was there to say but:
  Glory be to God?

And she half-believed her,
  For she knew her daughter;
And she saw the swan-down
  Tangled in her hair.
Though she knew how deeply
  Runs the stillest water,
How could she protect her
  From the winged air?

Why is it effects are
  Greater than their causes?
Why should causes often
  Differ from effects?

Why should what is lovely
    Fill the world with hardness?
And the most deceived be
    She who least suspects?

When the hyacinthine
    Eggs were in the basket,
Blue as at the whiteness
    Where a cloud begins;
Who would dream there lay there
    All that Trojan brightness;
Agamemnon murdered;
    And the mighty Twins?

JOHN MASEFIELD

From *Reynard the Fox*

[THE RUN TO MOURNE END WOOD]

The ducks flew up from the Morton Pond;
The fox looked up at their tailing strings,
He wished (perhaps) that a fox had wings.
Wings with his friends in a great V straining
The autumn sky when the moon is gaining;
For better the grey sky's solitude
Than to be two miles from the Mourne End Wood
With the hounds behind, clean-trained to run,
And your strength half spent and your breath half done.
Better the reeds and the sky and water
Than that hopeless pad from a certain slaughter.
At the Morton Pond the fields began –
Long Tew's green meadows; he ran, he ran.

First the six green fields that make a mile,
With the lip-ful Clench at the side the while,
With rooks above, slow-circling, showing
The world of men where a fox was going;
The fields all empty, dead grass, bare hedges,
And the brook's bright gleam in the dark of sedges.
To all things else he was dumb and blind;
He ran with the hounds a field behind.

At the sixth green field came the long slow climb

To the Mourne End Wood, as old as time;
Yew woods dark, where they cut for bows,
Oak woods green with the mistletoes,
Dark woods evil, but burrowed deep
With a brock's earth strong, where a fox might sleep.
He saw his point on the heaving hill,
He had failing flesh and a reeling will;
He felt the heave of the hill grow stiff,
He saw black woods, which would shelter – if
Nothing else, but the steepening slope
And a black line nodding, a line of hope –
The line of the yews on the long slope's brow,
A mile, three-quarters, a half-mile now.

A quarter-mile, but the hounds had viewed;
They yelled to have him this side the wood.
Robin capped them, Tom Dansey steered them;
With a 'Yooi! Yooi! Yooi' Bill Ridden cheered them.
Then up went hackles as Shatterer led.
'Mob him!' cried Ridden, 'the wood's ahead.
Turn him, damn it! Yooi! beauties, beat him!
O God, let them get him: let them eat him!
O God!' said Ridden, 'I'll eat him stewed,
If you'll let us get him this side the wood.'

But the pace, uphill, made a horse like stone;
The pack went wild up the hill alone.

Three hundred yards and the worst was past,
The slope was gentler and shorter-grassed;
The fox saw the bulk of the woods grow tall
On the brae ahead, like a barrier-wall.
He saw the skeleton trees show sky
And the yew-trees darken to see him die,
And the line of the woods go reeling back:
There was hope in the woods – and behind, the pack.

Two hundred yards and the trees grew taller,
Blacker, blinder, as hope grew smaller;
Cry seemed nearer, the teeth seemed gripping,
Pulling him back; his pads seemed slipping.
He was all one ache, one gasp, one thirsting,
Heart on his chest-bones, beating, bursting;
The hounds were gaining like spotted pards,
And the wood hedge still was a hundred yards.

The wood hedge black was a two-year, quick

Cut-and-laid that had sprouted thick
Thorns all over and strongly plied,
With a clean red ditch on the take-off side.

He saw it now as a redness, topped
With a wattle of thorn-work spiky cropped,
Spiky to leap on, stiff to force,
No safe jump for a failing horse;
But beyond it darkness of yews together,
Dark green plumes over soft brown feather,
Darkness of woods where scents were blowing –
Strange scents, hot scents, of wild things going,
Scents that might draw these hounds away.
So he ran, ran, ran to that clean red clay.

Still, as he ran, his pads slipped back,
All his strength seemed to draw the pack,
The trees drew over him dark like Norns,
He was over the ditch and at the thorns.

He thrust at the thorns, which would not yield;
He leaped, but fell, in sight of the field.
The hounds went wild as they saw him fall,
The fence stood stiff like a Bucks flint wall.

He gathered himself for a new attempt;
His life before was an old dream dreamt,
All that he was was a blown fox quaking,
Jumping at thorns too stiff for breaking,
While over the grass in crowd, in cry,
Came the grip teeth grinning to make him die,
The eyes intense, dull, smouldering red,
The fell like a ruff round each keen head,
The pace like fire, and scarlet men
Galloping, yelling, 'Yooi, eat him, then!'

He gathered himself, he leaped, he reached
The top of the hedge like a fish-boat beached.
He steadied a second and then leaped down
To the dark of the wood where bright things drown.

ALFRED NOYES

The Highwayman

I

The wind was a torrent of darkness among the gusty trees,
The moon was a ghostly galleon tossed upon cloudy seas,
The road was a ribbon of moonlight over the purple moor,
And the highwayman came riding –
      Riding – riding –
The highwayman came riding, up to the old inn-door.

He'd a French cocked-hat on his forehead, a bunch of lace at his chin,
A coat of claret velvet, and breeches of brown doe-skin;
They fitted with never a wrinkle: his boots were up to the thigh!
And he rode with a jewelled twinkle,
      His pistol butts a-twinkle,
His rapier hilt a-twinkle, under the jewelled sky.

Over the cobbles he clattered and clashed in the dark inn-yard,
And he tapped with his whip on the shutters, but all was locked and
    barred;
He whistled a tune to the window, and who should be waiting there
But the landlord's black-eyed daughter,
      Bess, the landlord's daughter,
Plaiting a dark red love-knot into her long black hair.

And dark in the old inn-yard a stable-wicket creaked
Where Tim the ostler listened; his face was white and peaked;
His eyes were hollows of madness, his hair like mouldy hay,
But he loved the landlord's daughter,
      The landlord's red-lipped daughter; –
Dumb as a dog he listened, and he heard the robber say –

'One kiss, my bonny sweetheart, I'm after a prize tonight,
But I shall be back with the yellow gold before the morning light;
Yet, if they press me sharply, and harry me through the day,
Then look for me by moonlight,
      Watch for me by moonlight,
I'll come to thee by moonlight, though hell should bar the way.'

He rose upright in the stirrups; he scarce could reach her hand,
But she loosened her hair i' the casement! His face burnt like a brand
As the black cascade of perfume came tumbling over his breast;
And he kissed its waves in the moonlight,
      (Oh, sweet black waves in the moonlight!)

Then he tugged at his rein in the moonlight, and galloped away to
  the west.

II

He did not come in the dawning; he did not come at noon;
And out o' the tawny sunset, before the rise o' the moon,
When the road was a gipsy's ribbon, looping the purple moor,
A red-coat troop came marching –
        Marching – marching –
King George's men came marching, up to the old inn-door.

They said no word to the landlord, they drank his ale instead,
But they gagged his daughter and bound her to the foot of her
  narrow bed;
Two of them knelt at her casement, with muskets at their side!
There was death at every window;
        And hell at one dark window;
For Bess could see, through her casement, the road that he would
  ride.

They had tied her up to attention, with many a sniggering jest,
They had bound a musket beside her, with the barrel beneath her
  breast!
'Now keep good watch!' and they kissed her.
        She heard the dead man say –
Look for me by moonlight;
        Watch for me by moonlight;
I'll come to thee by moonlight, though hell should bar the way!

She twisted her hands behind her; but all the knots held good!
She writhed her hands till her fingers were wet with sweat or blood!
They stretched and strained in the darkness, and the hours crawled by
  like years,
Till, now, on the stroke of midnight,
        Cold, on the stroke of midnight,
The tip of one finger touched it! The trigger at least was hers!

The tip of one finger touched it; she strove no more for the rest!
Up, she stood to attention, with the barrel beneath her breast,
She would not risk their hearing; she would not strive again;
For the road lay bare in the moonlight;
        Blank and bare in the moonlight;
And the blood of her veins in the moonlight throbbed to her love's
  refrain.

Tlot-tlot; tlot-tlot! Had they heard it? The horse-hoofs ringing clear;

Tlot-tlot, tlot-tlot, in the distance? Were they deaf that they did not
   hear?
Down the ribbon of moonlight, over the brow of the hill,
The highwayman came riding,
         Riding, riding!
The red-coats looked to their priming! She stood up, straight and still!

Tlot-tlot, in the frosty silence! *tlot-tlot*, in the echoing night!
Nearer he came and nearer! Her face was like a light!
Her eyes grew wide for a moment; she drew one last deep breath,
Then her finger moved in the moonlight,
         Her musket shattered the moonlight,
Shattered her breast in the moonlight and warned him – with her
   death.

He turned; he spurred to the westward; he did not know who stood
Bowed, with her head o'er the musket, drenched with her own red
   blood!
Not till the dawn he heard it, and slowly blanched to hear
How Bess, the landlord's daughter,
         The landlord's black-eyed daughter,
Had watched for her love in the moonlight, and died in the darkness
   there.

Back, he spurred like a madman, shrieking a curse to the sky,
With the white road smoking behind him and his rapier brandished
   high!
Blood-red were his spurs i' the golden noon; wine-red was his velvet
   coat;
When they shot him down on the highway,
         Down like a dog on the highway,
And he lay in his blood on the highway, with the bunch of lace at his
   throat.

And still of a winter's night, they say, when the wind is in the trees,
When the moon is a ghostly galleon tossed upon cloudy seas,
When the road is a ribbon of moonlight over the purple moor,
A highwayman comes riding –
         Riding – riding –
A highwayman comes riding, up to the old inn-door.

Over the cobbles he clatters and clangs in the dark inn-yard,
And he taps with his whip on the shutters, but all is locked and barred;
He whistles a tune to the window, and who should be waiting there
But the landlord's black-eyed daughter,
         Bess, the landlord's daughter,
Plaiting a dark red love-knot into her long black hair.

D. H. LAWRENCE

Snake

A snake came to my water-trough
On a hot, hot day, and I in pyjamas for the heat,
To drink there.

In the deep, strange-scented shade of the great dark carob-tree
I came down the steps with my pitcher
And must wait, must stand and wait, for there he was at the trough
    before me.

He reached down from a fissure in the earth-wall in the gloom
And trailed his yellow-brown slackness soft-bellied down, over the
    edge of the stone trough
And rested his throat upon the stone bottom,
And where the water had dripped from the tap, in a small clearness,
He sipped with his straight mouth,
Softly drank through his straight gums, into his slack long body,
Silently.

Someone was before me at my water-trough,
And I, like a second comer, waiting.

He lifted his head from his drinking, as cattle do,
And looked at me vaguely, as drinking cattle do,
And flickered his two-forked tongue from his lips, and mused a
    moment,
And stooped and drank a little more,
Being earth-brown, earth-golden from the burning bowels of the
    earth
On the day of Sicilian July, with Etna smoking.

The voice of my education said to me
He must be killed,
For in Sicily the black, black snakes are innocent, the gold are
    venomous.

And voices in me said, If you were a man
You would take a stick and break him now, and finish him off.

But must I confess how I liked him,
How glad I was he had come like a guest in quiet, to drink at my
    water-trough
And depart peaceful, pacified, and thankless,
Into the burning bowels of this earth?

Was it cowardice, that I dared not kill him?
Was it perversity, that I longed to talk to him?
Was it humility, to feel so honoured?
I felt so honoured.

And yet those voices:
If you were not afraid, you would kill him!

And truly I was afraid, I was most afraid,
But even so, honoured still more
That he should seek my hospitality
From out the dark door of the secret earth.

He drank enough
And lifted his head, dreamily, as one who has drunken,
And flickered his tongue like a forked night on the air, so black,
Seeming to lick his lips,
And looked around like a god, unseeing, into the air,
And slowly turned his head,
And slowly, very slowly, as if thrice adream,
Proceeded to draw his slow length curving round
And climb again the broken bank of my wall-face.

And as he put his head into that dreadful hole,
And as he slowly drew up, snake-easing his shoulders, and entered farther,
A sort of horror, a sort of protest against his withdrawing into that
    horrid black hole,
Deliberately going into the blackness, and slowly drawing himself after,
Overcame me now his back was turned.

I looked round, I put down my pitcher,
I picked up a clumsy log
And threw it at the water-trough with a clatter.

I think it did not hit him,
But suddenly that part of him that was left behind convulsed in
    undignified haste,
Writhed like lightning, and was gone
Into the black hole, the earth-lipped fissure in the wall-front,
At which, in the intense still noon, I stared with fascination.

And immediately I regretted it.
I thought how paltry, how vulgar, what a mean act!
I despised myself and the voices of my accursed human education.
And I thought of the albatross,
And I wished he would come back, my snake.

For he seemed to me again like a king,
Like a king in exile, uncrowned in the underworld,
Now due to be crowned again.

And so, I missed my chance with one of the lords
Of life.
And I have something to expiate;
A pettiness.

MURIEL STUART

In the Orchard

'I thought you loved me.' 'No, it was only fun.'
'When we stood there, closer than all?' 'Well, the harvest moon
Was shining and queer in your hair, and it turned my head.'
'That made you?' 'Yes.' 'Just the moon and the light it made
Under the tree?' 'Well, your mouth, too.' 'Yes, my mouth?'
'And the quiet there that sang like the drum in the booth.
You shouldn't have danced like that.' 'Like what?' 'So close,
With your head turned up, and the flower in your hair, a rose
That smelt all warm.' 'I loved you. I thought you knew
I wouldn't have danced like that with any but you.'
'I didn't know. I thought you knew it was fun.'
'I thought it was love you meant.' 'Well, it's done.' 'Yes, it's done.
I've seen boys stone a blackbird, and watched them drown
A kitten . . . it clawed at the reeds, and they pushed it down
Into the pool while it screamed. Is that fun, too?'
'Well, boys are like that . . . Your brothers . . .' 'Yes, I know.
But you, so lovely and strong! Not you! Not you!'
'They don't understand it's cruel. It's only a game.'
'And are girls fun, too?' 'No, still in a way it's the same.
It's queer and lovely to have a girl . . .' 'Go on.'
'It makes you mad for a bit to feel she's your own,
And you laugh and kiss her, and maybe you give her a ring,
But it's only in fun.' 'But I gave you everything.'
'Well, you shouldn't have done it. You know what a fellow thinks
When a girl does that.' 'Yes, he talks of her over his drinks
And calls her a – ' 'Stop that now. I thought you knew.'
'But it wasn't with anyone else. It was only you.'
'How did I know? I thought you wanted it too.
I thought you were like the rest. Well, what's to be done?'
'To be done?' 'Is it all right?' 'Yes.' 'Sure?' 'Yes, but why?'
'I don't know. I thought you were going to cry.

You said you had something to tell me.' 'Yes, I know.
It wasn't anything really . . . I think I'll go.'
'Yes, it's late. There's thunder about, a drop of rain
Fell on my hand in the dark. I'll see you again
At the dance next week. You're sure that everything's right?'
'Yes.' 'Well, I'll be going.' 'Kiss me . . .' 'Good night.' . . . 'Good
    night.'

WILFRED OWEN

The Sentry

We'd found an old Boche dug-out, and he knew,
And gave us hell, for shell on frantic shell
Hammered on top, but never quite burst through.
Rain, guttering down in waterfalls of slime
Kept slush waist-high that, rising hour by hour,
Choked up the steps too thick with clay to climb.
What murk of air remained stank old, and sour
With fumes of whizz-bangs, and the smell of men
Who'd lived there years, and left their curse in the den,
If not their corpses. . . .
                There we herded from the blast
Of whizz-bangs, but one found our door at last, –
Buffeting eyes and breath, snuffing the candles.
And thud! flump! thud! down the steep steps came thumping
And splashing in the flood, deluging muck –
The sentry's body; then, his rifle, handles
Of old Boche bombs, and mud in ruck on ruck.
We dredged him up, for killed, until he whined,

'O sir, my eyes – I'm blind – I'm blind, I'm blind!'
Coaxing, I held a flame against his lids
And said if he could see the least blurred light
He was not blind; in time he'd get all right.
'I can't,' he sobbed. Eyeballs, huge-bulged like squids',
Watch my dreams still; but I forgot him there
In posting next for duty, and sending a scout
To beg a stretcher somewhere, and floundering about
To other posts under the shrieking air.

Those other wretches, how they bled and spewed,
And one who would have drowned himself for good, –
I try not to remember these things now.
Let dread hark back for one word only: how

Half listening to that sentry's moans and jumps,
And the wild chattering of his broken teeth,
Renewed most horribly whenever crumps
Pummelled the roof and slogged the air beneath –
Through the dense din, I say, we heard him shout,
'I see your lights!' But ours had long died out.

F. L. LUCAS

Spain, 1809

All day we had ridden through scarred, tawny hills.
    At last the cool
Of splashing water. Then two blackened mills,
    A slaughtered mule.

And there, crag-perched, the village – San Pedro –
    We came to burn.
(Two convoys ambushed in the gorge below.
    They had to learn.)

Not a sound. Not a soul. Not a goat left behind.
    They had been wise.
Those death's-head hovels watched us, bleared and blind,
    With holes for eyes.

Down the one street's foul gutter slowly crawled
    Like blood, dark-red,
The wine from goatskins, slashed and hacked, that sprawled
    Like human dead.

From a black heap, like some charred funeral-pyre,
    Curled up, forlorn,
Grey wisps of smoke, where they had fed the fire
    With their last corn.

What hatred in that stillness! Suddenly
    An infant's cry.
Child, mother, bedrid crone – we found the three,
    Too frail to fly.

We searched their very straw – one wineskin there.
    We grinned with thirst.

And yet? – that Spanish hate! – what man would dare
    To taste it first?

Below, our captain called, 'Bring down the wench.'
    We brought her down –
Dark, brooding eyes that faced the smiling French
    With sullen frown.

'Señora, we are sent to burn the place.
    Your house I spare.'
Her proud chin nestled on her baby's face,
    Still silent there.

'Cold cheer you leave us! – one poor skin of wine!
    Before we sup,
You will honour us, Señora?' At his sign
    One filled a cup.

Calmly she took and, drinking, coldly smiled;
    We breathed more free.
But grimly our captain watched her – 'Now your child.'
    Impassively,

She made the small mouth swallow. All was well.
    The street was fired.
And we, by that brave blaze, as twilight fell,
    Sat gaily tired,

Laughing and eating, while the wine went round,
    Carefree, until
A child's scream through the darkness. At the sound
    Our hearts stood still.

Dumbly we glanced in one another's eyes.
    Our thirst was dead.
And in its place once more that grim surmise
    Upreared its head.

One dragged her to the firelight. Ashen–grey,
    She hissed – 'I knew
Not even the straw where an old woman lay
    Was safe from you.

'Now you are paid!' I never loved their wine,
    Had tasted none.
I will not tell, under that white moonshine,
    What things were done.

Twenty men mad with drink, and rage, and dread,
    Frenzied with pain –
That night the quiet millstream dribbled red
    With blood of Spain.

Under the moon across the gaunt sierra
    I fled alone.
Their balls whizzed wide. But in each tree lurked terror,
    In each stone.

Yes, men are brave. (Earth were a happier place,
    Were men less so.)
But I remember one pale woman's face
    In San Pedro.

STEVIE SMITH

Angel Boley

There was a wicked woman called Malady Festing
Who lived with her son-in-law, Hark Boley,
And her daughter Angel,
In a house on the high moorlands
Of the West Riding of Yorkshire
In the middle of the last century.

One day Angel
Overheard her mother, Malady, talking to Hark, her husband.
Hark, said Malady, it is time
To take another couple of children
Into our kitchen.
Hark laughed, for he too was wicked and he knew
For what purpose the little children
Were required.

But Angel, who was not happy and so
Lived out her life in a dream of absentmindedness,
In order not to be too much aware
Of her horrible relatives, and what it was
That happened every now and then
In the kitchen; and why the children who came
Were never seen again, this time
When she heard what her husband and mother said,
Came out of her absentmindedness and paid attention.

I know now, she said, and all the time I have known
What I did not want to know, that they kill all children
They lure to this house; and that is why, when I pass in the village,
The people look askance at me, and they whisper –
But not so that I cannot hear –

There goes the daughter of Mother Lure. And the stranger says:
Who is Mother Lure? And they answer: Mrs Festing and they make
    the sign
That is to protect them from evil. Selfish wretches, said Angel,
They do not mind about the children, that evil is not kept from *them*.
Angel wandered into the woods and she said: No more children
Are going to be murdered, and before they are murdered, tormented
And corrupted; no more children are going to be the victims
Of Mother Lure and my husband, Hark. Dark was the look then
On Angel's face, and she said: I am the Angel of Death.

Mrs Festing and Boley
Always left the cooking to Angel, they despised Angel but Angel
Could cook, and that they thought was all she was fit for,
To cook and keep house. And they realized
It was far from being to their disadvantage that Angel was,
As they thought, half-witted, and never knew
Or wanted to know, what was going on around her.

As soon as Angel
Said to herself: I am the Angel of Death
She became at once very practical and went out into the woods and
    fields
And gathered some A. Phalloides, commonly called the 'white' or
    deadly
Amanita, a mushroom of high toxicity. These poisonous fungi
She put into a soup, and this soup she gave
To Hark, and her mother, Malady, for supper, so that they died.

Angel then went to the police and said:
I have done evil, but I have saved many children.

The Judge said: Why did you not tell the police
That children were being destroyed? There was no proof, said Angel,
Because there were no bodies. I never could find out
What they did with the children after they had killed them.

So then the police searched hard, the wells, the rivers and the
    woodlands,
But never could they find out where

The children lay. Nor had the parents of the children
At any time done anything but weep. For they thought their children

Had been bewitched and done away with, and that
If they told their fears of Mother Lure and her wickedness
To the police, they would not believe them, and more children than
    ever
Would disappear.

From then onwards in the trial, Angel spoke
No word more, except to say: I am the Angel of Death.
So they put her in a lunatic asylum, and soon she died
Of an outbreak of typhoid fever. The people of the village
Now loved Angel, because she had delivered them from the fear

Of Mother Lure and Hark Boley, and had saved their
Little children from being tormented and slain by these wicked
    people.
So they wrote on her tombstone: 'She did evil that good
Might come'. But the Vicar said it was better not to put this but
Just her name and age, which was sixteen.
So he had the words
The villagers had written taken off the tombstone. But the next day
The words were again on the tombstone; so again the Vicar had them
Removed. And this time a watch was set on the grave,
A police constable and the village sexton watched there that night.

And no man came again to write on the tombstone
The forbidden words. Yet when morning came,
Again the words were on the tombstone.
So the Vicar said: It is the hand of the Lord.

And now in that graveyard, at that grave's head beneath the yew
    trees,
Still stands today the tombstone of Angel, with the words writ on it:
'She did evil that good might come'. May God be merciful.

C. DAY LEWIS

The 'Nabara'

*'They preferred, because of the rudeness of their heart,
to die rather than to surrender.'*

PHASE ONE

Freedom is more than a word, more than the base coinage
Of statesmen, the tyrant's dishonoured cheque, or the dreamer's mad
Inflated currency. She is mortal, we know, and made
In the image of simple men who have no taste for carnage
But sooner kill and are killed than see that image betrayed.
Mortal she is, yet rising always refreshed from her ashes:
She is bound to earth, yet she flies as high as a passage bird
To home wherever man's heart with seasonal warmth is stirred:
Innocent is her touch as the dawn's, but still it unleashes
The ravisher shades of envy. Freedom is more than a word.

I see man's heart two-edged, keen both for death and creation.
As a sculptor rejoices, stabbing and mutilating the stone
Into a shapelier life, and the two joys make one –
So man is wrought in his hour of agony and elation
To efface the flesh to reveal the crying need of his bone.
Burning the issue was beyond their mild forecasting
For those I tell of – men used to the tolerable joy and hurt
Of simple lives: they coveted never an epic part;
But history's hand was upon them and hewed an everlasting
Image of freedom out of their rude and stubborn heart.

The year, Nineteen-thirty-seven: month, March: the men, descen-
  dants
Of those Iberian fathers, the inquiring ones who would go
Wherever the sea-ways led: a pacific people, slow
To feel ambition, loving their laws and their independence –
Men of the Basque country, the Mar Cantábrico.
Fishermen, with no guile outside their craft, they had weathered
Often the sierra-ranked Biscayan surges, the wet
Fog of the Newfoundland Banks: they were fond of *pelota*: they met
No game beyond their skill as they swept the sea together,
Until the morning they found the leviathan in their net.

Government trawlers *Nabara*, *Guipuzkoa*, *Bizkaya*,
Donostia, escorting across blockaded seas
Galdames with her cargo of nickel and refugees
From Bayonne to Bilbao, while the crest of war curled higher

Inland over the glacial valleys, the ancient ease.
On the morning of March the fifth, a chill North-Wester fanned
    them,
Fogging the glassy waves: what uncharted doom lay low
There in the fog athwart their course, they could not know:
Stout were the armed trawlers, redoubtable those who manned them –
Men of the Basque country, the Mar Cantábrico.

Slowly they nosed ahead, while under the chill North-Wester
Nervous the sea crawled and twitched like the skin of a beast
That dreams of the chase, the kill, the blood-beslavered feast:
They too, the light-hearted sailors, dreamed of a fine fiesta,
Flags and their children waving, when they won home from the east.
Vague as images seen in a misted glass or the vision
Of crystal-gazer, the ships huddled, receded, neared,
Threading the weird fog-maze that coiled their funnels and bleared
Day's eye. They were glad of the fog till *Galdames* lost position
– Their convoy, precious in life and metal – and disappeared.

But still they held their course, the confident ear-ringed captains,
Unerring towards the landfall, nor guessed how the land lay,
How the guardian fog was a guide to lead them all astray.
For now, at a wink, the mist rolled up like the film that curtains
A saurian's eye; and into the glare of an evil day
Bizkaya, *Guipuzkoa*, *Nabara*, and the little
Donostia stepped at intervals; and sighted, alas,
Blocking the sea and sky a mountain they might not pass,
An isle thrown up volcanic and smoking, a giant in metal
Astride their path – the rebel cruiser, *Canarias*.

A ship of ten thousand tons she was, a heavyweight fighter
To the cocky bantam trawlers: and under her armament
Of eight- and four-inch guns there followed obedient
Towards Pasajes a prize just seized, an Estonian freighter
Laden with arms the exporters of death to Spain had sent.
A hush, the first qualm of conflict, falls on the cruiser's burnished
Turrets, the trawlers' grimy decks: fiercer the lime-
Light falls, and out of the solemn ring the late mists climb,
And ship to ship the antagonists gaze at each other astonished
Across the quaking gulf of the sea for a moment's time.

The trawlers' men had no chance or wish to elude the fated
Encounter. Freedom to these was natural pride that runs
Hot as the blood, their climate and heritage, dearer than sons.
Bizkaya, *Guipuzkoa*, knowing themselves outweighted,
Drew closer to draw first blood with their pairs of four-inch guns.

Aboard *Canarias* the German gun-layers stationed
Brisk at their intricate batteries – guns and men both trained
To a hair in accuracy, aimed at a pitiless end –
Fired, and the smoke rolled forth over the unimpassioned
Face of a day where nothing certain but death remained.

PHASE TWO

The sound of the first salvo skimmed the ocean and thumped
Cape Machichaco's granite ribs: it rebounded where
The salt-sprayed trees grow tough from wrestling the wind: it
    jumped
From isle to rocky isle: it was heard by women while
They walked to shrine or market, a warning they must fear.
But, beyond their alarm, as
Though that sound were also a signal for fate to strip
Luck's last green shoot from the falling stock of the Basques,
    Galdames
Emerged out of the mist that lingered to the west
Under the reeking muzzles of the rebel battleship:

Which instantly threw five shells over her funnel, and threw
Her hundred women and children into a slaughter-yard panic
On the deck they imagined smoking with worse than the foggy dew,
So that *Galdames* rolled as they slipped, clawed, trampled, reeled
Away from the gape of the cruiser's guns. A spasm galvanic,
Fear's chemistry, shocked the women's bodies, a moment before
Huddled like sheep in a mist, inert as bales of rag,
A mere deck-cargo; but more
Than furies now, for they stormed Galdames' bridge and swarmed
Over her captain and forced him to run up the white flag.

Signalling the Estonian, 'Heave-to', *Canarias* steamed
Leisurely over to make sure of this other prize:
Over-leisurely was her reckoning – she never dreamed
The Estonian in that pause could be snatched from her shark-shape
    jaws
By ships of minnow size.
Meanwhile *Nabara* and *Guipuzkoa*, not reluctant
For closer grips while their guns and crews were still entire,
Thrust forward: twice *Guipuzkoa* with a deadly jolt was rocked, and
The sea spat up in geysers of boiling foam, as the cruiser's
Heavier guns boxed them in a torrid zone of fire.

And now the little *Donostia* who lay with her 75's
Dumb in the offing – her weapons against that leviathan
Impotent as pen-knives –

Witnessed a bold manoeuvre, a move of genius, never
In naval history told. She saw *Bizkaya* run
Ahead of her consorts, a berserk atom of steel, audacious,
Her signal-flags soon to flutter like banderillas, straight
Towards the Estonian speeding, a young bull over the spacious
And foam-distraught arena, till the sides of the freight-ship screen her
From *Canarias* that will see the point of her charge too late.

'Who are you and where are you going?' the flags of *Bizkaya*
    questioned.
'Carrying arms and forced to go to Pasajes,' replied
The Estonian. 'Follow me to harbour.' 'Cannot, am threatened.'
Bizkaya's last word – 'Turn at once!' – and she points her peremptory
    guns
Against the freighter's mountainous flanks that blankly hide
This fluttering language and flaunt of signal insolence
From the eyes of *Canarias*. At last the rebels can see
That the two ships' talk meant a practical joke at their expense:
They see the Estonian veering away, to Bermeo steering,
Bizkaya under her lee.

(To the Basques that ship was a tonic, for she carried some million
    rounds
Of ammunition: to hearts grown sick with hope deferred
And the drain of their country's wounds
She brought what most they needed in face of the aid evaded
And the cold delay of those to whom freedom was only a word.)
Owlish upon the water sat the *Canarias*
Mobbed by those darting trawlers, and her signals blinked in vain
After the freighter, that still she believed too large to pass
Into Bermeo's port – a prize she fondly thought,
When she'd blown the trawlers out of the water, she'd take again.

Brisk at their intricate batteries the German gun-layers go
About death's business, knowing their longer reach must foil
The impetus, break the heart of the government ships: each blow
Deliberately they aim, and tiger-striped with flame
Is the jungle mirk of the smoke as their guns leap and recoil.
The Newfoundland trawlers feel
A hail and hurricane the like they have never known
In all their deep-sea life: they wince at the squalls of steel
That burst on their open decks, rake them and leave them wrecks,
But still they fight on long into the sunless afternoon.

– Fought on, four guns against the best of the rebel navy,
Until *Guipuzkoa*'s crew could stanch the fires no more
That gushed from her gashes and seeped nearer the magazine. Heavy

At heart they turned away for the Nervion that day:
Their ship, *Guipuzkoa*, wore
Flame's rose on her heart like a decoration of the highest honour
As listing she reeled into Las Arenas; and in a row
On her deck there lay, smoke-palled, that oriflamme's crackling
    banner
Above them, her dead – a quarter of the fishermen who had fought
    her –
Men of the Basque country, the Mar Cantábrico.

PHASE THREE

And now the gallant *Nabara* was left in the ring alone,
The sky hollow around her, the fawning sea at her side:
But the ear-ringed crew in their berets stood to the guns, and cried
A fresh defiance down
The ebb of the afternoon, the battle's darkening tide.
Honour was satisfied long since; they had held and harried
A ship ten times their size; they well could have called it a day.
But they hoped, if a little longer they kept the cruiser in play,
Galdames with the wealth of life and metal she carried
Might make her getaway.

Canarias, though easily she outpaced and out-gunned her,
Finding this midge could sting
Edged off, and beneath a wedge of smoke steamed in a ring
On the rim of the trawler's range, a circular storm of thunder.
But always *Nabara* turned her broadside, manoeuvring
To keep both guns on the target, scorning safety devices.
Slower now battle's tempo, irregular the beat
Of gunfire in the heart
Of the afternoon, the distempered sky sank to the crisis,
Shell-shocked the sea tossed and hissed in delirious heat.

The battle's tempo slowed, for the cruiser could take her time,
And the guns of *Nabara* grew
Red-hot, and of fifty-two Basque seamen had been her crew
Many were dead already, the rest filthy with grime
And their comrades' blood, weary with wounds all but a few.
Between two fires they fought, for the sparks that flashing spoke
From the cruiser's thunder-bulk were answered on their own craft
By traitor flames that crawled out of every cranny and rift
Blinding them all with smoke.
At half-past four *Nabara* was burning fore and aft.

What buoyancy of will
Was theirs to keep her afloat, no vessel now but a sieve –
So jarred and scarred, the rivets starting, no inch of her safe

From the guns of the foe that wrapped her in a cyclone of shrieking
    steel!
Southward the sheltering havens showed clear, the cliffs and the surf
Familiar to them from childhood, the shapes of a life still dear:
But dearer still to see
Those shores insured for life from the shadow of tyranny.
Freedom was not on their lips; it was what made them endure,
A steel spring in the yielding flesh, a thirst to be free.

And now from the little *Donostia* that lay with her 75's
Dumb in the offing, they saw *Nabara* painfully lower
A boat, which crawled like a shattered crab slower and slower
Towards them. They cheered the survivors, thankful to save these
    lives
At least. They saw each rower,
As the boat dragged alongside, was wounded – the oars they held
Dripping with blood, a bloody skein reeled out in their wake:
And they swarmed down the rope-ladders to rescue these men so
    weak
From wounds they must be hauled
Aboard like babies. And then they saw they had made a mistake.

For, standing up in the boat,
A man of that grimy boat's-crew hailed them: 'Our officer asks
You to give us your bandages and all your water-casks,
Then run for Bermeo. We're going to finish this game of *pelota*.'
Donostia's captain begged them with tears to escape: but the Basques
Would play their game to the end.
They took the bandages, and cursing at his delay
They took the casks that might keep the fires on their ship at bay;
And they rowed back to *Nabara*, trailing their blood behind
Over the water, the sunset and crimson ebb of their day.

For two hours more they fought, while *Nabara* beneath their feet
Was turned to a heap of smouldering scrap-iron. Once again
The flames they had checked a while broke out. When the forward
    gun
Was hit, they turned about
Bringing the after gun to bear. They fought in pain
And the instant knowledge of death: but the waters filling their riven
Ship could not quench the love that fired them. As each man fell
To the deck, his body took fire as if death made visible
That burning spirit. For two more hours they fought, and at seven
They fired their last shell.

Of her officers all but one were dead. Of her engineers
All but one were dead. Of the fifty-two that had sailed

In her, all were dead but fourteen – and each of these half killed
With wounds. And the night-dew fell in a hush of ashen tears,
And *Nabara*'s tongue was stilled.
Southward the sheltering havens grew dark, the cliffs and the green
Shallows they knew; where their friends had watched them as
    evening wore
To a glowing end, who swore
Nabara must show a white flag now, but saw instead the fourteen
Climb into their matchwood boat and fainting pull for the shore.

Canarias lowered a launch that swept in a greyhound's curve
Pitiless to pursue
And cut them off. But that bloodless and all-but-phantom crew
Still gave no soft concessions to fate: they strung their nerve
For one last fling of defiance, they shipped their oars and threw
Hand-grenades at the launch as it circled about to board them.
But the strength of the hands that had carved them a hold on history
Failed them at last: the grenades fell short of the enemy,
Who grappled and overpowered them,
While *Nabara* sank by the stern in the hushed Cantabrian sea.

*

They bore not a charmed life. They went into battle foreseeing
Probable loss, and they lost. The tides of Biscay flow
Over the obstinate bones of many, the winds are sighing
Round prison walls where the rest are doomed like their ship to rust –
Men of the Basque country, the Mar Cantábrico.
Simple men who asked of their life no mythical splendour,
They loved its familiar ways so well that they preferred
In the rudeness of their heart to die rather than to surrender . . .
Mortal these words and the deed they remember, but cast a seed
Shall flower for an age when freedom is man's creative word.

Freedom was more than a word, more than the base coinage
Of politicians who hiding behind the skirts of peace
They had defiled, gave up that country to rack and carnage:
For whom, indelibly stamped with history's contempt,
Remains but to haunt the blackened shell of their policies.
For these I have told of, freedom was flesh and blood – a mortal
Body, the gun-breech hot to its touch: yet the battle's height
Raised it to love's meridian and held it awhile immortal;
And its light through time still flashes like a star's that has turned to
    ashes,
Long after *Nabara*'s passion was quenched in the sea's heart.

W. H. AUDEN

Miss Gee

Let me tell you a little story
   About Miss Edith Gee;
She lived in Clevedon Terrace
   At Number 83.

She'd a slight squint in her left eye,
   Her lips they were thin and small,
She had narrow sloping shoulders
   And she had no bust at all.

She'd a velvet hat with trimmings,
   And a dark grey serge costume;
She lived in Clevedon Terrace
   In a small bed-sitting room.

She'd a purple mac for wet days,
   A green umbrella too to take,
She'd a bicycle with shopping basket
   And a harsh back-pedal brake.

The Church of Saint Aloysius
   Was not so very far;
She did a lot of knitting,
   Knitting for that Church Bazaar.

Miss Gee looked up at the starlight
   And said, 'Does anyone care
That I live in Clevedon Terrace
   On one hundred pounds a year?'

She dreamed a dream one evening
   That she was the Queen of France
And the Vicar of Saint Aloysius
   Asked Her Majesty to dance.

But a storm blew down the palace,
   She was biking through a field of corn,
And a bull with the face of the Vicar
   Was charging with lowered horn.

She could feel his hot breath behind her,
   He was going to overtake;
And the bicycle went slower and slower
   Because of that back-pedal brake.

Summer made the trees a picture,
　Winter made them a wreck;
She bicycled to the evening service
　With her clothes buttoned up to her neck.

She passed by the loving couples,
　She turned her head away;
She passed by the loving couples
　And they didn't ask her to stay.

Miss Gee sat down in the side-aisle,
　She heard the organ play;
And the choir it sang so sweetly
　At the ending of the day,

Miss Gee knelt down in the side-aisle,
　She knelt down on her knees;
'Lead me not into temptation
　But make me a good girl, please.'

The days and nights went by her
　Like waves round a Cornish wreck;
She bicycled down to the doctor
　With her clothes buttoned up to her neck.

She bicycled down to the doctor,
　And rang the surgery bell;
'O, doctor, I've a pain inside me,
　And I don't feel very well.'

Doctor Thomas looked her over,
　And then he looked some more;
Walked over to his wash-basin,
　Said, 'Why didn't you come before?'

Doctor Thomas sat over his dinner,
　Though his wife was waiting to ring,
Rolling his bread into pellets;
　Said, 'Cancer's a funny thing.

'Nobody knows what the cause is,
　Though some pretend they do;
It's like some hidden assassin
　Waiting to strike at you.

'Childless women get it,
    And men when they retire;
It's as if there had to be some outlet
    For their foiled creative fire.'

His wife she rang for the servant,
    Said, 'Don't be so morbid, dear';
He said: 'I saw Miss Gee this evening
    And she's a goner, I fear.'

They took Miss Gee to the hospital,
    She lay there a total wreck,
Lay in the ward for women
    With the bedclothes right up to her neck.

They laid her on the table,
    The students began to laugh;
And Mr Rose the surgeon
    He cut Miss Gee in half.

Mr Rose he turned to his students,
    Said, 'Gentlemen, if you please,
We seldom see a sarcoma
    As far advanced as this.'

They took her off the table,
    They wheeled away Miss Gee
Down to another department
    Where they study Anatomy.

They hung her from the ceiling,
    Yes, they hung up Miss Gee;
And a couple of Oxford Groupers
    Carefully dissected her knee.

CHARLES CAUSLEY

Balaam

King Balak sat on his gaudy throne
    His eyes like bits of glass
At the sight of the Children of Is-ra-el
    Camped on the river grass.
        Hee-haw, said the ass.

Balak called his princes,
   Stood them in a silver row.
'Go fetch me a conjuring man,' he said,
   'Who will melt them away like snow.'
     Said the donkey, *I don't think so.*

Three princes stopped at Balaam's gate,
   They tinkled at the bell.
'King Balak bids you curse,' they said,
   'The Children of Is-ra-el.'
     Said the cuddy, *Just wait a spell.*

Balaam watched and Balaam prayed,
   He lifted his head and spoke.
'The Children of Israel must be blessed
   For they are God's chosen folk.'
     Quite right, said the moke.

Three princes rode to Balak,
   Told him what had come to pass.
'I know what I'll do,' King Balak said.
   'I'll line his pockets with brass.'
     A waste of time, said the ass.

King Balak sent his money-box
   But Balaam shook his head.
'Forgive me, brother,' he cried, 'But I
   Must listen to the Lord instead.'
     Me too, the donkey said.

Early in the morning
   Before the black sun rose,
Jehovah spoke to Balaam,
   Told him to put on his clothes.
     Said the donkey, *The mystery grows!*

'Ride, ride to Moab,'
   The donkey heard Jehovah say,
But before he knew what deed he should do
   Balaam was up and away.
     The cuddy said, *Master, stay!*

They hadn't gone but one mile
   Over river and mire,
When an angel with a burning sword
   Stood as tall as a spire.
     Said the ass, *There's a man on fire!*

Balaam's eyes were heavy,
    His thoughts were as thick as lead
As the donkey galloped off the road
    And into a field of bread,
        Crying, *I spy trouble ahead!*

Balaam beat old Jenny
    Towards the mountain pass,
Didn't see the angel by the grape-yard wall
    Ready with the *coup de grâce*.
        He's here again! said the ass.

Jenny twisted, Jenny turned,
    Knew they were heading for a fall,
Crushed her master's grape-white foot
    Against the vineyard wall.
        Said, *It isn't my fault at all!*

Balaam took his oaken stick,
    Used it with a will.
Can't you see that bird-man? Jenny cried.
    Watch it, or we'll take a spill.
        I think he's aiming to kill!

The donkey carried Balaam
    Under the mountain stack.
When the angel came on for the third time
    She couldn't go fore nor back.
        Said, *This is the end of the track.*

Jenny fell down in the roadway.
    Balaam went over her head.
He saw ten thousand shooting stars.
    'Am I living,' he cried, 'or dead?'
        But the donkey turned and said,

Master, why do you seize your staff
    To tan my hide of grey?
Don't you see that man with the sword in his hand
    Standing in the king's highway?
        He'd have killed us both today.

Balaam opened his silent eyes.
    The angel blazed like a tree.
'Balaam,' he said, 'I would have slain,
    But the donkey would have gone free.'
        Said the ass, *That's news to me.*

'Then I have sinned,' said Balaam,
  'And I must homeward steer.'
'Go forward,' said the angel.
  'Speak God's word, loud and clear.'
    The donkey said, *Hear, hear!*

King Balak stood on the hilltop,
  Israel like sand below.
Balaam lifted up his arms,
  Blessed them where they did go.
    The donkey cried, *Bravo!*

Balaam stood on the mountain,
  Israel was like the sea.
He stretched his hand on the waters
  And blessed what they should be.
    Said the ass, *At last we agree.*

Balaam walked over the mountain,
  The donkey by his side.
He laughed, he wept, he suddenly sneezed,
  'Bless you, my friend,' he cried.
    Bless YOU, the ass replied.

I Saw a Jolly Hunter

I saw a jolly hunter
  With a jolly gun
Walking in the country
  In the jolly sun.

In the jolly meadow
  Sat a jolly hare.
Saw the jolly hunter.
  Took jolly care.

Hunter jolly eager –
  Sight of jolly prey.
Forgot gun pointing
  Wrong jolly way.

Jolly hunter jolly head
  Over heels gone.
Jolly old safety catch
  Not jolly on.

Bang went the jolly gun.
  Hunter jolly dead.
Jolly hare got clean away.
  Jolly good, I said.

JOHN HEATH-STUBBS

The Ballad of Don and Dave and Di

Don and Dave and Di –

Dave
Was an artist (no man's slave);
But Don
Always got on;
And Di
Was anybody's apple-pie.

Don loved Dave, and Dave
Loved Don
(I wonder why)
And both loved Di,
But Di
Looked after Di.

Di married Dave
(God save
The mark, she thought he'd save
Her from her inner lie.)

But Don
Got on, got on,
And off with Di.
She saw the point of pie
Not in the sky.

Dave hated Don,
But he forgave
(I wonder why).

But Don could crave
No hatred then for Dave:

Don still had Di,
And he caressed her thigh.

Said Dave:
'One of us three must die;
And if it's Don
I'm bound to sigh
Over his early grave;
And if it's Di
I know I'll cry.'

Don still had Di.
She was his slave.
Till, by and by,

Don killed Dave
(I wonder why).
It was an unmarked grave.

Don still had Di,
He still got on.
Till Di
Drove him to an early grave.
(God knows why.)

ACKNOWLEDGEMENTS

W. H. AUDEN 'Miss Gee' reprinted by permission of Faber and Faber Ltd from *Collected Poems* by W. H. Auden.

HILAIRE BELLOC 'Jim' reprinted by permission of the Peters Fraser and Dunlop Group Ltd from *Complete Verse*.

CHARLES CAUSLEY 'Balaam' and 'I Saw a Jolly Hunter' reprinted by permission of Macmillan London Ltd from *Collected Poems* and *Figgie Hobbin* respectively.

ROBERT FROST 'Paul's Wife' reprinted by permission of the Estate of Robert Frost from *The Poetry of Robert Frost* edited by Edward Connery Lathem and published by Jonathan Cape Ltd.

JOHN HEATH-STUBBS 'The Ballad of Don and Dave and Di' reprinted by permission of Carcanet Press Ltd from *Collected Poems*

CECIL DAY LEWIS 'The Nabara' reprinted by permission of Jonathan Cape Ltd from *Collected Poems*, 1954.

F. L. LUCAS 'Spain, 1809' reprinted by permission of The Bodley Head from *Many Times and Many Lands*.

JOHN MASEFIELD Extract from 'Reynard the Fox' reprinted by permission of The Society of Authors as the literary representative of the Estate of John Masefield.

ALFRED NOYES 'The Highwayman' reprinted by permission of John Murray (Publishers) Ltd from *Collected Poems*.

OLIVER ST JOHN GOGARTY 'Leda and the Swan' reprinted by permission of Oliver D. Gogarty.

ROBERT SERVICE 'The Shooting of Dan McGrew' reprinted by permission of Dodd Mead and Co. © Dodd Mead and Co., 1910.

STEVIE SMITH 'Angel Boley' reprinted by permission of James MacGibbon from *The Collected Poems of Stevie Smith* published by Penguin Books Ltd.

MURIEL STUART 'In the Orchard' reprinted by permission of the Estate of Muriel Stuart from *Selected Poems* published by Jonathan Cape Ltd.

INDEX OF AUTHORS

INDEX OF FIRST LINES AND TITLES